Experiment in Republicanism

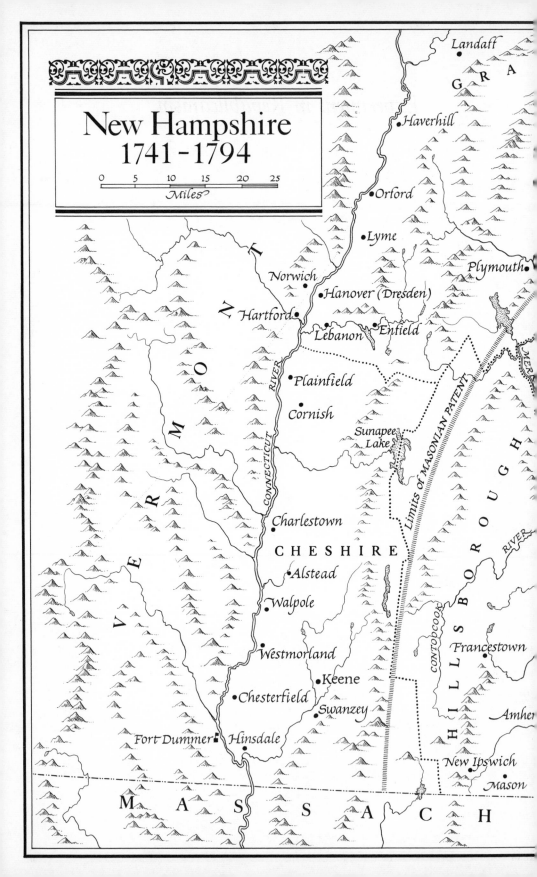

New Hampshire
1741–1794

0   5   10   15   20   25
Miles

Landaff

G R A

Haverhill

Orford

Lyme

Plymouth

Norwich

Hanover (Dresden)

Hartford

Lebanon   Enfield

Plainfield

Cornish

Sunapee
Lake

V E R M O N T

CONNECTICUT RIVER

Charlestown

C H E S H I R E

Alstead

Walpole

Westmorland

Keene

Chesterfield

Swanzey

Fort Dummer   Hinsdale

Limits of MASONIAN PATENT

H I L L S B O R O U G H

MER

CONTOOCOOK

RIVER

Francestown

Amher

New Ipswich

Mason

M A S S A C H

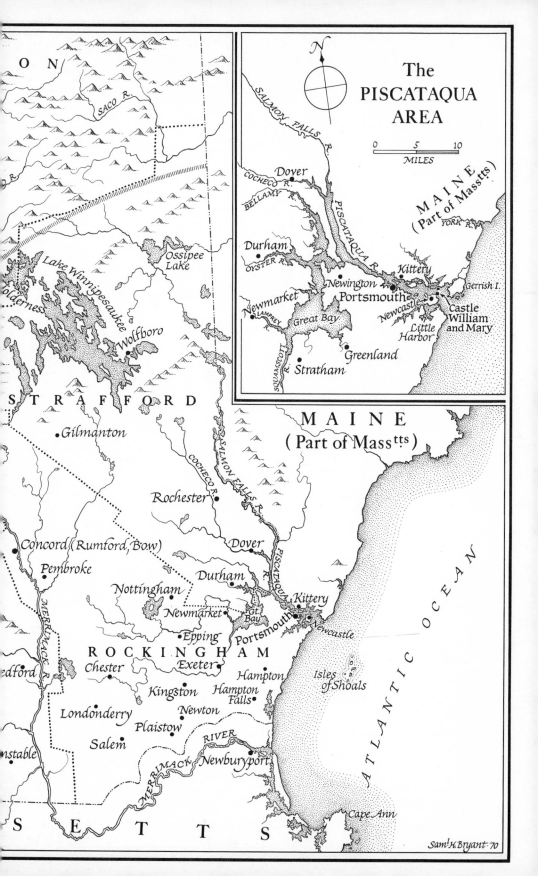

The
PISCATAQUA
AREA

0   5   10
MILES

N

MAINE
(Part of Mass^tts)

SALMON FALLS R.

COCHECO R.

BELLAMY R.

Dover

PISCATAQUA R.

YORK R.

Durham

OYSTER R.

Kittery

Newington

Gerrish I.

Newmarket

Portsmouth

LAMPREY R.

Great Bay

Newcastle

Castle
William
and Mary

Little
Harbor

SQUAMSCOTT R.

Stratham

Greenland

ON

SACO R.

Ossipee
Lake

Lake Winnipesaukee

Holderness

Wolfboro

STRAFFORD

Gilmanton

SALMON FALLS R.

COCHECO R.

Rochester

MAINE
(Part of Mass^tts)

Concord (Rumford, Bow)

Dover

Pembroke

Durham

PISCATAQUA R.

Nottingham

Kittery

MERRIMACK R.

Newmarket

Gt.
Bay

Epping

Portsmouth

Newcastle

ROCKINGHAM

Chester

Exeter

Hampton

ATLANTIC OCEAN

Kingston

Hampton
Falls

Isles
of Shoals

Londonderry

Newton

Salem

Plaistow

MERRIMACK RIVER

edford

Newburyport

stable

Cape Ann

S   E   T   T   S

Saml H. Bryant. 70

Experiment in Republicanism

New Hampshire Politics and

the American Revolution, 1741–1794

Jere R. Daniell

Harvard University Press

Cambridge, Massachusetts

1970

To Elena

Contents

Illustrations

Preface

Twenty years ago historians were in general agreement about the
nature of the American revolution. Events between 1765 and 1788,
they felt, were part of an intense and constant struggle between
groups of conservatives and radicals. Conservatives—eastern merchants, southern planters, and other men of wealth—considered
themselves aristocrats and tried to create a political system to serve
their class interests. Radicals, identified with the people as a whole,
believed in a more democratic form of government and found support among debtors and small farmers. Both groups had their mo-
ments of triumph. The radicals gained control of political processes
sometime after the Stamp Act crisis, led the movement for independence, and dominated both the Continental Congress and the
state governments during the war. Ratification of the federal Constitution climaxed the conservative resurgence, which began as soon
as the war ended. This broad interpretation was rarely questioned:
virtually all the scholarly literature about the revolution published
since the turn of the century had provided detailed evidence to
support it.

Today no such consensus exists. A massive and highly effective
attack has been made on the scholarship of the most influential of
the earlier works, Charles Beard's *Economic Interpretation of the
Constitution*. State and local studies have shown that in many areas
political divisions did not reflect a pattern of conflict between rich
and poor, creditor and debtor, merchant and farmer. We now
know that most revolutionists, even those who led the movement

for independence, thought that men of wealth, education, and so-cial prestige should manage public affairs and had no desire to cre-ate a "democratic" form of government. Many writers have reacted against explanations of individual and group behavior cast solely in terms of economic self-interest by emphasizing ideology as a deter-minant of political action. Others insist that the main weakness of the old interpretation lay in its failure to consider adequately the way in which local conditions affected politics, not in its assumptions about the nature of human motivation.

What the literature since World War II adds up to is far from clear. Evidence presented by regional historians appears too com-plex and idiosyncratic to permit any but the vaguest generalizations about the relationship between socio-economic status and political commitment on specific issues. It seems clear that "conservatism" and "radicalism" have outlived their usefulness as unifying concepts, but there is no agreement on the terms in which revolutionary poli-tics might more accurately be discussed. The differences between those emphasizing the economic sources of political behavior and those impressed by the degree to which the revolutionists acted in accordance with their political beliefs cannot be resolved; they are too deeply rooted in incompatible concepts of human psychology among historians themselves. Given all this, it is not surprising that writers adept at criticizing their predecessors have failed to produce a fresh interpretation of the revolutionary era as a whole.

The present study may add to the confusion. To begin with, it presents additional proof of the way in which purely local circum-stances affected the course of political development in late-eigh-teenth-century America. The immense influence of the Wentworth family gave New Hampshire a uniquely stable governmental struc-ture in the years before 1774. Constitutional conditions in the colonial period, especially the lack of broad representation in the as-sembly, accentuated the degree to which revolution disrupted the pattern of state authority. Population growth, from about 40,000 at mid-century to over 140,000 in 1790, created a host of problems for both imperial and revolutionary magistrates. The presence of three major river systems intensified sectional attitudes and made political integration difficult.

Furthermore, the history of New Hampshire tends to validate claims of both older writers and their critics. Some political struggles did pit merchants against farmers, debtors against creditors, and easterners against inhabitants in the interior. Some New Hampshiremen did see the revolution as a vehicle for destroying the power of the rich and wellborn and reacted in the 1780s against what they thought was a systematic attempt by these same men to deprive the people as a whole of the benefits of political independence. The revolutionists may not have believed in democracy, but they introduced many reforms which we would consider democratic: qualifications for voting and officeholding were reduced, participation in state politics became more widespread, and rulers found it more difficult to ignore popular criticism. On the other hand, the case of New Hampshire reveals fully the inadequacies of the earlier conceptual framework. The terms "radical" and "conservative" have little meaning unless applied to specific issues. State politics reflected what William Nesbit Chambers has called the "indigenous, deeply-rooted, conflicting pluralism" of American life as a whole. Kinship patterns, sectional interests, personal ambition, the desire for social order, constitutional beliefs, disappointed expectations, and irrational fears all influenced political behavior. Each of these ingredients plays an important role in my description and explanation of events.

My study does, however, illustrate certain phenomena I consider true of late-eighteenth-century America as a whole. The experience of New Hampshire's colonial rulers in the decade after 1765 was in many ways "typical"; therefore, the process described in Chapter 2 may have broader application as an interpretation of the coming of revolution. Moreover, the revolution in New Hampshire had an impact on politics similar to that in many other colonies. It weakened the effective power of those whose economic, political, and social interests were bound up within the imperial system and resulted in the greater distribution of authority among local elites. It made possible the creation of a constitutional structure consistent with the needs of a rapidly expanding population of men accustomed to a high degree of communal autonomy. It involved a dramatic shift in assumptions about the nature of government and the relationship between individual citizens and that government. It necessitated the development of political techniques rarely employed in the colonial period. Finally, my story should remind us that the American revolution was much more than a movement for national independence. The revolutionists themselves considered national affairs of secondary importance. Before the late 1780s they assumed that state and local institutions would be able to satisfy their basic governmental needs, and they accepted the federal constitution partly because it left the management of most affairs in the hands of locally elected officials. We cannot understand what the revolution meant to those who lived through it until we learn more about their experience at the state and local level.

This study could not have been completed without the help of others. Bernard Bailyn not only taught me much of what I know about colonial history but guided by research efforts and offered constant critical advice. William Abbott suggested important revisions in Chapter 1, as did Phillip Benjamin for Chapter 4. Michael Kammen gave me several bibliographical references I might otherwise have missed. D. H. Watson located useful manuscript collections in England. Sally Daniell helped with writing style and typed more versions of the manuscript than either she or I care to remember; Donna Musgrove typed the final draft. Staff members in the various document repositiories were thoroughly cooperative. I would also like to thank Dartmouth College for the research assistance and the faculty fellowship which allowed me to complete my work.

Chapter 1 appeared, in virtually the same form, as "Politics in New Hampshire under Governor Benning Wentworth, 1741–1767," *William and Mary Quarterly*, 3rd series, 23 (1966), 76–105, and is reprinted with permission. Sir William Ramsden has allowed me to quote from the Rockingham Letters deposited in Sheepscar Library, Leeds, England. I have modernized the spelling and punctuation of quotations throughout the book.

Jere R. Daniell

Hanover, New Hampshire
September 1969

Experiment in Republicanism

Abbreviations

BLDC	Baker Library, Dartmouth College, Hanover, N.H.
HSP	Historical Society of Pennsylvania, Philadelphia
LC	Library of Congress, Washington
MHS	Massachusetts Historical Society, Boston
NEHGR	*New England Historical and Genealogical Register*
NHA	New Hampshire Archives, Concord
NHHS	New Hampshire Historical Society, Concord
NHSL	New Hampshire State Library, Concord
NHSP	*New Hampshire Provincial and State Papers*
NYHS	New-York Historical Society, New York
NYPL	New York Public Library, New York
PA	Portsmouth Athenaeum, Portsmouth, N.H.
PCSM	*Publications of the Colonial Society of Massachusetts*
PRO	Public Record Office, London
WMQ	*William and Mary Quarterly*

Part I
Colonial Politics
and the
Coming of Revolution

Benning Wentworth (1696–1770). Portrait by Joseph Blackburn painted in 1760.

1

The Administration of
Governor Benning Wentworth
1741–1767

When John Wentworth arrived at Portsmouth in the summer of 1767 to assume the governorship of New Hampshire, the selectmen of the second largest provincial town, Londonderry, published a welcoming address in which they noted the "kind patronage" of Wentworth's grandfather, John, and of his uncle, Benning, who had preceded him in office. They thought it "a hopeful presage of much future good" that "an amiable branch, sprung from such ancestors," had "come to fill the chief seat in the government" and concluded with a prayer "that the name of Wentworth" be made "hereditary." Others in the province were less pleased with Wentworth's appointment, for it perpetuated an administration which a bitter opponent had once accused of leaving the province like "a field of battle after the fight is ended; the common people being compared to the carcasses, and those who are the chief in power to the vultures and ravens glutting on the carnage."[1] Whatever his reaction to the new governor, the individual inhabitant knew that the Wentworths, their relatives, and their friends had monopolized the key positions of political authority in New Hampshire since Benning Wentworth became governor in 1741.[2]

---

1. *New Hampshire Gazette* (Portsmouth), July 10, 1767; Richard Waldron to Jonathan Belcher, Sept. 24, 1747, in Nathaniel Bouton, ed., *Documents and Records relating to the Province of New Hampshire* (Manchester, 1872–1943), VI, 41. Titles, editors, and places of publication vary in this 40–volume series; hereafter all volumes will be cited *NHSP*.
2. Benning's father John had been lieutenant governor during the 1720s, but during the thirties Governor Belcher had kept the Wentworth influence in check. See

The rewards of political preference were most apparent to inhabitants of the provincial capital, Portsmouth. There the wealthy and intermarried Atkinson, Jaffrey, Peirce, Rindge, Warner, and Wentworth families led an exclusive social life, met weekly in their own Anglican chapel, and occupied most provincial offices of profit and honor. Just south of the capital Benning Wentworth resided in a fifty-two-room mansion built with the rewards of his governorship. Members of the provincial government—many of them wardens or vestryment in Queen's Chapel—traveled regularly to the governor's mansion where until 1758 the council held its meetings, conveniently near the gaming and billiard rooms.[3]

Even those who lived elsewhere in the colony witnessed the authority and wealth of the provincial aristocracy. As most of settled New Hampshire lay within a day's travel of Portsmouth, many had seen the bustling port themselves. The capital was the commercial center of New Hampshire and the only place where provincial courts met. Inhabitants who did not travel had indirect contact with the "clan," as its critics labeled the family group. Large sections of virtually every township in the province were owned by members of the oligarchy. Governor Wentworth exercised special authority in the interior as Surveyor of the King's Woods, charged with the responsibility of preserving provincial forests from wasteful lumbering.

The Wentworth family maintained its political power from 1741 until the outbreak of revolution; between 1752 and the early 1770s it reigned virtually unchallenged.[4] A complex pattern of personal, social, economic, and constitutional relationships linked the family interests to the interests of others concerned with provincial government. The crown, individual British administrators, assembly representatives and their fellow townsmen, even the inhabitants of

Jeremy Belknap, *The History of New Hampshire* (Philadelphia, 1784–1792), II, 1–157. As one of 14 children, Benning Wentworth had no trouble finding relatives to reward: John Wentworth, *The Wentworth Genealogy* (Boston, 1878), I, 99–101.

3. For a description of Portsmouth society see Mary C. Rogers, *Glimpses of an Old Social Capital* (Boston, 1923), and "Benning Wentworth" in Clifford K. Shipton, *Biographical Sketches of Those Who Attended Harvard College* (*Sibley's Harvard Graduates*, vols. IV–XIV [Boston, 1933–   ]), VI, 114. Of the seven wardens and vestrymen in 1762, five were councilors, another was soon to become one, and the seventh was the governor's brother: Society for the Propagation of the Gospel Papers, transcript vol. 79, NHHS, hereafter cited as SPG Papers; Belknap, *History*, II, 487. The governor's mansion is described in Charles W. Brewster, *Rambles about Portsmouth* (Portsmouth, 1859), I, 99.

4. For the decline and fall of the Wentworths, see chaps. ii and iii below.

unrepresented communities, felt, for the most part, satisfied with the existing political structure. From an imperial point of view, the administration operated as effectively as any in prerevolutionary America.

Few provincial administrations could remain long in power without dependable and influential friends in England to see that the right people were appointed to the governorship and to other imperial offices. The Wentworths were represented at court by John Thomlinson—merchant, mast contractor, deputy paymaster of His Majesty's troops in North America, and political associate of Thomas Pelham-Holles, Duke of Newcastle.[5] As a young and aggressive London Merchant, in the 1730s Thomlinson had developed a trade with many leading Piscataqua merchants, among them Theodore Atkinson and the Wentworth brothers, Benning and Mark.[6] Familiar with the commerce of the province, he obtained near the end of the decade his first mast contract from the Navy Board; and from then until the mid-sixties he and his merchant friends conducted a lucrative mast trade with Mark Wentworth and Theodore Atkinson— the governor's brother-in-law and the provincial secretary—acting as their New England subcontractors.[7] Thomlinson was also the assembly-appointed agent for the province of New Hampshire, a remunerative position he obtained in the 1730s while Atkinson and Wentworth were members of the house. His association with the province provided an opportunity for him to assist the growth of Anglicanism; as a devoted member of the Society for the Propagation of the Gospel, the provincial agent manifested an almost paternal concern for the welfare of the Queen's Chapel and its "missionary" minister, the Reverend Arthur Browne.[8]

5. See Robert M. Howard, ed., *Records and Letters of the Family of the Longs of Longville, Jamaica, and Hampton Lodge, Surrey* (London, 1925), I.

6. Joshua Peirce Letter Book and Daniel Rindge Letter Book, Wendell Collection, Baker Library, Harvard Business School, Boston, Mass.; Thomlinson to Moffatt, Oct. 16, 1745, Moffatt, Whipple, and Mason Papers, NHHS; Thomlinson-Atkinson correspondence, *NHSP*, XVIII, *passim*.

7. Atkinson to Thomlinson, Nov. 26 and Dec. 20, 1740, *NHSP*, XVIII, 165, 166; Joseph J. Malone, *Pine Trees and Politics: The Naval Stores and Forest Policy in Colonial New England, 1691–1775* (Seattle, 1964), 124–133; Peter Livius to Henry Muilman, Feb. 6, 1764, Livius Letter Book, 19, NHHS.

8. See Atkinson to Thomlinson, May 19, 1742, *NHSP*, XVIII, 175; and SPG Papers, 39–85.

Thomlinson obtained leverage to serve his adopted province through extensive political relationships. By the 1750s he had become friendly enough with the Duke of Newcastle to write him directly when he wanted favors more rapidly than the Privy Council and Board of Trade could provide. Earlier he was supported by a member of the Board of Trade itself, Martin Bladen, who handled such a large portion of its business that he was referred to as "trade" while the other members were only "board."[9] After Bladen's death in 1746 Thomlinson relied on the board's powerful secretary, John Pownall; in 1753, when Thomlinson began to tire of his work as agent, it was Pownall whom he recommended to the governor and assembly as his replacement.[10] Thomlinson had worked with Ferdinand John Paris, one of the most successful solicitors in England and a skilled and powerful colonial agent, to obtain a separate governor for New Hampshire after Jonathan Belcher's removal from the joint governorship of Massachusetts and New Hampshire in 1741, and Paris continued to represent provincial interests at Whitehall.[11] Furthermore, the New Hampshire agent was an important member of the group which had supported William Shirley as Belcher's replacement in Massachusetts. Thomlinson lent Shirley £1,000 on condition that Shirley ask his patron Newcastle to seek Wentworth's appointment; shortly thereafter Newcastle announced that Benning Wentworth would be appointed governor. Elsewhere, in Parliament, at the treasury, the Navy Board, and the Board of Ordinance, the ubiquitous merchant had his contacts. Robert Morris wrote of Thomlinson and John Hanbury, Thomlinson's partner in the business of supplying specie to the British army in America, that he "knew of no two

9. Thomlinson to Newcastle, Colonial Office Papers, Class 5, X, 143 (73), PRO (hereafter cited as C.O.); Jack P. Greene, "Martin Bladen's Blueprint for a Colonial Union," *WMQ*, 3d ser., 17 (1960), 517. See also John A. Schultz, *William Shirley: King's Governor of Massachusetts* (Chapel Hill, 1961), 34; Atkinson to Thomlinson, May 19, 1744, *NHSP*, XVIII, 187.

10. James Nevin to Atkinson, Nov. 14, 1761, *NHSP*, XVIII, 543; Thomlinson to Atkinson and others, Mar. 3, 1753, New Hampshire Miscellaneous Manuscripts, LC; *NHSP*, VI, 219; Thomlinson to Assembly, Oct. 9, 1753, Belknap Papers, NHHS. Franklin B. Wickwire, "John Pownall and British Colonial Policy," *WMQ*, 3d ser., 20 (1963), 543–554, discusses Pownall's influence with the Board of Trade.

11. John A. Schultz, "Succession Politics in Massachusetts, 1730–1741," *WMQ*, 3d ser., 15 (1958), 508–520; *NHSP*, XVIII, 64–115, 151–162; Thomlinson to Atkinson and others, Mar. 3, 1753, New Hamp. Misc. MSS; same to same, May 21, 1754, Miscellaneous Bound, XII, MHS. For details on Paris see Mabel P. Wolff, *The Colonial Agency of Pennsylvania, 1712–1757* (Philadelphia, 1933), 39–40 and *passim*, and Davis to Thomlinson, 1755, Province Papers, Correspondence, II, 317, NHA.

6

merchants in London that have such personal weight and interest with the ministry."[12]

Thomlinson's service to Wentworth, Atkinson, and their merchant friends was continuous and varied. He obtained the mandamuses placing them and their children in office and advised them what they should do to maintain those offices; any criticism of the governor and his officers heard in London coffeehouses or the ministry he relayed to Wentworth without delay. Acting as their commercial agent, Thomlinson and his business partners sold their shipments and forwarded English goods for sale and use in New Hampshire. At Whitehall, the center of political activity, he represented the interests of the Piscataqua merchants, as well as the entire merchant community of New England, in disputes with West Indian planters. So intimate were his relations with at least two New Hampshire merchants, Atkinson and George Jaffrey, that Thomlinson selected some of their clothing.[13]

Thomlinson's influence and his understanding of imperial politics were particularly important to the governor. Before 1752 frequent disputes marked Governor Wentworth's relationship with the House of Representatives. Sometimes Wentworth sympathized with assembly demands but hesitated to disobey royal instructions which ordered him not to conform to those demands; on such occasions he sought the aid of Thomlinson or Governor Shirley in obtaining from the ministry either formal or informal permission to make concessions to the assembly. When, on the other hand, Wentworth disapproved of demands by the house or felt they would infringe upon royal prerogative, he asked Thomlinson to obtain an additional instruction to support him in his resistance to house action. If internal disputes threatened to embarrass the governor at Whitehall, Thomlinson either defended the governor or used his "interests" to keep

12. Schutz, *William Shirley*, 34–35, 56–57, 71–73; Thomlinson to Atkinson, Feb. 6, 1740/I, NHSP, XVIII, 169; NHSP, V, 255; Henry W. Foote *et al.*, eds., *Annals of King's Chapel from the Puritan Age of New England to the Present Day* (Boston 1882–1940), II, 143; Robert Morris to P. V. B. Livingston and [John] Stevens, Apr. 12, 1756, Boggs Papers, Rutgers University Library, New Brunswick, N.J., quoted in Beverly McAnear, ed., "An American in London, 1735–1736: The Diary of Robert Hunter Morris," *Pennsylvania Magazine of History and Biography*, 64 (1940), 358n.

13. Thomlinson-Atkinson correspondence, NHSP, XVIII, 161–164, 174–182, 312, 385, 549, and Misc. Bound, XII; Nevin to Atkinson, Nov. 14, 1761, NHSP, XVIII, 543; Daniel Rindge Letter Book, Wendell Collection, *passim*.

the matter from being heard before the Privy Council or the Board of Trade.[14]

But Thomlinson did not confine his support to Wentworth and the "clan." As assembly-appointed agent for the province and a business associate of numerous Portsmouth merchants, he could not play favorites. Through the years of intense struggles between governor and house he did everything in his power, as he told Atkinson, "to reconcile things for the benefit of the province." He scolded Wentworth after the governor had arbitrarily reduced in militia rank certain of his personal enemies, and he saw to the restoration of their commissions. The only time house members formally requested Wentworth's dismissal, Thomlinson, so he claimed, presented their complaint to ministry officials. When he reported his action to Henry Sherburne, Jr., he explained that he was as much a friend "to you and every other gentleman in the province" as to the governor. Although Sherburne may not have been convinced—his brother later led an unsuccessful effort to appoint a different agent—others were: Thomlinson retained both the agency and the confidence of provincial inhabitants until his death in 1767.[15]

Most of the time apologies were unnecessary, for Thomlinson's efforts on behalf of New Hampshire benefited both governor and assembly. The appointment of Benning Wentworth as governor in 1741 was only one part of an elaborate scheme which among other things resulted in the settlement in New Hampshire's favor of its longstanding boundary dispute with Massachusetts.[16] In imperial eyes the settlement saved valuable naval stores in the contested areas from the unruly citizens of the Massachusetts charter government; but Massachusetts men saw their dreams of landed wealth evaporate

14. *NHSP*, V, 238–242, 336, 654; Albert S. Batchellor and Henry H. Metcalf, eds., *Laws of New Hampshire* (Manchester and elsewhere, 1904–1920), III, 631–634; Atkinson to Thomlinson, June 28, 1758, *NHSP*, XVIII, 472; Shirley to Wentworth, Sept. 25, 1744, *NHSP*, XVIII, 210; Thomlinson to Atkinson and others, Mar. 3, 1753, New Hamp. Misc. MSS; Wentworth to Thomlinson, Oct. 21, 1743, in Howard, ed., *Records*, I, 207.

15. Thomlinson to Atkinson, Aug 10, 1749, *NHSP*, VI, 887; *NHSP*, XVIII, 332–335; Thomlinson to Henry Sherburne, Jr., Nov. 13, 1749, *NHSP*, VI, 888; John Sherburne to John Huske, Feb. 9 and Aug. 20, 1754, New Hamp. Misc. MSS.

16. So effective were Thomlinson and his aids that the decision gave New Hampshire even more than it had claimed. Most of the documents pertaining to the boundary controversy are in *NHSP*, XVIII, 42–171, and XIX, 177–646.

in an instant and immediately dispatched Thomas Hutchinson to present their grievances. The New Hampshire agent helped ensure the failure of Hutchinson's mission. Later, when a group which had settled in Rumford (now Concord) under a Massachusetts charter, appealed to the Privy Council for reversal of a decision in New Hampshire courts awarding part of the town to New Hampshire men, Thomlinson argued against the appeal. Throughout the period of his agency, he collected and invested specie due the province from the treasury.[17]

The actions of Benning Wentworth himself reinforced the influence stemming from Thomlinson's political interests; stubborn, at times vindictive, but neither aloof nor uncompromising, the governor was well suited to the task of maintaining internal political harmony while presenting a picture of administrative competence to his English superiors. As surveyor general he did almost nothing to enforce the laws for preserving mast trees, yet wrote to London convincingly of efforts to prevent wanton destruction of the American forests. He informed the Board of Trade that no illegal commerce existed in New Hampshire—"the place of my residence is within a mile of . . . the harbour," he wrote, "and no vessel can come into port without coming within my sight, which . . . has contributed in a great measure to the chastity of the port"—at a time when Piscataqua was notorious for smuggling.[18] He continuously asked the Duke of Newcastle's colonial favorite, Governor Shirley, for advice and treated the Massachusetts magistrate with such deference that reports of it undoubtedly reached the minister's ears. When New Hampshire troops performed well and willingly in both the Louisbourg expedition and later campaigns, the governor made certain that his part in such operations became known to military leaders in America and to officials in England. In all his official correspondence, Wentworth gave the impression that his devotion to the royal prerogative and to his gubernatorial instructions was absolute and inflexible, and that primarily through his stubborn

17. *Ibid.*, V, 180, 846, VI, 144, 544, XVIII, 135, XIX, 475, 510–536.
18. Malone, *Pine Trees and Politics*, 128–134. The quotation is from Wentworth to Board of Trade, Mar. 4, 1764, Sparks Manuscripts, no. 43, IV, 2, Houghton Library, Harvard University, Cambridge, Mass. Byron Fairchild, *Messrs. William Pepperrell: Merchants at Piscataqua* (Ithaca, 1954), 190 and *passim*, describes smuggling in the Portsmouth area.

loyalty to the crown, New Hampshire had become a productive and peaceful part of the British empire.[19]

The governor went even further in his efforts to please those whose pleasure would be of use to him. He supported Anglicanism, recommended the creation of an American bishopric, and offered to grant land for its financial support. In each new township he set aside a lot for the Society for the Propagation of the Gospel, and after 1760 an additional one for the first settled Anglican minister. Furthermore, Wentworth courted the interest of the Earl of Strafford, Lord Rockingham, Baron Monson, the Duke of Grafton, Admiral Boscawen, Thomas and John Pownall, and dozens of other important cival and military officials by naming townships after them. The men so honored were frequently presented with grants of land, sometimes without having to bear any of the proprietary fees.[20]

Jonathan Belcher once wrote of Wentworth, "guts sometimes can do more than brains."[21] Belcher without doubt underestimated his antagonist's political wisdom; but he did understand the governor's political technique. How much actual support Wentworth gained through his actions and how seriously English officials took the governor's image of himself is impossible to measure. Yet with Thomlinson as the ministry's primary source of information about the province, those whose responsibility it was to judge the effectiveness of New Hampshire's provincial government remained ignorant of much that went on in the colony. Since the Thomlinson-Wentworth team functioned smoothly until the early 1760s, it is not difficult to understand how Benning Wentworth retained his governorship for twenty-five years—longer than any other colonial governor in British North America.

19. Schutz, *William Shirley*, 64–66; *NHSP*, V, 933–950; Wentworth-Amherst correspondence, War Office Papers, 34, XXIV, *passim*, PRO (photostats in LC); Robinson to Wentworth, Nov. 11, 1757, New Hamp. Misc. MSS; Wentworth to Lords of Trade, Mar. 23, 1750/1, *NHSP*, XVIII, 396.

20. Wentworth to the Secretary of the SPG, Additional Manuscripts no. 32704, fol. 135, British Museum, London (transcript in LC); Arthur Browne correspondence, SPG Papers, *passim*; John F. Looney, "The King's Representative: Benning Wentworth, Colonial Governor, 1741–1767," unpub. diss. Lehigh University, 1961, 105; Elmer Hunt and Robert A. Smith, "The English Background of Some of the Wentworth Town Grants," *Historical New Hampshire*, 6 (1950), 2–52; C.O. 5/925, *passim*. Both Browne and Wentworth felt that support of the Church of England played an important role in keeping the governor in office.

21. Belcher to Waldron, Jan. 13, 1741/2, Belcher Papers, III, no. 112, NHHS.

The trade in masts ensured Thomlinson's continued political cooperation with the Wentworths. The successful English mast contractor needed widespread political connections in both England and the colonies. He had to purchase a license from the Privy Council before contracting with the admiralty, obtain affidavits from the surveyor general, governor, and naval officer of the province where he procured his masts, get certificates from customs commissioners and dockyard officials attesting that his masts met contract specifications and qualified for premium payments, and have connections in the treasury to hasten the notoriously slow process of payment for masts delivered to the admiralty. In addition he needed dependable colonial agents to purchase masts of the quality to meet rigid naval standards.[22] Politically well-connected in England and New Hampshire, wealthy enough to participate in a business requiring heavy initial capital outlay, and certain of his colonial subcontractors, Thomlinson enjoyed a secure and profitable situation: no one could seriously challenge his control of the mast trade from New Hampshire while Wentworth remained in power.[23]

Thomlinson's control of this trade was highly satisfactory from the Wentworths' point of view. As long as Thomlinson continued to deliver masts, admiralty and Board of Trade officials were apt to remain satisfied with the provincial government. Moreover, the existing arrangement ensured family domination of the mast business in New Hampshire. Peter Livius, a well-to-do Englishman who came to Portsmouth in the sixties to manage the American estate of his father-in-law John Tufton Mason, was obviously disappointed to discover that masting was "in the hands of a few associated gentlemen of very large fortunes," who had the surveyor general "entirely at their devotion" and opposed any interference in their affairs.[24]

22. Malone, *Pine Trees and Politics*, 47–51.
23. There may have been some competition between Thomlinson and the powerful mast contractor Joseph Gulston in the early forties, but I have encountered no evidence of any after that. The other leading contractor was John Henniker, who worked in close cooperation with Thomlinson. See Atkinson to Thomlinson, Dec. 20, 1740, *NHSP*, XVIII, 167, and unsigned note, Dec. 1, 1757, Wentworth Papers, NHHS; Peter Livius to Henry Muilman, Feb. 6, 1764, Livius Letter Book, 19; Robert G. Albion, *Forests and Sea Power: The Timber Problem of the Royal Navy, 1652–1862* (Cambridge, Mass., 1926), 56, 235.
24. Livius to John Raymond, June 18, 1765, Livius Letter Book, 59. For biographical details on Livius see *ibid.*, *passim*; Langdon Papers, 23, HSP; "Peter Livius" in Shipton, *Biographical Sketches*, XIII, 261–270.

Livius had good cause to lament that such conditions made masting "too perilous" for him to attempt, for he had some idea how profitable the trade could be. The exact terms of the naval contracts, he found, were "kept profound secrets" in Portsmouth "in order to deter anyone from attempting the contract;" nevertheless, even those who wanted "to diminish any opinion of their being very large" acknowledged the profits exceeded 100 per cent. Livius was not exaggerating. In 1764 a mast of twenty-four inches in diameter which cost a Portsmouth agent £6 5s. was worth about £35 to the contractor in England; a thirty-inch mast cost £25 10s. and sold for about £75; and a thirty-six-inch mast could be obtained for less than £100 while selling for about £180.[25] Benning Wentworth was bankrupt when he was appointed governor—indeed his appointment was largely a product of the political influence of his creditors—and his cut in the mast trade combined with his salary and his fees as governor and surveyor general made him in time a wealthy man. The mast agent Mark Hunking Wentworth in 1754 was by far the largest taxpayer in Portsmouth, paying 3 per cent of the town's entire tax. Masting was without doubt, as Livius concluded, "a business where the profits are very great, morally certain and attended with very little trouble."[26]

The Wentworths' influence in England gave them control over royal appointments in New Hampshire and allowed them to dominate the mast trade. It did not, however, guarantee them the cooperation and approval of their fellow provincial inhabitants. To be sure, men who lived in mid-eighteenth-century America expected that wealth, social superiority, and political preferment would go hand in hand and thus were conditioned to respect any governing aristocracy. But in some colonies royal officials commanded little allegiance. They found their effective authority undermined by their inability to reward those whose political support was necessary to the successful conduct of everyday governmental affairs. The oligarchy

25. Livius to Raymond, June 18, 1765, and Livius to Henry Muilman, May 14, 1764, Livius Letter Book, 38, 59; Malone, *Pine Trees and Politics*, 147. In his letter to Muilman, Livius reports mast costs to colonial agents; Malone in his Appendix B has charted mast prices from information in admiralty ledgers. Prices in general doubled between 1740 and 1758, then began to decline.

26. Portsmouth Tax Records, City Hall, Portsmouth, New Hampshire; Livius to Muilman, May 14, 1764, Livius Letter Book, 36.

in New Hampshire, however, suffered from no such inability. Circumstances in the province gave the Wentworths opportunity to construct a broad economic and political foundation on which their provincial authority could rest. They took every advantage of their opportunity.

Prerevolutionary New Hampshire depended economically on the export of masts, ships, and lumber, which were marketed in England, Spain, Newfoundland, and the West Indies in exchange for specie, raw materials, or finished goods. All of settled New Hampshire engaged in the trade. In the Great Bay area and up what is now Salmon Falls River, hundreds of lumbermen provided the raw materials for building vessels near Portsmouth and for their future cargoes; along the Merrimack, woodsmen worked to supply ships at Newburyport. Indeed, so many men were engaged in lumbering that provincial merchants had to import grain and other foodstuffs. And there was little reason to think the trade would decline; even in the 1750s the forests of New Hampshire seemed to provide an endless supply of timber.[27]

But one threat to the lumber trade did exist. The imperial government considered New Hampshire an important source of naval stores. Fearful that colonists would destroy American forests in their eagerness to build up trade, the admiralty had urged Parliament and the ministry to enact regulations protecting American forests from waste, and by the time Wentworth became governor of New Hampshire, Parliament had prohibited the cutting of any white pine trees on public property, and pines on private property which were twenty-four inches or more in diameter two feet from the base.[28] Had the colonists been forced to obey the regulations, their trade might well have been destroyed. White pine boards constituted nearly all their export shipments.

As surveyor general charged with the enforcement of the white pine policy, Benning Wentworth made certain that nothing disturbed the lumber trade. Richard Waldron, searching in 1748 for a

---

27. Fairchild, *William Pepperrell*, 61–66; Samuel J. McKinley, "Economic History of Portsmouth," unpub. diss. Harvard University, 1931, *passim*; Livius to Muilman, Jan. 9, 1764, Livius Letter Book, 6; Nathaniel Adams, *Annals of Portsmouth* (Portsmouth, 1825), 258; Belknap, *History*, III, 203–212.

28. Malone, *Pine Trees and Politics*, chaps. 5, 6; Bernhard Knollenberg, *Origin of the American Revolution: 1759–1766* (New York, 1960), 127–128; Albion, *Forests and Sea Power*, 241–256.

way to undermine the ministry's good opinion of Wentworth, wrote that there was "one thing, which if rightly represented . . . would break the Don[29] in pieces; that is the waste of the King's timber." But Waldron knew that "hardly a man in the province would mention it, either as a complaint or a witness, as most of the people" made "earnings out of the unrighteous indulgence." They made their earnings because the mast agent agreed to accept all good-quality masts tendered to him, regardless of current contract demands, and the surveyor licensed all who supplied masts to the agent. The arrangement meant that Mark Wentworth had a "dock of masts always ready to supply the wants of those . . . in need, at his own price . . . and the countrymen cut what trees they please, making masts of the best . . . and converting the rest into mill logs for their own use." Only a court of inquiry, Waldron lamented, could expose the "affair . . . and moving in it would be one of the most unpopular things in the world." During Wentworth's governorship there were about a dozen seizures of illegally cut timber —the logs were sometimes bought back at auctions by the same people from whom they had been seized—and no successful prosecutions of millmen. No wonder Richard Waldron had difficulty exciting the inhabitants of the colony about the iniquities of Wentworth's administration.[30]

There were other reasons for acquiescence in family rule. The ambitious colonist identified wealth with land ownership, and when he needed land for lumbering, farming, settlement, or speculation, he wanted to get it cheaply. Land was plentiful in New Hampshire and its cost reasonable. But if a man cooperated with those in power, he might acquire a huge estate with little expense at all, for the members of the clan had absolute control over vast areas of ungranted territory in the province.

The Wentworths exercised control in part through the Masonian proprietorship. Late in the 1730s John Thomlinson had arranged for the New Hampshire assembly to purchase John Tufton Mason's

29. Waldron had a variety of names for Governor Wentworth, who often boasted of his former exploits in Spain.

30. Waldron to Belcher, Sept. 16, 1748, in John Farmer and Jacob B. Moore, eds., *Collections, Historical and Miscellaneous*, III (Concord, 1824), 256. See also Malone, *Pine Trees and Politics*, 131–132. The only complaint I have found came after Wentworth began to assess an informal fee of "five of the best logs" on each company of cutters; he wanted the timber to build his mansion. See Nathaniel Rolfe to B. Rolfe, Mar. 12, 1756, State Papers, 1620–1789, NHA.

claim to ownership of all wastelands within sixty miles of New Hampshire's coast. But the house members in 1744 balked at payment unless disposal of the lands was left to them—a demand to which neither governor nor council would agree. While the assembly bickered, a group of twelve Portsmouth merchants led by Atkinson and Mark Wentworth secretly paid Thomlinson for the purchase and began to organize their proprietorship.[31] Their move astounded even the governor: he contemplated instituting proceedings against the proprietors to recover the land for the crown and informed his ministerial superiors that he felt the proprietors' power should be contained.[32] But when officials at Whitehall said nothing, Wentworth pursued the matter no further.

Although the legality of the purchase and the validity of Mason's title were both questionable, provincial inhabitants made little complaints against the proceedings. The Masonian proprietors were quick to confirm all actual settlers in their possessions and to issue quitclaim deeds to the existing towns in the purchase. Furthermore, it soon became evident that the proprietors' terms for granting unsettled lands were so generous that objection would have been ridiculous. Rather than attempting direct sale in a province where money was scarce and liquid capital mostly in their own hands, the proprietors simply gave town charters to those who met with their approval, offered an additional one hundred acres for each settled European immigrant, and reserved plots in each township for themselves. Their profits came from the increase in value of their own plots resulting from the settlement they encouraged.[33]

Those who sought land grants outside the Masonian patent had to deal with a governor and council they found equally accommodating. Wentworth had a seemingly endless supply of townships at his disposal. As far as he was concerned, the settlement of the boundary dispute with Massachusetts gave New Hampshire jurisdiction over all land north of the boundary as far west as what is now New York. Much of the territory which before settlement of the bound-

31. *NHSP,* V, 409–470. The family relationship of the various proprietors has been tabulated by Otis G. Hammond, "The Mason Title and Its Relations to New Hampshire and Massachusetts," in *Proceedings of the American Antiquarian Society,* 26 (1916), 256–257. It provides an excellent history of the proprietorship.
32. Wentworth to Board of Trade, Mar. 23, 1750/1, *NHSP,* XVIII, 390–400; Looney, "The King's Representative," 76–81.
33. *NHSP,* VI, 896–904; Hammond, "The Mason Title," 258–262.

ary dispute had been granted to influential Massachusetts men he regranted to the same men. They and new grantees found quitrents nominal and fees moderate; in some cases Wentworth may have asked no fees at all.[34] And although the governor did require that some of his friends be included as proprietors of townships; that schools, the first settled minister, the Society for the Propagation of the Gospel, and the Church of England be reserved one share each; and that a large plot, usually 500 acres but sometimes as much as 800 acres, be reserved for His Majesty's royal governor, no one complained.[35] There was land enough for all. By 1765 Wentworth had granted 124 townships, and few men of means and ambition in New Hampshire had failed to increase their estates.[36]

Wentworth had still another way of repaying the faithful or punishing the recalcitrant: as governor of New Hampshire he had no trouble finding offices to distribute or to withhold. Richard Waldron informed Isaac Royall, when encouraging him in 1748 to seek the governorship, that as chief magistrate he would appoint "Judges and Justices . . . the Secretary, Treasurer, Sheriff, Register of Probate and the military officers" and recommend appointment of clerks to the courts. Waldron knew how effective patronage could be. Under Belcher he had been secretary of the province, judge of the inferior and probate courts, councilor, justice of the peace, and for nearly a decade the governor's unofficial lieutenant in charge of New Hampshire; by 1743 Wentworth had stripped him of every office, and Belcher was surprised that the treasurer, the sheriff, and the clerk

34. George P. Anderson's paper, "Land Grants Made in New Hampshire by Governor Benning Wentworth to Boston Men," in *PCSM*, XXV: *Transactions* (1922–1924), 33–38; Atkinson to Thomlinson, Nov. 19, 1752, *NHSP*, VI, 161; Charles B. Kinney, Jr., *Church and State: The Struggle for Separation in New Hampshire, 1630–1900* (New York, 1955), 69; William H. Fry, *New Hampshire as a Royal Province* (New York, 1908), 290–324; *NHSP*, XXIV–XXVI, *passim*; Matt B. Jones, *Vermont in the Making, 1750–1777* (Cambridge, Mass., 1939), 52–53.

35. Some astounding paper fortunes were accumulated in this way. Wentworth himself owned close to 100,000 acres. Friends John Nelson, John Temple, and James Nevin had shares in from 19 to 46 townships; brothers Mark and John and cousin Theodore were equally well treated. See Roy H. Akagi, *Town Proprietors of the New England Colonies: A Study of Their Development, Organization, Activities and Controversies, 1620–1770* (Philadelphia, 1924), 212; Joseph B. Walker, "The Controversy between the Proprietors of Bow and Those of Penny Cook, 1727–1789," in *Proceedings of the New Hampshire Historical Society*, 3 (1895–1899), 269; *NHSP*, XXIV–XXVI, *passim*.

36. For a typical example, see William H. Brown, *Colonel John Goffe* (Manchester, 1950).

of courts had "stood so long."[37] But the governor showed more interest in courting friends than in punishing enemies. Wentworth bestowed justice-of-the-peace commissions so prodigally that by the sixties they had become objects of ridicule. If Jeremy Belknap's information was correct, there were but twenty-five justices in the entire province when Wentworth arrived, and he appointed that many again from Portsmouth alone. In 1765 a local wag described Wentworth's administration as "the happy silver age/ When magistrates, profoundly sage/ O'erspread the land; and made it seems/ Justice run down the streets in streams."[38]

If the governor ran out of civil commissions, there were always military honors to bestow. Atkinson was a full colonel in the militia, as were Nathaniel Meserve of Portsmouth and Thomas Wallingford of Dover (both Masonian proprietors), Joseph Blanchard of Dunstable (surveyor for the Masonian proprietors), John Goffe of Bedford, and Meshech Weare of Hampton Falls. Most of these and other appointees were capable and effective military leaders, but Wentworth's selection of his own young sons and a ten-year-old nephew as officers can hardly have improved the military efficiency of the province. Such appointments irritated his enemies, particularly since Wentworth simultaneously cashiered or failed to promote Waldron's son Thomas and others, like John Sherburne and Peter Gilman of the Exeter family which had strongly supported Belcher, whom he felt he could not trust. Wentworth had been serious in his observation when extending commissions that "as the power is absolutely in me, I can remove at pleasure if there is any occasion."[39]

Most royal governors in colonial America possessed the same official powers as did Benning Wentworth, yet found themselves unable to control the behavior of provincial judicial and legislative

37. Waldron to Royall, Sept. 16, 1748, *NHSP,* VI, 60; "Richard Waldron," in Shipton, *Biographical Sketches,* V, 655–656; Wentworth to Board of Trade, Mar. 23, 1750/1, *NHSP,* XVIII, 397; Belcher to Waldron, Apr. 3, 1742, *Collections of the New Hampshire Historical Society* (Concord, 1824–1939), IV, 99.
38. Belknap, *History,* II, 340; *Portsmouth Mercury,* Oct. 7, 1765, printed in Belknap, *History,* II, 341.
39. Weare Papers, II, 82, NHA; Batchellor and Metcalf, eds., *Laws of New Hampshire,* II, 595; Waldron to Belcher, Sept. 24, 1747, *NHSP,* VI, 40; Waldron to Royall, Apr. 22, 1748, *NHSP,* VI, 48; Waldron to Belcher, July 1, 1748, in Farmer and Moore, eds., *Collections,* III, 238; Wentworth to Thomlinson, Oct. 21, 1743, Howard, ed., *Records,* I, 207.

officials. The effectiveness of royal government in New Hampshire, however, was never seriously compromised during Wentworth's administration. Councilors, judges, and house representatives remained for the most part loyal to their appointed ruler; and the one serious challenge to family and royal government, which came in the late 1740s, met with decisive defeat. In fact, the pattern of influence which the merchant oligarchy developed through their extensive connections in England and their distribution of political and economic rewards made Wentworth's management of provincial political institutions a relatively easy task.

The council presented no problems at all. Wentworth's dismissal of Waldron warned those already on the council that if they wished to retain the social prestige and influence over land grants and political patronage that membership provided they had better cooperate with the governor. Furthermore, the support of Thomlinson and Wentworth at Whitehall was necessary before any candidate for appointment could obtain his mandamus; when vacancies occurred, friends and relatives of the governor found themselves in an enviable position. Of the twelve councilors chosen between 1741 and 1764, all except William Temple—a nonresident friend of the governor— were Portsmouth merchants, and most were Anglicans. In 1753 a Congregational minister complained that the council had become an Anglican stronghold; a decade later the Reverend Arthur Browne, as chaplain of the council, offered prayers with a group which included a brother, a brother-in-law, a nephew, and five other relatives of the governor.[40]

Once the Belcher men had been weeded out or silenced, the council had no reason to disagree with its governor except for the rare cases when Wentworth's vindictiveness seemed insupportable even to his merchant associates. As the members of the upper house of the legislature, the councilors consistently backed their benefactor in disputes with the lower house. They voted against taxes on unimproved lands, supported Wentworth's financial and military plans, and helped persuade reluctant representatives to comply with the governor's legislative requests. When the house and governor came

40. Wentworth to Board of Trade, Mar. 23, 1750/1, and Atkinson to Thomlinson, Jan. 28, 1758, *NHSP*, XVIII, 398, 473; John Odlin to Dr. Avery, June 1753, in NHHS, *Collections*, IX, 22. Councilors are listed in Belknap, *History*, II, 487. Brewster, *Rambles*, and Wentworth, *Wentworth Genealogy*, I, contain scattered information on most colonial council members.

to such an impasse that the assembly went without meeting for more than three years, the councilors continued to assist Wentworth in his administration.[41] As his sworn advisers it was their legal duty; as his friends and relatives it was their inclination.

Cooperation between governor and council meant family domination of the court system. Not only were judicial appointments made by Wentworth and the councilors, but together they acted without jury as a final court of appeals on matters both civil and criminal. Understandably the Court of Appeals alienated some people. Belknap, who moved to New Hampshire in the mid-sixties, reported that "frequent complaints were made of partiality," particularly in cases where council members had earlier sat as judges in the decisions being appealed. John Sherburne, son of a prominent Congregational merchant, became enraged at the situation: as primary legatee of his father's will he saw the will disallowed because the Court of Appeals would not accept the testimony of Portsmouth's leading Congregational ministers, Samuel Haven and Samuel Langdon. Sherburne possessed the wealth and patience to seek a reversal in England. But few others could afford to fight decisions of the Court of Appeals.[42]

Family influence in the superior, inferior, and probate courts was no less obvious. As Belknap noted, "members of the Council" and others "devoted to the interest of the governor or personally related to him" filled court offices. When Wentworth became governor the situation had been different. Actually he made no wholesale purge; but he was determined to see that judges remained loyal to his personal rule. In 1754 he forced the resignation of Chief Justice Ellis Huske, who a few years before had been an accomplice of Waldron in the attempt to oust Wentworth from the governorship, and replaced him with Atkinson. When the house refused to vote Atkinson a salary, Wentworth agreed to pay it himself. And as other judges resigned or died, Wentworth put friends and relatives in office.[43]

The influence of the merchant oligarchy reached even deeper into

41. NHSP, V, 126, 458, and *passim*, and VI, 341, 448–486; Jackson T. Main, *The Upper House in Revolutionary America, 1763–1788* (Madison, 1967), 63–67.
42. Fry, *New Hampshire*, 119–127, 458; Belknap, History, III, 256; Add. MSS no. 36218, fols. 147–150 (transcripts in LC); John Huske to [John Sherburne], Apr. 11, 1765, New Hamp. Misc. MSS; Joseph H. Smith, *Appeals to the Privy Council from the American Plantations* (New York, 1950), 667–670.
43. Belknap, *History*, III, 256; NHSP, VI, 339, 418, 721, and XVIII, 496; Charles H. Bell, *The Bench and Bar of New Hampshire* (Boston, 1894), 18.

the judicial system. Those who had interest with court officials could sometimes obtain a hearing out of court. The practice of "watering the jury"—the phrase is Belknap's—was familiar, and since all courts met in Portsmouth, it was not difficult to find jurors sympathetic to royal government. Wentworth had no intention of disturbing the situation. In 1737 the Privy Council had disallowed a law locating courts in Exeter, on the ground that inland juries would be biased in cases involving illegal lumbering. The argument seemed so sound that Wentworth used it to justify his refusal in 1760 to go along with an assembly plan to divide the province into counties and organize a county court system. "I hope your lordships will think I am as well qualified to judge" as the assembly when such a division should be made, he wrote to the Board of Trade, "and my sentiments are fixed that this is the most improper time to make any alteration."[44]

Yet in spite of family influence in the courts, there was no widespread disapproval of the judicial system. Wentworth's associates were better educated and more qualified for judicial posts than all but a few men in the province. And the governor did not restrict judicial appointments to his merchant relatives. Meshech Weare, for example, a Harvard graduate whose father and grandfather had been provincial political leaders and who himself had become town moderator of Hampton Falls early in his twenties, had no particular family connection with the governor and was not a merchant; yet he was a permanent justice of the Superior Court of Common Pleas from 1747 to 1776, as well as a trusted militia leader.[45] In an age when it was generally assumed that justice would be meted out by "the better sort of people," exclusiveness on the bench did not trouble the ordinary citizen, who, in any case, rarely carried legal matters further than the local justice of the peace.

One specific legal problem in which the interests of New Hampshire as a whole were involved made family influence in the court system seem to some a positive good. The problem involved a con-

44. Belknap, *History*, III, 256; James Munro, ed., *Acts of the Privy Council of England, Colonial Series* (London, 1908–   ), III, 453; *NHSP*, VI, 454, 722–726, 749, and 766; Wentworth to Board of Trade, Aug. 13, 1760, C.O. 5/928.
45. "Theodore Atkinson," in Shipton, *Biographical Sketches*, VI, 221–231, and "Meshech Weare," *ibid.*, IX, 590–596. A more recent study of Weare is Avery J. Butters, "New Hampshire History and the Public Career of Meshech Weare, 1713 to 1786," unpub. diss. Fordham University, 1961.

troversy between the proprietors of the township of Rumford and the proprietors of the township of Bow. Years before settlement of the Massachusetts–New Hampshire boundary dispute, a group of Bay State Congregationalists under the leadership of their minister, Timothy Walker, had created a prospering agricultural community near the junction of the Contoocook and Merrimack rivers. The deed to their township of Rumford had been granted by Massachusetts in 1727, but much of the same land was shortly thereafter granted as the township of Bow by Lieutenant Governor John Wentworth. During the 1740s Walker and his congregation were allowed to run their affairs as a district of New Hampshire and were even sent a precept for the assembly election of 1748. In 1749, however, the Bow proprietors, who included Wentworth, three of his brothers, Atkinson, and Jaffrey, brought suit in the New Hampshire courts against settlers under the Rumford deed, and the courts decided in their favor. Walker, armed with a grant from the Massachusetts General Court and letters of introduction from Jonathan Mayhew and the New Hampshire convention of ministers, sailed to England with a petition for redress.[46]

The Rumford proprietors sent Walker because they had no hope of redress in New Hampshire courts. The fact that "the Governor and most of the Council" were "proprietors of Bow" and responsible for appointing judges was only part of the trouble. The petitioners felt that any New Hampshire jury would manifest "prejudices by reason of relations, favor or interest in similar causes." The people of New Hampshire, they lamented, are "generally disaffected to your petitioners on account of their deriving their titles from the Massachusetts." The proprietors described the situation accurately, for a determination in favor of the Rumford claim would have threatened anyone holding title in New Hampshire to land also claimed under a Massachusetts deed. Waldron, the Exeter Gilmans, and hundreds of others held such titles. When the New Hampshire assembly learned of Walker's departure, they voted to lend the Bow proprietors £100 to finance Thomlinson's defense against Walker's appeal. The Rumford-Bow case helps explain why the provincial assembly in 1767

46. Two competent summaries are Walker, "The Controversy," 261–292, and Akagi, *Town Proprietors*, 165–174. Documents concerning the dispute are scattered: see Add. MSS no. 36218, fols. 181–192 (transcripts in LC); Walker Papers, I, NHHS; New Hampshire Miscellaneous, box 1, NYPL; *NHSP*, IX, 134–139, 349–358, and 354; Waldron to Belcher, Feb. 9, 1753, Waldron Papers, II, no. 115, NHHS.

made a point of thanking Benning Wentworth particularly for his "steady administration of justice."[47]

Prevailing economic conditions, the kinship structure of Portsmouth's merchant community, and the accepted constitutional framework of provincial government made it possible for Benning Wentworth and his associates to maintain control of New Hampshire's executive and judicial institutions, as long as they retained their influence in England. Different circumstances prevailed in the lower house of the legislature. Members of the House of Representatives were elected in town meetings by freeholders over whom the Wentworths had little direct influence. As elected representatives they customarily felt more responsible to their local constituents than to imperial interests or the needs of the merchant aristocracy. In the house, therefore, the Wentworths could not expect to dominate as they did in the council and courts.

The goal of the Wentworths in the house, however, was not complete political domination. Quite to the contrary, they expected house members to assume independent responsibility for many of New Hampshire's internal affairs. The house appointed excise collectors, handled petitions from individuals and communities, and determined the outcome of disputes between the units of local government. In addition the governor and councilors depended often on representatives to make recommendations for local judicial and military posts. The arrangements satisfied most elected representatives. They had sought or accepted election in part because membership gave them access to those sources of authority over local affairs lodged in the provincial government. Many representatives, an observer noted, were so limited in their concerns that they "never find they have anything to do in the House when there is nothing on the tapis in which the town or borough which chose them is not immediately concerned."[48] The governor and his advisers had neither the need nor the desire to become involved in such local business.

What Benning Wentworth did expect from the house was that it help him fulfill his responsibilities as New Hampshire's royal

47. Walker Papers, I, 27, printed in Walker, "The Controversy," 278–281; "A State of a Case . . ." New Hamp. Misc., box 1, NYPL; *NHSP*, VI, 294, IX, 67–68, and VII, 116.

48. *New Hampshire Gazette*, (Portsmouth), Nov. 3, 1758. Vols. IX and XI–XIII of *NHSP* contain records of petitions handled in the assembly.

governor. If the house threatened in any way to prevent him from obeying what he considered to be his duty, or from pleasing those who at any time could remove him from his offices, then Wentworth could no longer afford to let its members act without interference. Furthermore, the governor understood that the House of Representatives provided those with wealth and ambition a convenient place for maneuvering in the game of imperial politics. During the 1740s the house contained only twenty members. Since most of these members, Wentworth explained to his superiors at Whitehall, "were very little acquainted with men of the world," any house member with education and acknowledged social superiority—including the governor's personal enemies—automatically commanded great influence. Such circumstances, Wentworth continued, made it possible for "two or three designing persons, under pretence of defending the liberties of the people and opposing the King's Governor, to obtain followers." He wrote from experience: in the 1730s he and Atkinson as house representatives had been able to harness resentment against royal authority in their efforts to embarrass Governor Belcher.[49] From the beginning of his administration, then, Wentworth acted upon his knowledge that house opposition was most dangerous when led by those capable of replacing him in his position of political authority.

As governor, Wentworth could utilize both the prerogative and his royal instructions as constitutional weapons in disagreements with his house. He had the right to convene, adjourn, prorogue, or dissolve the assembly at any time. He could veto legislation, negative the choice of house speaker, and if necessary attempt to change personnel in the house by calling for new elections. Existing laws worked to the advantage of the governor in such elections. In the first place, representatives were required to have £300 of ratable estate: men of such wealth, particularly in frontier communities, were apt to have gained their wealth through dealing with the Wentworths in the masting business, or through receiving land grants from the governor. In addition the governor claimed the right to issue precepts to previously unrepresented communities, many of

49. Wentworth to Board of Trade, Mar. 23, 1750/1, *NHSP*, XVIII, 396; same to same, Nov. 8, 1747, C.O. 5/926; *NHSP*, IV, 794, 802. The struggles between Governor Belcher and the House of Representatives are described in Belknap, *History*, II, 101–157.

which he could be reasonably certain would return representatives friendly to his administration. The house members naturally claimed the right to control their own representation and challenged Wentworth's use of his other constitutional powers. But they were unsuccessful.[50]

The general circumstances of Wentworth's administration helped him in his efforts to prevent the house from obstructing his exercise of royal authority. He held office during wartime in a province continuously threatened by encroachments from the French and Indians. When he demanded appropriations to support British military policy in America, the assembly usually complied with his requests; as individuals they benefited from supply contracts and as representatives of the people they sought protection of the frontiers. Moreover, the only way to finance war was to issue paper money backed by future taxes. Since provincial residents and their elected representatives found business easier to conduct with paper currency than without, they encouraged their chief magistrate to permit emissions and applauded his success in obtaining royal permission for what in peacetime would not have been allowed.[51]

The financial independence of the governor further strengthened his hand in dealing with the house. To be sure, Wentworth did not hesitate to seek an adequate salary; and in the early part of his administration he needed the money to pay debts.[52] But as his fortune accumulated, his dependence on the assembly decreased. By the time organized resistance to his rule had developed in the house, Wentworth had sufficient wealth to go without salary for nearly four years. He could afford, a few years later, to pay Atkinson as chief justice of the superior court when the house refused to make an appropriation for his salary.

Wentworth and the council could, in addition, reward cooperative house members directly. "I suppose," wrote Waldron in 1742 after the governor had been voted a salary even he considered adequate, "our Assembly expect to be landlords of thousands and thousands of acres, esteeming but reasonable, for generous grants of money, to have a return of as generous grants of land, *huzza, huzza, huzza.*"

50. *NHSP*, VI, 94; Fry, *New Hampshire*, 66–208.
51. *NHSP*, V and VI, *passim*; *New Hampshire Gazette*, Jan. 21, 1757, and Mar. 23, 1758. For a list of paper money issues see B. V. Ratchford, *American State Debts* (Durham, 1941), 26–28.
52. For a typical salary controversy see *NHSP*, V, 136–153.

Wentworth did not disappoint them. His generosity, particularly in the fifties, became so lavish that of the thirty-one representatives in the house which met in 1764, all but three new members had been granted land in from one to eleven towns. The next year, during the Stamp Act crisis, he granted an entire township to the house members. The distribution of political patronage and military supply contracts could be used to serve the same purpose.[53] And the possibility that Wentworth might as surveyor general institute proceedings against those who were engaged in illegal lumbering may also have deterred some representatives from opposing their royal governor.

The normal activity of the assembly reflected the degree to which the political management of New Hampshire was in the hands of Governor Wentworth. Except in times of military crisis, there was little for the house to do. Sometimes it went six months without meeting, and when it did meet, it often lacked a quorum. Those members who attended worked in small committees appointed to consider local and personal petitions. When they met as a house it was not for general debate but rather to listen to the governor speak or to hear a bill which had been prepared by Wentworth, Atkinson, and their associates in the assembly. House leaders worked closely with their executive; as a result political disagreements often were compromised before reaching the floor of the house. Wentworth contributed to this harmony by omitting sessions during planting and harvesting, and by inviting representatives to Little Harbour to drink the King's health.[54]

It is not surprising then that for much of Wentworth's administration relations between the governor and house remained relatively amicable. The terms of the boundary settlement, the establishment of an independent governorship, and the redistribution of patronage and land grants all helped to prevent serious conflicts during the first few years of Wentworth's administration. Between 1752 and Wentworth's resignation fifteen years later the house and governor

53. Waldron to Pepperrell, Mar. 26, 1742, *NEHGR*, 19 (1865), 223; Looney, "The King's Representative," 141; *NHSP*, VII, 56; "Meshech Weare," in Shipton, *Biographical Sketches*, IX, 593; Belknap, *History*, II, 277.

54. *NHSP*, VI, 158, 169, 248, 321, 790, 830, and VII, 49–50; Wentworth to Amherst, Mar. 27, 1761, and June 18, 1762, War Office, 34, XXVII (photostats in L.C.); Wentworth to Atkinson, Mar. 24, 1755, Province Papers, Correspondence, II, 177.

got along equally well. The usual disputes concerning salary, the sources of tax revenue, the raising of troops and supplies for war all were compromised, although Wentworth, like other colonial governors, complained constantly about house control of financial appropriations. The controversy over judges' salaries and the proposed division into counties was dropped before animosities became intense. Even during the Stamp Act crisis the royal governor and his assembly reached agreement on what should be done: the house forwarded a protest to Thomlinson, but it refused to send a representative to the Stamp Act Congress.[55]

One major struggle, however, did take place between the governor and house. Trouble first appeared in 1744 and four years later exploded with such intensity that Wentworth and the legislature remained at loggerheads until 1752. The issues which precipitated the conflict were both constitutional and personal. When it was all over, Wentworth had succeeded in defending royal prerogative, had completely eliminated the immediate threat to family government, and had demonstrated the basic strength of his administration so plainly that no one in New Hampshire dared challenge his authority again.[56]

The original dispute in 1744 arose when the house, led by former supporters of Governor Belcher, refused to vote supplies for Fort Dummer, a Connecticut Valley outpost so distant from existing provincial settlements that representatives felt it offered no military protection to New Hampshire residents. The opposition justified its conduct in constitutional terms. "We think ourselves at liberty," they explained, "fully and freely to remonstrate against any part of your Excellency's public conduct, which we apprehend affects the privileges of the House or the people we represent." As free men and representatives of free men they argued that the king's governor, "however much he may be exalted above us by the honor he receives from His Majesty's commission, is yet liable to mistakes and errors in his conduct, and may do wrong though his royal master cannot." Wentworth defended his conduct as defense of the royal

55. John Sherburne to John Huske, Feb. 9, and Aug. 20, 1754, New Hamp. Misc. MSS; *NHSP*, VI, *passim*; Belknap, *History*, II, 277; Looney, "The King's Representative," 131–141.

56. One minor qualification to this last statement should be made. In 1761, House Speaker Henry Sherburne successfully urged the assembly to send the ministry a formal complaint against Wentworth, but the ministry refused to consider it. See James Nevin to Atkinson, Nov. 14, 1761, *NHSP*, XVIII, 543.

prerogative—he had been given specific instructions to have Fort Dummer supplied—and then dissolved the assembly and called for new elections.[57]

Wentworth did not leave the results of the new elections to chance. He issued election precepts to several communities in the Merrimack Valley where he knew men supporting his legislative demands would be elected. At the same time he used what influence he had in communities already represented in the legislature to obtain the election of sympathetic candidates. In Dover, Thomas Wallingford, a Masonian proprietor and local selectman, engineered the election of a delegation favorable to Wentworth; the governor undoubtedly received similar assistance elsewhere. The disputed issue itself tended to help the governor, for the threat of war with France made Wentworth's argument for protecting the frontier difficult for voters to resist. Of the twenty assembly members returned, nine were new; eight of these voted to supply Fort Dummer. When the house refused to seat members elected in newly represented communities, Wentworth did not press the issue. He had gained his main objective and did not want to run the risk of alienating a house which continued to support him when he asked for troops and supplies for the attack on Louisbourg and defense of the province.[58]

By 1748, when the governor was required by the provincial triennial act to call for new elections, antagonism to Wentworth and his associates had increased. Many had been angered by the governor's military appointments. Those whose political cooperation with Wentworth during the war had resulted more from the military threat than from any fondness for their executive again questioned the wisdom of supplying Fort Dummer. Most important, the opposition now had an effective leader, Richard Waldron, who planned to use the assembly elections in furthering his plans "to oust Diego" from the governorship.[59]

Ever since Wentworth's appointment Waldron had yearned to rid the province of those who were responsible for his own political

57. Documents concerning the Fort Dummer controversy are in *NHSP*, V, 226–339, esp. 301–339; the quotation is from 307.

58. *NHSP*, V, 260–265, 304–339, and XI, 515–516.

59. *NHSP*, V, 478–480, and XVIII, 332–353; Waldron to Belcher, July 1, 1748, in Farmer and Moore, eds., *Collections*, III, 227. Much correspondence from Waldron's plot has been preserved in the Waldron Papers and the Belcher Papers, III. Some of the letters have been printed in *NHSP*, VI, 39–68, and Farmer and Moore, eds., *Collections*, III.

ruin. His correspondence with Belcher included frequent suggestions on the strategy he and his kinsman might employ to turn the tables on the Wentworth clan. Belcher's interest waned after his appointment as governor of New Jersey, but throughout the forties Waldron's increased. A New Light Congregationalist, he felt that Anglican officials who scorned Puritanism (the Wentworths had taken no part in the religious revival inspired by George Whitefield) and flaunted traditional standards of public morality by conducting "balls," "parties," and "other gay scenes of life," were corrupting his native province.[60] A series of personal misfortunes, capped by the accidental death of his first son, further embittered the former councilor. After Wentworth blocked the military and political advancement of Thomas, the only remaining son, Waldron could contain himself no longer. Destruction of family government became the consuming ambition of his life.[61]

Waldron found others prepared to join in his scheme. In Portsmouth, fellow New Lights Ellis Huske and Henry Sherburne disliked the religious and political orientation of their rulers. Malcontents in Exeter—where Whitefield had been surprised to find that the "power of God" was manifest "chiefly among the rich"—were even easier for Waldron to locate, for Wentworth had alienated the politically prominent Gilman family. Similarly, Dover and Hampton contained men of sufficient wealth and prestige to feel the loss of patronage Belcher's dismissal had meant. Waldron was doubtless aware that these four towns supplied eleven of the twenty house members.[62]

For support outside the assembly, Wentworth's antagonist sought help from a number of sources. Ellis Huske aspired to the governorship and possessed some influence through his brother, a lieutenant general in the British army. Waldron felt that Isaac Royall, a wealthy and ambitious Massachusetts merchant, would prove a better replacement for Wentworth, mostly because Royall expressed

60. Belcher-Waldron letters, Belcher Papers, III, nos. 112 to 141; Arthur Browne to SPG, July 24, 1742, in Rogers, *Glimpses*, 23. The quotations are from Waldron to Nicholas Gilman, Aug. 3, 1733, and Waldron to Greenwood, 1752, *NHSP*, XVIII, 50, 406.

61. Waldron to Belcher, Sept. 24, 1747, and Apr. 15, 1748, *NHSP*, VI, 39, 47; letters from Richard Waldron to Thomas Waldron, Miscellaneous Manuscripts, NYHS; Waldron-Belcher letters in Waldron Papers and Belcher Papers.

62. Earnest E. Ells, "An Unpublished Journal of George Whitefield," *Church History*, 7 (1938), 312, 338, 341; "Nicholas Gilman," in Shipton, *Biographical Sketches*, VII, 338–344; *NHSP*, V, 322, 330.

willingness to contribute £600 to the cause. Excited at the possibility of preferment, Royall obtained the services of Slingsby Bethell, a member of parliament from London, and offered to enlist the aid of Admiral Peter Warren, Admiral Edward Hawke, and George White-field himself. Governor Belcher refused to take an active part but contributed constant advice. Belcher considered the Kittery merchant William Pepperrell, hero of the Louisbourg expedition and an old merchant rival of the Wentworths, a stronger gubernatorial candidate than either Huske or Royall; Pepperrell seemed willing to replace Wentworth, who had accused him of military mismanagement. Pepperrell's son-in-law, Nathaniel Sparhawk, encouraged him and offered up to £12,000 for the surveyorship should he succeed. A few of Belcher's friends in Massachusetts joined forces as opposition to Wentworth grew.[63]

The members of Waldron's party close to the situation in New Hampshire expected that the impending assembly dissolution and elections would, as Royall commented, "prove great helps toward effecting our scheme." They knew that Wentworth had lost support among provincial voters, and that the governor had been unable to force house acceptance of members elected from communities to which he had sent election precepts. What they did not know, however, was that since the election of 1745 Wentworth had obtained through Thomlinson an additional instruction confirming his right to extend representation to deserving communities. Six new groups of towns received precepts for the 1748 election; they returned, among others, Thomas Packer, who was the governor's brother-in-law and the provincial sheriff, and Joseph Blanchard, the surveyor of the Masonian proprietors. When the assembly convened, Wentworth and Waldron—now the Hampton representative—clashed openly. Waldron controlled a majority of delegates from the old towns. Packer, Blanchard, and the other new representatives were refused house membership on the ground that only the house could extend its own representation; the old members then elected Waldron Speaker. Wentworth in turn disallowed the house's choice of

---

63. Belcher-Waldron and Royall-Waldron letters, *NHSP*, VI, 41–52, and Farmer and Moore, eds., *Collections*, III, 226, 254, 323; Waldron letters to Pepperrell, Waldron Papers, I, nos. 133, 136, 137; Sparhawk to Pepperrell, Sept. 24, 1749, and Mar. 8, 1750/1, in Usher Parsons, *Life of Sir William Pepperrell, Bart., The Only Native of New England Who Was Created a Baronet During Our Connection with the Mother Country* (Boston, 1855), 214–219; Fairchild, *William Pepperrell*, 179.

Speaker because delegates from the new towns had not been allowed to vote.[64]

Following the initial confrontation Waldron organized a massive assault on the Wentworth administration. His associates described the political crisis to the Massachusetts assembly agent, Richard Partridge, and asked his help in obtaining redress. Henry Sherburne, Jr., and perhaps Waldron himself, wrote directly to Thomlinson—they had no idea that Wentworth and the house agent were so intimate—and pleaded with him to do something. An assembly address to the citizens of New Hampshire exposing the need for a change in government was prepared. Meanwhile, as chairman of a house committee to present grievances to the crown, Waldron readied a formal petition of protest and sent it to Slingsby Bethell in London.[65]

The formal petition included only a statement of the malcontents' constitutional argument. The assembly possessed, it asserted, the privilege of determining its own representation and its own speaker; the governor had denied these rights by issuing election precepts and by rejecting Waldron; the normal political processes of the province had been brought to a standstill by the governor's actions. In a letter to Bethell, Waldron exhibited no such restraint. The iniquities and depredations of the governor he described in detail. Wentworth had made "arbitrary attempts on our civil and religious privileges" and had been disrespectful to Congregational ministers; he had flaunted the assembly and threatened it with the prerogative; he had misused funds and made unjust civil and military appointments which favored those related to him. In short, the inhabitants of New Hampshire could be redeemed from what Waldron had earlier labeled their "Spanish bondage" only if His Majesty would "place a gentleman of better abilities, and a different disposition" in the governor's chair.[66]

64. Royall to Waldron, Apr. 11, 1748, *NHSP*, VI, 46; *ibid.*, 69–126, and XVIII, 339; Batchellor and Metcalf, eds., *Laws of New Hamp.*, II, 653; Thomlinson to Atkinson, Mar. 2, 1752, *NHSP*, XVIII, 403.

65. Thomlinson to Henry Sherburne, Jr., Nov. 13, 1749, *NHSP*, VI, 889; Waldron to Thomlinson, undated draft, Waldron Papers, II, no. 155; *NHSP*, VI, 63–64, 89–93, 99. Thomlinson told Sherburne he had nothing to do with the additional instructions.

66. Waldron *et al.* to Bethell, Apr. 13, 1749, *NHSP*, VI, 63–64; Waldron to Belcher, Mar. 10, 1748/9, in Farmer and Moore, eds., *Collections*, III, 226.

Even as those complaints were sent, Waldron must have suspected there would be no redemption. Wentworth had made known his possession of the additional instruction just at the time the house felt it had gained the upper hand. If Waldron remained hopeful in spite of the instruction, the reaction of those in England undoubtedly sobered his enthusiasm. Thomlinson read the petition and wrote back that if the "address was calculated and designed to turn out the Governor . . . in favor of a Massachusetts man," as he had been told, "it would not have been in your power, or in the power of the most sanguine of his enemies to remove him." If the controversy had taken place when New Hampshire was under the Massachusetts governor, Thomlinson pointed out, the assembly "might have been indulged." But one reason for separating the two had been to strengthen royal government where the crown's best supply of mast trees grew, and the Lords of Trade were in no mood to support the provincial assembly. In any case the assembly's constitutional position was weak. Why should New Hampshire demand fewer representatives when all the other provinces sought more? Thomlinson was not the only one to criticize the petition. John Thorpe informed Bethell that, if anything, the assembly petition would fix Wentworth "firmer in his seat" since he was acting in accordance with specific instructions. Another contact in London, Samuel Storke, wrote that Ferdinand Paris advised the assembly to draw up "a new petition against the Governor for illegal acts he may have committed" as it was the chancellor's opinion that Wentworth had power to negative its choice of speaker.[67]

Wentworth's enemies, however, were not convinced that constitutional issues would determine the outcome of their campaign. "Wishers and woulders are but poor house builders," Waldron was advised by Belcher; "a good soliciter at home with a pocket full of yellow dust might do something; but alas, where is such a one to be found?" Waldron thought he knew. An influential candidate for the governorship might obtain such a solicitor and, as Belcher recognized, Royall did not have the necessary interest; Sir William Pepperrell, still basking in the prestige of his Louisbourg victory, was far

67. *NHSP*, XVIII, 339; Thomlinson to Henry Sherburne, Jr., Nov. 13, 1749, *NHSP*, VI, 888–893; John Thorpe to Slingsby Bethell, July 5, 1749, *NHSP*, VI, 65; letter from Samuel Storke, Mar. 9, 1750/1, Weare Papers, II, NHA.

more powerful. After the fruitlessness of pushing Royall became evident, Waldron obtained a house address asking Sir William to seek the appointment. For a time it appeared he would accept, and the assemblymen warned their English supporters to prepare for a second assault. But late in 1750 Pepperrell informed Waldron he was not qualified to fill "the breach made in your state affairs."[68]

Pepperrell's refusal to seek the governorship meant the disintegration of Waldron's party. Belcher had once written that "the body [of New Hampshire] merchants are such a divided herd that it is to be feared they'll not be enough united to withstand the torrent that's going to be let loose from your province." In 1748 enough Portsmouth merchants had backed Waldron to return sympathetic candidates to the assembly. But their enthusiasm for his cause waned as Wentworth's strength became apparent. Henry Sherburne announced in February 1750 that he could no longer see his "way clear to be concerned"; and others like Daniel Warner became "very cool in the affair." Elsewhere those who had participated in the scheme to rid New Hampshire of Wentworth domination decided to come to terms with the governor.[69]

As soon as Wentworth sensed victory, he called for new elections and issued precepts to the same six groups of towns whose representatives the house had rejected before. This time there was little serious trouble. Although all but four of the rebellious representatives elected in 1748 returned to the new assembly, when it met the house voted to admit the new members and then elected a speaker—Meshech Weare—acceptable to the governor. Wentworth celebrated the house action, Belknap commented later, by making a "liberal distribution of commissions, civil and military," which inaugurated "an era of domestic reconciliation." The possibility of further disputes was reduced when Waldron resigned early in 1753 and died a few months later. Soon thereafter Waldron's political associate John Sherburne lamented that the house would make "no com-

---

68. Belcher to Waldron, Aug. 7, 1749, in Farmer and Moore, eds., *Collections*, III, 324; Assembly to Pepperrell, Dec. 19, 1749, Belknap Papers, 61.C.96, MHS; letter from Samuel Storke, Mar. 9, 1750/1, Weare Papers, II, NHA; Pepperrell to Waldron, Nov. 29, 1750, in Parsons, *Life of Pepperrell*, 231.

69. Belcher to Waldron, Sept. 10, 1743, Belcher Papers, III, no. 141; Waldron to Belcher, Apr. 15, 1748, *NHSP*, VI, 46; Henry Sherburne to Waldron, Feb. 13, 1750/1, Dreer Collection, Albany Convention, HSP; *NHSP*, VI, 127.

plaints at the Governor, do what he will." Wentworth had completely repulsed the legislative threat to his government.[70]

Benning Wentworth and his relatives and friends dominated New Hampshire politics from 1741 to 1767. Not only did they occupy most of the important appointive offices because they possessed "interest" in England, but through control of the council and effective use of their constitutional powers they also influenced the behavior of elected officials. They even interfered successfully in local elections when such interference seemed necessary to prevent the weakening of their authority.

The success of the Wentworths in maintaining their political ascendancy provided New Hampshire with both stable and effective government. Family control inhibited development of the type of factionalism which in many colonies undermined royal authority. It provided a system of personal influence which reinforced the formal constitutional structure. Furthermore, family government pleased the vast majority of provincial inhabitants, who shared with their rulers the benefits of existing economic and political conditions. When Benning Wentworth resigned his commission as governor, the assembly of New Hampshire thanked him for "the steady administration of justice, the quiet enjoyment of property, the civil and religious liberties and privileges his Majesty's good subjects of this province have experienced and possessed during this period."[71]

70. *NHSP*, VI, 127–130, 178–181; Belknap, *History*, II, 277; Sherburne to Huske, Aug. 20, 1754, New Hamp. Misc. MSS.
71. *NHSP*, VII, 116.

John Wentworth (1737–1820), New Hampshire's last royal governor. Copy by U. D. Tenney from a pastel drawn by John Singleton Copley in 1769.

2

Family and Royal
Authority under Attack,
1760–1773

The extraordinary web of political interests which sustained Benning Wentworth in office and provided New Hampshire with effective, stable, and popular government during the last fifteen years of his "reign" remained to some degree intact during the eight-year administration of his nephew and successor, John Wentworth. The new governor, through "interest" with politically influential men in England, managed to keep his two offices—he was also Surveyor of the King's Woods—until revolution forced him from the province. Family and friends benefited as well. Atkinson continued as secretary, chief justice, and the most influential member of the council. Other relatives of the governor and many of his personal associates who were not relatives received offices of profit and honor which enabled them to exercise political authority and participate in what John Adams once labeled "the pomps and vanities and ceremonies of that little world, Portsmouth."[1]

Furthermore, John Wentworth and his associates, at least compared to royal officials in other mainland colonies, exercised a good deal of influence over provincial politics. Cooperation between governor and assembly was the rule rather than the exception for much of his administration. New Hampshire's response to the Townshend duties was so moderate that officials in Whitehall congratulated

---

1. *Diary and Autobiography of John Adams*, ed. Lyman H. Butterfield (Cambridge, 1961), I, 355. See Lawrence S. Mayo, *John Wentworth, Governor of New Hampshire, 1767–1775* (Cambridge, 1921), and "John Wentworth" in Shipton, *Biographical Sketches*, XIII, 650–681, for general descriptions of Wentworth's administration.

Wentworth on his success in maintaining royal authority. When a disaffected councilor launched a massive assault on Wentworth from England, the House of Representatives remained quiet, and towns throughout the province passed resolutions praising their royal governor. As late as January 1774 the inhabitants of Londonderry publicly expressed "sentiments of gratitude and affection" for their governor's "person and administration."[2] On the surface it might have seemed that both family and royal government were still on a sound footing.

Beneath the surface, however, the Wentworths were in deep trouble. Developments in England and in New Hampshire had seriously weakened the political foundations of the family oligarchy. Conflict within the empire had both undermined the effectiveness of New Hampshire's royal government and accentuated the Wentworths' political problems. By the end of 1773 a few of the best-informed political observers in the province suspected that the entire structure of government might soon collapse.

Unfortunately for the Wentworths, John Thomlinson and those among his associates who had an interest in New Hampshire lost most of their political influence in the early 1760s. In part the problem was simply one of the passage of time. Ferdinand John Paris, who had been the New Hampshire agent's chief legal counsel, died in 1759. Thomlinson's health failed too; in 1761 a provincial resident traveling in England reported him so "broken down and past his labor" that he rarely visited London. Other friends of the family, including Mark Hunking Wentworth's son John, who went overseas in 1763 as his father's commercial agent, later confirmed the report.[3]

In response the New Hampshire Assembly, at Benning Wentworth's request, made Thomlinson's son, John Jr., joint agent with his father. But the arrangement did not work out well. Thomas Martin, a Portsmouth ship captain, wrote that "the young one's want of application hinders our being served from that quarter, and what is still against it is the small degree of intimacy subsisting between the two gentlemen." Martin may have misinterpreted what

2. Correspondence from the Earl of Hillsborough to John Wentworth, Apr. 4, 1768 to July 3, 1771, *NHSP*, VII, 343–344. The Londonderry statement is republished in Mayo, *Wentworth*, 85–86.

3. James Nevin to Atkinson, Nov. 14, 1761, *NHSP*, XVIII, 543; John Wentworth to Daniel Peirce, Feb. 15 and Mar. 1, 1766, Peirce Papers, PA.

he witnessed, for at least in 1764 young Thomlinson was working energetically for what he called in one letter to his father "our province." In any case, whatever influence the new agent possessed soon faded. He, too, became ill; he died early in 1767.[4]

The Wentworths, however, faced more serious problems than those stemming from Thomlinson's retirement. Their basic trouble lay in the simple fact that after the accession of George III Newcastle and his supporters had fallen from power and their replacements had little at stake in continued Wentworth rule. Furthermore, one influential man in England had a positive interest in seeing the Wentworths removed. John Huske, nephew of a lieutenant general in the British army and son of the man Benning Wentworth had forced to resign as Chief Justice of New Hampshire in 1755, had long yearned to help his friends and relatives in the colony. Earlier he had sought, without success, to replace Thomlinson as agent and aided Timothy Walker in his ill-fated attempt to battle the Wentworths in the case of *Rumford* v. *Bow*. Now Huske's position made him more effective. Early in 1763 Charles Townshend, his political patron, became president of the Board of Trade. Wentworth's antagonist also had the ear of the new first lord of the treasury, George Grenville, and the new chief justice, William Murray, the Earl of Mansfield. Huske himself became a member of Parliament in 1764.[5]

These developments soon disrupted the political calm which Benning Wentworth had enjoyed since the early 1750s. For some years the governors of New York had been complaining that the land in what is now the state of Vermont belonged under their jurisdiction, not Wentworth's. In 1763 the Board of Trade began hearings on the dispute. News of the board's action shocked the governor, for he had recently granted dozens of townships in the disputed area and owned over 30,000 acres there himself. But his urgent letters requesting that

4. *NHSP*, VI, 856, 868; Thomas Martin to Daniel Rindge, Dec. 24, 1765, Masonian Papers, III, 37, NHA; Louis B. Namier, *England in the Age of the American Revolution* (London, 1930), 286; Thomlinson Jr. to Thomlinson Sr., Mar. 26, 1764, in Howard, ed., *Records*, I, 226.

5. J. Steven Watson, *The Reign of George III, 1760–1815* (Oxford, 1960), 67–110; William L. Sachse, "John Huske's Proposals for Improving American Trade," *PCSM*, XLII: *Transactions* (1952–1956), 474–487; John Sherburne to Huske, Aug. 20, 1754, New Hamp. Misc. MSS; Daniel Peirce and others to Thomlinson, Aug. 6, 1761, Misc. MSS, MHS; Lawrence C. Wroth, *An American Bookshelf, 1755* (Philadelphia, 1934), 132–137; Charles R. Ritcheson, *British Politics and the American Revolution* (Norman, Okla., 1954), 23.

New Hampshire's possession of the territory be confirmed had no effect. The board first ordered him to stop all surveying west of the Connecticut River, and then, in July 1764, recommended to the Privy Council that the land become part of New York. Although Wentworth protested the decision vigorously and let it be known in the *New Hampshire Gazette* that as far as he was concerned his grants were valid, the Privy Council accepted the board's recommendation. John Wentworth provided a blunt explanation for the calamity: "Your province," he wrote to Daniel Peirce, "is near a fourth part of it given to New York because no one said a word to the contrary."[6]

Meanwhile Wentworth had become mired in even deeper trouble. The hearings before the Board of Trade blossomed into a full-scale investigation of royal authority in New Hampshire, and the results of the investigation were far from favorable. In its report to the Privy Council the board accused Wentworth of "negligence, misconduct and disobedience." His land grants had been "in every particular totally inconsistent" with the mode of settlement prescribed in his instructions and had been made "with a view more to private interest than public advantage." They found that the governor had allowed "the most absurd, incongruous and unjust" laws to go into effect because he had approved them without suspending clauses and had failed to send the records to Whitehall. They further noted, basing their information in part on the testimony of John Fisher, a well-connected English gentleman who had married a niece of the governor, that Wentworth used his authority to line his own pockets and reward his relatives with posts of honor. Benning Wentworth, they concluded, should be dismissed.[7]

Full reports on the turn of events soon reached Portsmouth. Huske wrote gleefully in April 1765 that a formal list of charges

6. Benning Wentworth to Board of Trade, Aug. 14, 1763 to June 10, 1766, C.O. 5/938; *New Hampshire Gazette*, Mar. 23, 1764; Board of Trade to Wentworth, Oct. 21, 1764, Nov. 8, 1765, and Board of Trade to Privy Council, July 10, 1764, C.O. 5/942; *NHSP*, VII, 62; John Wentworth to Daniel Peirce, Feb. 15, 1766, Peirce Papers.
7. Board of Trade to Privy Council, July 10, 1764, C.O.5/942. Charles Townshend, though no longer president of the Board of Trade, may have been the driving force behind the proceedings. In his papers there is a list of all Wentworths who had received land grants, and a lengthy history of New Hampshire critical of the Masonian proprietorship. See Buccleuch and Queensberry Muniments: The Charles Townshend Papers, introd. [and ed.] by T. C. Smoot (East Ardsley, Yorkshire: Micro Methods, 1964), box 6, paper no. 17.

including not only the complaints of the Board of Trade but evidence of judicial irregularities had been drawn up. Chief Justice Mansfield especially had been amazed at what Huske and others reported about appeal procedures in New Hampshire. Wentworth's dismissal was a foregone conclusion—even his friends had given up —and most of the council "no doubt" would be replaced as soon as the new governor was appointed. John Wentworth corroborated Huske's information and added that proceedings might be instituted against the Masonian proprietors. On the general question of New Hampshire's influence at Whitehall, Wentworth noted simply, "It is notorious that we are scarcely known and not considered but in the most diminutive way, and as a province . . . have no rights or interests."[8]

Wentworth, however, exaggerated. The influence of New Hampshire had declined, but it had not been destroyed. Indeed the governor's nephew had spent much of his time and energy in England in a successful effort to shore up the crumbling walls of his family's political fortunes. Soon after his arrival he visited his distant kinsman, Charles Watson-Wentworth, the Marquis of Rockingham, to whom many of Newcastle's former associates had turned for patronage. The two young men—Rockingham was thirty-four and Wentworth twenty-seven—quickly became close friends and prepared a petition in Governor Wentworth's behalf which Rockingham promised to present at Whitehall, though he doubted it would have any effect.[9] Wentworth also consulted with Barlow Trecothick, who had become head of Thomlinson's commercial firm in 1759 when the New Hampshire agent retired from business. Trecothick's wife was Grizell Apthorp, from the Boston family which had close commerical and kinship connections with both Rockingham's supporters and the American Wentworths. The interest of Trecothick, the Apthorps, the Wentworths, and Rockingham in the Society for the Propagation of the Gospel further cemented what in any case was a natural political association.[10]

8. Huske to [John Sherburne], London, Apr. 11, 1765, New Hamp. Misc. MSS; John Wentworth to Daniel Peirce, Feb. 15 and Mar. 1, 1766, Peirce Papers.

9. Watson, *George III*, 110–112; Mayo, *Wentworth*, 15–17; Wentworth to Rockingham, Mar. 10, 1765, NHSP, XVIII, 560–567; Wentworth to Jeremy Belknap, May 15, 1791, *Belknap Papers, MHS Collections*, 6th ser., IV (1891), 498.

10. D. H. Watson, "Barlow Trecothick and Other Associates of Lord Rockingham during the Stamp Act Crisis, 1765–1766," unpub. M.A. thesis Sheffield University, 1958, 20–74; Theodore D. Jervey, "Barlow Trecothick," *South Carolina Historical*

These connections proved invaluable when in July 1765, as a result of the Stamp Act crisis, Rockingham replaced Grenville as head of the ministry. John Wentworth had already left for home via the continent when he heard "of a general change of men and measures" and rushed back to England. There William Legge, Earl of Dartmouth and new president of the Board of Trade, promised him "any favor" the board could dispense. Even better, Rockingham and Dartmouth offered him the governorship of New Hampshire; he declined only long enough "to escape taking an oath to enforce the Stamp Act" and to induce his uncle "to save his honor" by a timely resignation. While awaiting confirmation of his appointment Wentworth advised his friends in Portsmouth to have Trecothick made permanent agent. Trecothick, Rockingham, and Wentworth then obtained the council appointments they desired and quashed proceedings against the Masonian patent.[11] Soon after his commissions as governor and surveyor general were published, John Wentworth set out for America, undoubtedly well pleased with his accomplishments and deeply grateful to his patron, Lord Rockingham.[12]

Unhappily for the Wentworths, Rockingham remained in power only thirteen months; after his eclipse the family influence in England began again to decline.

Governor John Wentworth expected Trecothick to perform the same services for him that Thomlinson had performed for his uncle. Trecothick, however, could not. Mast contracts were let to others whose politics gave them more interest at court. Decisions at White-

---

and Genealogical Magazine, 32 (1931), 157–169; Foote *et al.*, eds., *Kings Chapel*, II, 91, 143; Wendell D. Garrett, *Apthorp House* (Cambridge, Mass., 1960), 6–8; SPG Papers, *passim*, NHHS. Watson has published some of his material in "Barlow Trecothick," *Bulletin of the British Association for American Studies*, September 1960, 36–49, and March 1961, 29–39.

11. Watson, *George III*, 110–113; Wentworth to Peirce, undated, Feb. 15, and Mar. 1, 1766, Peirce Papers; Wentworth to Rindge, Nov. 29, 1765, Masonian Papers, III, 36; Wentworth to Belknap, May 15, 1791, *Belknap Papers, MHS Collections*, 6th ser., IV (1891), 498. Wentworth also helped Trecothick and Rockingham in obtaining repeal of the Stamp Act: Watson, "Trecothick and Other Associates," 13–18.

12. Wentworth had other irons in the fire. Before the governorship proposal he arranged to be appointed deputy postmaster in the colonies; even after he was reasonably certain of becoming his uncle's successor, he successfully sought the New Hampshire agency and served briefly with Trecothick before leaving for America. See Jervey, "Trecothick," 159; NHSP, XVIII, 574; Wentworth to Peirce, Feb. 15, Mar. 1, and Sept. 10, 1766, Peirce Papers.

hall affecting royal government in New Hampshire were made in spite of his opposition. By the early 1770s Trecothick and Rockingham could not even control provincial council appointments.[13] At the same time the new agent's economic ties to New Hampshire and northern New England in general weakened. Withdrawal of English troops after the French defeat at Quebec meant the end of lucrative contracts for providing specie to troops; what contracts there were went to others. Loss of the mast contracts and a gradual erosion of mast prices further reduced his American trade. Understandably, Trecothick turned his attention elsewhere. He failed to secure Wentworth's admission to the Society for the Propagation of the Gospel and defended the governor's conduct to the ministry only half-heartedly. Declining health further diluted the agent's effectiveness.[14] In 1775 it was reported that Trecothick had "withdrawn himself from all business" and had become totally useless as representative of the province and its governor.[15]

As soon as Wentworth began to understand the danger of relying too heavily on Trecothick, he took steps elsewhere to bolster his political position. He courted the new mast contractors—Anthony Bacon and John Durand, both Grenville supporters—with land grants and asked their help in getting laws passed which would make his execution of white pine policy more effective. When Wills Hill, Earl of Hillsborough and the new Secretary of State for the American Colonies, asked that a friend be appointed agent for New Hampshire, Wentworth promised to recommend the change as soon as Trecothick retired. The new governor, like his uncle, named towns and counties after important English politicians and maintained a constant flow of official correspondence in which he catalogued his

13. Wentworth to John Henniker, Jan. 12, 1769, and Wentworth to Trecothick and Apthorp, Apr. 10, 1769, Wentworth Letter Book no. 1, pp. 178, 216, NHA; Namier, *England*, 281, 283; George Boyd to John Wendell, June 27 and December 1774, *Proceedings MHS*, 48 (1914–1915), 336–341; Wentworth to Rockingham, Nov. 9, 1774, NEHGR, 23 (1869), 274.

14. Arthur Browne to Dr. Burton, Nov. 6, 1767, and Nov. 15, 1770, SPG Papers, 97, 109; Wentworth to Henry Bellew, Apr. 8, 1775, Wentworth Letter Book no. 3, p. 83. Trecothick became a London alderman.

15. Letter from Paul Wentworth, Jan. 13, 1775, NHSP, XVIII, 658. Two other problems helped to weaken Trecothick's relationship with the Wentworths. In the 1760s he sued Benning Wentworth's brother Samuel for breach of contract but lost the case in the New Hampshire courts; Trecothick may also have known that John Wentworth wanted him replaced by Paul Wentworth as agent. Watson, "Trecothick and Other Associates," 63–66.

accomplishments as royal governor.[16] But for the most part Wentworth had to rely on his Whig connections. He sent Rockingham gifts (including of all things a moose), reports on American affairs, and advice on how imperial administration could be improved. He even asked permission to name his children after the marquis and his wife.[17] At the same time Wentworth kept up his association with Paul Wentworth, a member of parliament who supported Rockingham and had influence with Henry Howard IV, the Earl of Suffolk. When Paul Wentworth, who already represented a group of settlers west of the Connecticut seeking to have the boundary decision reversed, asked to replace Trecothick as provincial agent, the governor replied, "If I can only get that commission into your hands—and our friends be established in power at St. James I should think myself perfectly happy, and would not willingly change my situation for the government of Jamaica."[18] But Rockingham never regained the ministry; and the assembly refused to make Paul Wentworth agent.

The danger of dependence on men out of power became evident when in the early 1770s Peter Livius—the councilor who earlier had been astonished at the profit potential of the mast trade—organized a scheme to oust the governor. Livius, whom John Wentworth had dismissed from his provincial judicial post and whose criticisms of family government in the council had been systematically ignored, traveled to England and petitioned the Board of Trade. He accused Wentworth of making illegal land grants, of using public taxes for private purposes, of changing judges in provincial courts until he gained favorable decisions, and of disguising his activities by failing to send official records to England. Wentworth, when he learned of the petition, asked Trecothick and Paul Wentworth to defend him against Livius and sent his secretary

16. Fols. 21 and 47, Peirce Papers; Hunt and Smith, "English Background," 2–52; Wentworth to Hillsborough, May 2, 1769, and Wentworth to Durand and Bacon, July 17, 1769, Wentworth Letter Book, no. 1, pp. 230, 259; Province and Revolutionary Papers, 66, NHA; C.O. 5/928, 937–939, *passim*.

17. Wentworth's correspondence to Rockingham may be found in Wentworth Letter Books no. 1 and no. 3 and in Wentworth-Woodhouse Muniments, Rockingham Papers, Sheffield City Library, Sheffield, England, hereafter referred to as Rockingham Papers.

18. John Wentworth to Paul Wentworth, Wentworth Letter Books nos. 1 and 3, *passim*: the quotation is from a letter written Sept. 17, 1769, Letter Book no. 1, 269. See also Julien P. Boyd, "Silas Deane: Death by a Kindly Teacher of Treason," *WMQ*, 16 (1959), 178 and 320n; *NHSP*, VII, 298, 350, and VIII, 658; Watson, "Trecothick and Other Associates," 256–257.

Thomas McDonough to assist them. But in May 1773 the Board of Trade recommended Wentworth's dismissal.[19]

Only a massive effort by the governor's friends saved him. Mc-Donough, Paul Wentworth, and Sir Thomas Wentworth (a well-connected kinsman of Rockingham who held office as the High Sheriff of Yorkshire) successfully petitioned for a rehearing before the Privy Council. Rockingham remained officially behind the scenes but wrote personally to Lord Mansfield in the governor's defense and hired two influential lawyers, John Lee and Sir John Skynner, to defend the case. McDonough armed the lawyers with depositions from the province attesting to the popularity of Wentworth's administration and copies of letters from the secretary of state complimenting Wentworth on his conduct as governor and surveyor general. Impressed with this evidence and unwilling to condemn the one royal servant who had kept his province from joining the nonimportation movement, the Privy Council—which included Paul Wentworth's patron Lord Suffolk—refused to accept the Board of Trade's recommendation and exonerated Wentworth.[20]

The victory was by no means complete. Livius had gained the ear of Lord Dartmouth, now both Secretary of State for the American Colonies and the president of the Board of Trade but no longer a member of the Rockingham faction, and obtained a commission to replace Atkinson as Chief Justice of New Hampshire.[21] He also recommended that Woodbury Langdon, a Portsmouth merchant bitterly critical of his governor, be appointed to the council. Meanwhile another Portsmouth resident, the wealthy shipbuilder George Boyd, had traveled to London and been introduced, perhaps by Livius, to Frederick North (Earl of Guilford and first lord of the

19. *The Memorial of Peter Livius* ([London], 1773), NHSP, XVIII, 623–650; Atkinson to Trecothick, Dec. 28, 1772, New Hamp. Misc. MSS; Wentworth to Henry Bellew, Apr. 8, 1775, Wentworth Letter Book no. 3, p. 83. Wentworth blamed the decision on Trecothick's failure to protect him; the agent's bill for expenses at the Board of Trade indicates, however, that the governor underestimated his role: New Hamp. Misc. MSS.

20. The most voluminous records of this defense are in the Rockingham Papers. See also NHHS, *Collections*, IX (1889), 304–363; New Hamp. Misc., box 1, NYPL; Munro, ed., *Acts of the Privy Council*, V, 370–375, and VI, 529–536.

21. William Lee to Sam Adams, Apr. 10, 1775, Adams Papers, NYPL; Peter O. Hutchinson, comp., *Diary and Letters of His Excellency Thomas Hutchinson* (Boston, 1884), 187; Atkinson to Earl of Louden, May 5, 1774, Photostat Misc. MSS, MHS. Livius refused to return to New Hampshire unless he was given an independent salary.

treasury), Dartmouth, and "several other great people." Boyd quickly gained the impression that "Governor Wentworth . . . has but little interest here" and reported, "I am sure mine at this time is more than his is now or ever was this side of the water." He purchased a council commission, reactivated the complaint against "the family compact," and promised his merchant friends in Portsmouth —some of whom were already seeking imperial office through their own connections—that they would be included in the new council which he expected would be chosen.[22] Rockingham and Paul Wentworth could do nothing to prevent these developments. It is quite possible that the revolution, which destroyed the Wentworth oligarchy, rescued it from a less honorable demise.

John Wentworth once warned a friend against embarking on a career in English politics with the comment that "the uncertainty of success seems very great."[23] In one sense he was living proof that success was possible, for he did retain the governorship of New Hampshire until the outbreak of revolution and later became lieutenant governor of Nova Scotia. Yet his was never a secure position. Far more than his uncle, John Wentworth had to worry about the English sources of the family's political power.

In New Hampshire itself John Wentworth experienced a different set of problems. His predecessor had been able to construct a political system which prevented the development of effective internal opposition to family rule. But in the years following the end of the French and Indian War, that system began to collapse. By 1774 complaints about the family compact circulated in all parts of the province, and the effectiveness of New Hampshire's royal officials had been seriously reduced.

Ironically, this decline took place while the province was ruled by a sensitive, energetic, and politically imaginative chief magistrate. As governor, John Wentworth did everything in his power to share the benefits of family rule with his fellow colonists. Much of his behavior—the judicious distribution of offices and the awarding of land

22. Wentworth to Rockingham, Nov. 9, 1774, *NEHGR*, 23 (1869), 274; Boyd to John Wendell, June 27 and December 1774, *Proceedings MHS*, 48 (1914–1915), 336–341; Wendell to Hope and Co., Jan. 18, 1774, Wendell Family Papers, Wendell Collection.
23. Wentworth to Joshua Loring, Feb. 18, 1769, Wentworth Letter Book no. 1, p. 193.

grants to men of local influence—aped the techniques employed so successfully by his uncle. But in many ways the new governor went further. He courted old enemies in the Waldron, Gilman, and Sherburne families by offering them high posts in provincial government. He responded to demands for judicial and administrative reform by supporting a plan for division of the province into counties, each of which would have its own court system. He attempted to mollify the growing anxiety of congregationalists about the growth of Anglicanism by helping to establish Dartmouth College. Wentworth also had an affable personal manner and a flair for publicizing his good deeds, both of which made him popular with the men he ruled.[24] But his popularity, however well deserved, could not stem the tide of internal opposition.

Two processes, independent in origin but mutually reinforcing in impact, undermined the political position of family-dominated oligarchy. One grew out of a series of developments that destroyed the economic and political foundations on which Benning Wentworth's political success had rested. The other stemmed from antagonism to all royal government generated by the enactments of Parliament and the alternations in administrative procedures adopted by the various ministries following the accession of George III.

(1) The governor's loss of influence at Whitehall adversely affected his ability to control matters in New Hampshire. In the first place, it reduced the number of rewards he had at his disposal. Mark Hunking Wentworth lost the mast agency to other merchants who had connections with the new contractors in England; as a result the family no longer controlled the distribution of subcontracts to woodsmen in the interior. The boundary decision in favor of New York reduced by two thirds the territory available for land grants at a time when the demand for land was increasing. To make matters worse, inhabitants deprived of holdings in Vermont sought additional grants; some began to think that another governor might be able to obtain a reversal of the 1764 decision. One more source of rewards—the ability to control provincial appointments made in England—had been closed off when Rockingham lost power. While

---

24. See especially the characterizations drawn by Mayo, *Wentworth*, and Wilbur C. Abbott, *Conflicts with Oblivion* (New Haven, 1924), 183–219, and the depositions used to defend Wentworth before the Privy Council printed in NHHS, *Collections*, IX (1889), 309–363.

Wentworth governed, councilors, customs officials, and deputy surveyors were selected without his approval.[25]

The attitudes of those who replaced Newcastle and his associates cut the governor's political leverage even further. One of Benning Wentworth's great strengths had been his ability to ignore instructions from England when obedience would have jeopardized his local position. When trouble arose, Thomlinson took care of things. John Wentworth, however, could not afford to regard his official responsibilities so lightly, for those in power insisted that royal administration everywhere in the colonies, including New Hampshire, be strengthened. Wentworth, as a result, had little room in which to maneuver. When, consistent with his responsibilities as surveyor general, he made a serious effort to enforce the white pine policy, protests arose throughout the northern colonies; in 1772 lumbermen and millowners in Weare manhandled a sheriff attempting to examine recently cut logs.[26] The first time Wentworth flagrantly disobeyed instructions—by signing the assembly bill which violated a recent act of Parliament—the new secretary of state, Lord Hillsborough, sent him a stiff warning. His comments on the episode to Paul Wentworth reflected his frustration. "Good God," the governor asked, must a colonial magistrate act as "verbatim ·instructed," and so alienate his subjects that "his windows are demolished and his chariot overset" before he can hope to be supported?[27] He paid closer attention to orders from England after this, but his obedience, particularly when it meant enforcing new colonial regulations, undermined his popularity in New Hampshire.

Developments within the province also weakened the governor's political hand. During Benning Wentworth's tenure New Hampshire had been so economically dependent on the mast trade, lumbering, and shipbuilding that resistance to rulers who permitted the exploitation of forest resources would have been foolish. The old governor had benefited equally from the artificial economic stimulation of war, which not only raised the price of naval stores but also

25. See citations in n. 13, and Wentworth to Rockingham, July 23, 1771, Rockingham Papers.

26. Correspondence in Wentworth Letter Book no. 1, pp. 295–392, and no. 2, *passim; New Hampshire Gazette*, May 8, 1772. Wentworth, naturally, de-emphasized this resistance in his official correspondence.

27. Wentworth to Rockingham, Sept. 17, 1769, Wentworth to Wentworth, Sept. 17, 1769, and Wentworth to Hillsborough, Sept. 1769, Wentworth Letter Book no. 1, pp. 266–269.

gave him the opportunity to distribute military commissions and supply contracts to those who cooperated with him. All this changed in the 1760s.

For a variety of reasons the mast trade went into a gradual but serious decline. Forest fires in 1762 destroyed much timber. The rapid cutting of the previous two decades had consumed all the resources near the coast and most of the large trees near the Merrimack and Salmon Falls rivers; timber cut in the interior cost much more to transport to the seacoast. The demand for masts declined once the Treaty of Paris had brought an end to the war. With prices dropping and profit margins reduced, cutters looked elsewhere for supplies. In 1772 Falmouth for the first time shipped more masts for His Majesty's navy than did Portsmouth.[28]

Those engaged in the lumbering and shipbuilding industries also found their costs rising at a time when demand for their products was falling. One writer complained in 1764: "We have so overstocked the West India Islands with lumber . . . that they despise it, and many times get it for less than it costs." England suffered such a glut of ships that in 1768 an agent for Trecothick and Apthorp reported there had not been a single offer to buy their vessels in the past year. There were other changes, too. The presence of the English navy in the Caribbean curtailed American smuggling operations in the French islands. Merchants who had prospered while supplying the military suffered when the fighting moved south. Everyone engaged in trade found himself hampered by a lack of specie in the province and by imperial regulations which prevented the legislature from emitting paper currency.[29] Commercial activities, of course, continued, allowing men like Woodbury Langdon and George Boyd to build their personal fortunes.[30] But the Ports-

28. *New Hampshire Gazette*, Aug. 13, 1762; Watson, *George III*, 103; Malone, *Pine Trees and Politics*, 147; Wentworth to Henniker, Jan. 12, 1769, and Wentworth to Trecothick and Apthorp, Apr. 10, 1769, Wentworth Letter Book no. 1, pp. 178, 216; Albion, *Forests and Sea Power*, 271–276.

29. Anthony Dehom [Trecothick's agent] to Montgomery and Wentworth, August 1768, fol. 166, Larkin Papers, PA; Livius correspondence, Livius Letter Book, *passim;* Wentworth to Shelburne, Mar. 25, 1768, Wentworth Letter Book no. 1, p. 94; *New Hampshire Gazette*, 1764–1768, *passim*. The quotation is from the *Gazette*, Aug. 17, 1764.

30. Howard T. Oedel, "Portsmouth, New Hampshire: The Role of the Provincial Capital in the Development of the Colony (1700–1775)," unpub. diss. Boston University, 1960, 662–668; Boyd Letter Book, *passim*, NHHS; Lawrence S. Mayo, *John Langdon of New Hampshire* (Concord, 1737), 22–28. Boyd's success was spec-

mouth merchants, who by controlling forest product exports had dominated the provincial economy in the 1750s, now found their trade reduced.

The political implications of these changes were many. Dissatisfaction with the ruling oligarchy spread easily among the economically distressed. Peter Livius, for example, blamed his commercial reverses on the Wentworths and never forgave them for what he considered their monopolization of profitable trade. Equally as significant, those who did manage to succeed were not dependent on the Wentworths. Woodbury Langdon traded mostly through Lane and Sons, Fraser, not through Trecothick. George Boyd sold his ships to men whom Wentworth did not know. John Wendell moved to Portsmouth when an uncle in Massachusetts procured the mast agency. Wendell's brother-in-law, Joshua Wentworth (a distant kinsman of the governor), became prosperous although unrewarded by the clan.[31] It was not accidental that Livius, Langdon, Boyd, and Joshua Wentworth led the opposition to family government in the years before the revolution.

The 1760s witnessed still another dramatic change of economic and political importance. During the war New Hampshire's population growth slowed, and new settlement in the areas near Canada stopped altogether. The capture of Quebec, however, ushered in an era of rapid expansion. Benning Wentworth granted dozens of new towns. Farmers from the overcrowded provinces in southern New England rushed to take advantage of the opportunity, urged on by the enthusiastic advertisements of land speculators. The signing of the Treaty of Paris, which gave England permanent possession of Canada, further fueled the migration. A minister delivering a sermon entitled "Thanksgiving for Peace" predicted that with "none to molest them" Americans would turn the "howling wilderness" into "a pleasant and fruitful field." Walpole, a town on the eastern

tacular. In 1761 he paid about 1 per cent of Portsmouth's taxes; in 1774 he paid about 6 per cent and was worth, in his own words, at least a thousand guineas a year. See Portsmouth Tax Records, City Hall, Portsmouth, and Boyd to John Cruger, Nov. 1, 1773, Boyd Letter Book.

31. See citations in n. 22 and n. 30, and Livius to John Raymond, June 18, 1765, Livius Letter Book, 51. On Wendell and Joshua Wentworth see Wentworth to Edmund Wendell, Feb. 18, 1769, Wentworth Letter Book no. 1, p. 192; and "John Wendell," in Shipton, *Biographical Sketches* XII, 592–597.

bank of the Connecticut River, contained four families in 1759; by 1775 the number had increased to 658. Nearby towns grew almost as quickly. The population of New Hampshire as a whole rose from about 40,000 to over 82,000 in the same period.[32]

This growth, although promoted by the officials of royal government, threatened to undermine their authority. As early as 1768 John Wentworth acknowledged that the "order, peace and obedience of the province" depended "on extending the power of government into the new settlements," whose people, he predicted, would otherwise "increase in dangerous strength of ungovernable disorder, licentiousness and disregard of government."[33] To prevent this from happening the governor advocated construction of roads to connect the three major river systems in the province, fought for the division of New Hampshire into counties, began to build a country estate in the area north of Lake Winnipesaukee, and supported the establishment of Dartmouth College. Each of these programs was designed to bolster royal authority. The roads would channel trade to Portsmouth, thus providing economic integration on which effective government could rest.[34] Each of the counties would have its own court system; the governor and his associates could control appointments.[35] The estate at Wolfboro would provide visible proof that Wentworth, unlike his predecessor, wanted to represent more than seaboard aristocracy. The college served a

32. Belknap, *History*, III, 234; Paine Wingate, "Thanksgiving for Peace," quoted in Charles E. L. Wingate, *Life and Letters of Paine Wingate* (Medford, Mass., 1930), I, 79; Henry W. Bellows, *Historical Sketch of Colonel Benjamin Bellows* (New York, 1855), 61; Bunker Gay, *The Accomplished Judge; or a Compleat Dress for Magistrates* (Portsmouth, 1773), 25; Dudley Papers, 37, NHHS.

33. Wentworth to Trecothick and Apthorp, May 23, 1768, Wentworth Letter Book no. 1, p. 115.

34. *NHSP*, VII, 232–306, and XVIII, 584, 605, 613, 643; Wentworth to Hugh Hall Wentworth, Dec. 23, 1768, Wentworth Letter Book no. 1, p. 188; James W. Goldthwait, "The First Province Road; the Road from Durham to Co-os," *New Hampshire Highways*, April 1931, 2. The program provided one important side benefit. Wentworth promised that if landowners paid their quitrents he would use the money locally in road construction. In 1773 over £700 was collected: Wentworth to Shelburne, Mar. 25, 1768, Wentworth Letter Book no. 1, p. 111; Wentworth to Board of Trade, draft of intended letter, December 1774, Wentworth Papers.

35. *NHSP*, VII, 129–276; Batchellor and Metcalf, eds., *Laws of New Hamp.*, III, 542; Wentworth to Nathaniel Rogers, Dec. 19, 1768, Wentworth to Shelburne, Mar. 25, 1768, Wentworth to Trecothick and Apthorp, May 23, 1768, and Wentworth to Hector Cramahe, Apr. 5, 1768, Wentworth Letter Book no. 1, pp. 169, 104, 115, 91.

dual function: to soothe the Congregational clergy and to provide the west with royal officials—Eleazar Wheelock and his associates became justices of the peace—dependent on their eastern counterparts.[36] It was a well-conceived plan, but it didn't work.

The road-building program hardly got off the ground. The assembly balked at providing funds, and townsmen more interested in improving their land than in promoting external trade hesitated to commit their energies to the governor's projects. Even when roads were built, trade continued to flow through Newburyport, Salem, Boston, and Hartford rather than Portsmouth. Water transportation was cheaper; in any case the newcomers preferred to maintain commercial relationships with their friends and relatives in provinces to the south.[37] The division into counties proved a mixed blessing. Royal authority did increase, but in many places it produced more resentment than allegiance. Immigrants from Connecticut, Rhode Island, and Massachusetts, all charter colonies with strong traditions of local autonomy, feared the new arrangement might bring upon them "a swarm of pettifoggers, who like the Egyptian locusts" would "destroy all before them." The privileges assumed by some of the new officials confirmed such anxieties.[38] The college served its intended purposes, but only in the Hanover area. Congregational ministers elsewhere continued to fear Anglican interference; many regretted the inclusion of so many Anglicans on the college board of trustees. Proprietors in Haverhill and other Connecticut Valley communities became angry when Wentworth approved Hanover as the college site. Only in the eastern interior, where Wentworth concentrated his personal attention and the major river system fed trade

36. Wentworth to Thomas Waldron, Oct. 25, 1774, *Belknap Papers, MHS Collections,* 6th ser., IV (1891), 56; Wentworth to Wheelock, Mar. 21, 1768, Wentworth Papers, box 1; Wentworth to Bishop of London, Apr. 28, 1770, fol. 770278.1, BLDC; *NHSP,* VII, 17.

37. James W. Goldthwait, "The Governor's Road, from Rochester to Wolfboro," and "The Road to Conway and the Upper Cohos," *New Hampshire Highways,* May 1931, 2–5, and August 1931, 1–5; *New Hampshire Gazette,* Oct. 18, 1771; Wentworth to Board of Trade, draft of intended letter, December 1774, Wentworth Papers; Belknap, *History,* III, 207. Aaron Storrs of Hanover complained that Wentworth was "bitter against carrying trade out of this province" and continued to ship his goods down the Connecticut: Storrs to Wheelock, Aug. 10, 1771, fol. 771460, BLDC.

38. John L. Rice, "Dartmouth College and the State of New Connecticut," *Papers and Proceedings of the Connecticut Valley Historical Society,* 1 (1876–1881), 152–158; *NHSP,* IX, 21, 329. The quotation is from the *New Hampshire Gazette,* Feb. 19, 1768.

into Portsmouth, did the governor's efforts meet with general approval.[39]

The growth of settlement caused political problems for Wentworth among seaboard residents, too. Ambitious easterners barraged him with requests for land grants and appointments which would enable them to benefit from the provincial expansion: he could satisfy only a few. Many of his friends and relatives obstructed his efforts to integrate the province. They wanted the courts to remain in Portsmouth and saw little sense in building roads which could not alter the flow of commerce. At least a few feared that newcomers from other provinces would "send such a number of representatives . . . as will outvote the original inhabitants." Peter Livius argued that "the province has so increased . . . it is now of great importance to dissolve a family combination which has already been productive of so much injustice." For others the concern was more general. "Laws and regulations which prove very effectual for small communities," wrote one worried *Gazette* correspondent, "by no means answer the same good ends when they . . . become more extensive." He urged provincial rulers to initiate a far-reaching program of legal reform.[40]

John Wentworth's task as governor, then, was much more difficult than that of his uncle. Changing political conditions in England and postwar economic adjustments in New Hampshire reduced the leverage he could bring to bear on men potentially dissatisfied with family rule. The expansion of settlement produced sectional attitudes which further divided his subjects and provided fertile ground for political opposition. Yet, in spite of the seriousness of these developments, to Wentworth himself they were of secondary importance. While he governed New Hampshire, a more fundamental challenge to his rule emerged.

(2) That challenge was directed at the governor because he represented a system of political authority which the colonists increasingly distrusted. No matter how judiciously Wentworth acted, he

39. Frederick Chase, *The History of Dartmouth College and the Town of Hanover*, ed. John K. Lord (Cambridge, 1891), 90–155; NHHS, *Collections*, III, 386; *New Hampshire Gazette*, July 13, 1770, and Oct. 8, 1773.
40. *NHSP*, VII, 129–306. For Livius' remark see Munro, ed., *Acts of the Privy Council*, VI, 535; the other quotations are from *New Hampshire Gazette*, Oct. 11, 1771, and Feb. 25, 1774.

could not avoid identification with those who were responsible for the passage and enforcement of unpopular legislative and administrative measures. Antagonism to royal government throughout the colonies inevitably weakened the ability of New Hampshire's provincial officials to command personal allegiance and to maintain civil order.

When John Wentworth assumed office in 1767, the ruling oligarchy still possessed a reputation for protecting local citizens against arbitrary acts of the home government. Benning Wentworth's habit of ignoring those parts of his instructions which, if enforced, might threaten the peace and quiet of his province had prevented trouble during the Stamp Act crisis. The aging governor made no effort to stop protests organized in Portsmouth; instead, he informed the Board of Trade that "nothing can be done here to enforce obedience to this Act . . ." When the stamp collector, George Meserve, delivered his commission into Wentworth's custody for safekeeping, Wentworth just as quickly handed it back and later excused his behavior by explaining he had never been officially notified of the act's passage. Meanwhile the governor's associates had begun fighting for repeal, for they had been hurt just as much by the decline in trade as Portsmouth's less influential merchants and had little affection for a ministry which threatened their political power.[41] John Wentworth cooperated closely with Rockingham and Trecothick in England. In Portsmouth, Councilor Daniel Warner and two other relatives of the governor, Daniel Rindge and Daniel Peirce, helped frame the town remonstrance against the act. Their cooperation led Samuel Langdon, a radical Congregational minister, to report gleefully: "in these parts at present there are no open opponents to these our resolutions and . . . we have no reason to be apprehensive of any opposition." In the celebration that followed repeal, Governor Wentworth was among the first to be toasted.[42]

41. Wentworth to Board of Trade, Oct. 5, 1765 and Jan. 10, 1766, Wentworth Papers, box 2. One council member, John Nelson, was, as he put it, "leveled . . . to the ground" and left New Hampshire altogether. He ended up taking charge of Thomlinson and Trecothick's estate on Grenada: Nelson to Hugh Wentworth, Nov. 1, 1764, fol. 37, Larkin Papers; Wentworth to Margaret Thomlinson, Mar. 5, 1772, Howard, *Records*, I, 245.

42. Watson, "Trecothick and Other Associates," 13–18; John Wentworth to Rindge, Nov. 29, 1765, Masonian Papers, III, 36; Brewster, *Rambles*, I, 234; Looney, "The King's Representative," 134–136; Meserve to John Wentworth, Sept. 29, 1765, Peirce Papers; [Samuel Langdon] to the Boston Sons of Liberty, Feb. 8, 1766, Belknap Papers, 61.c.112, MHS; *New Hampshire Gazette*, May 30, 1766.

The provincial response to the Stamp Act did, however, reveal some distrust of the ruling oligarchy. The resolutions referred to by Langdon had been sponsored by Portsmouth citizens who, in part because they distrusted established leaders, had formed a local Sons of Liberty organization to assure full New Hampshire participation in resistance to the unpopular measure. The Portsmouth Sons of Liberty included Henry Sherburne, Woodbury Langdon, Samuel Cutts, and many other "tradesmen of reputation . . . occasionally assisted," Belknap later noted, "by lawyers, clergymen and other persons of literary ability." In addition to pressuring the town to petition for repeal, they organized protest demonstrations, forced the stamp collector to resign his commission, held quasi-judicial proceedings to judge those accused of using the hated stamps, and in general encouraged what Meserve called a "Damned Rebellious Spirit."[43] One of their most effective devices was publishing the *Portsmouth Mercury*, a newspaper occasionally critical of the Wentworths and consistently critical of "men who . . . artfully make themselves acceptible to both sides." The *Mercury* engaged in a running feud with the more conservative *Gazette*, which printed little information about dissension in other colonies and ignored the Stamp Act Congress completely. Many radicals, not without reason, accused the publisher of the *Gazette* of being under the influence of men in power.[44]

Criticism of New Hampshire's royal officials increased after John Wentworth made it apparent he would fight any provincial effort to oppose the Townshend duties. His decision was logical despite its consequences. In the first place, the new governor was in no position to alienate a ministry in which Rockingham and Trecothick had little influence. Secondly, he probably thought the tax just. He had recently returned from England, where much political discussion focused on the financial problems of the government and few questioned the need for colonial taxation; on the matter of constitutionality, even opponents of the ministry, Rockingham included, agreed

43. *New Hampshire Gazette*, Apr. 2, 1765 to May 30, 1766; Belknap, *History*, II, 333–334; Belknap Papers, 61.c.111 through 61.c.129; Meserve to John Wentworth, Sept. 27, 1765, Peirce Papers. The quotation is from Belknap, *History*, II, 333.

44. *Portsmouth Mercury*, Jan. 21, 1765 to Sept. 29, 1766; *New Hampshire Gazette*, Jan. 17, 1766; [Samuel Langdon] to Thomas Young, undated, Belknap Papers, 61.c.144, MHS. The quotation is from the first issue of the *Mercury*. There is no direct proof the Sons of Liberty sponsored the *Mercury*, but the paper was definitely supported by their advertisements.

that Parliament had been within its legal rights in authorizing the duties.[45] Finally, in New Hampshire itself Wentworth received encouragement for his stand. Most Portsmouth merchants, whether beneficiaries of family rule or not, feared the effect that adopting nonimportation measures might have on the precarious provincial economy. Some undoubtedly expected to prosper from a traffic in goods unloaded in New Hampshire and smuggled overland into southern New England. Even in 1770, after every other major seaport in the colonies had adopted some form of import control and Boston merchants had voted to cut off all exports to New Hampshire, the Portsmouth town meeting voted overwhelmingly not to pass any resolutions against the duties. Wentworth reported to Hillsborough that the margin had been "about ten to one" and interpreted the vote as both a vindication of his policy and an expression of general opinion in the province as a whole.[46]

Unfortunately for the governor, his assessment was inaccurate. Even among men who voted against local import controls there were many who wanted to adopt other means of protesting the duties. In 1768 Langdon, Cutts, Boyd, and a number of merchants outside the orbit of family preference sponsored a petition instructing Portsmouth's house representatives to have the assembly cooperate in petitioning for repeal. Wentworth's opposition to such cooperation and even to an isolated petition from New Hampshire seemed to them arbitrary and unnecessary. Many other inhabitants felt the colony should join the nonimportation agreement. Samuel Langdon claimed that "the independent part of the province" [he meant those not under the influence of governor and council] was "as patriotic . . . as any part of the continent" and implied that towns other than Portsmouth would be happy to join their fellow Americans in refusing to consume English goods. After the Boston Massacre both Exeter and New Ipswich passed formal nonimportation resolutions, other communities participated informally, and the house forwarded a petition for repeal to Trecothick. In the Connec-

45. Ritcheson, *British Politics,* 50–66. At no point did Wentworth defend colonial taxation publicly. His private correspondence, however, makes it clear that he accepted it in principle. See especially Wentworth to Belham, Aug. 9, 1768, Wentworth Letter Book no. 1, p. 130.

46. Belknap Papers, 61.c.136, MHS; *New Hampshire Gazette,* July 17, Nov. 20, 1767, Aug. 19, Sept. 30, 1768, Apr. 15, June 22, July 6, 13, 1770; Wentworth to Hillsborough, June 25, Nov. 7, 1768, and Oct. 28, 1770, Wentworth Letter Book no. 1, pp. 123, 164, 384. The quotation is from the letter written Oct. 28, 1770.

ticut Valley the Walpole Sons of Liberty complained that the entire seaboard area behaved in too moderate a fashion. Opposition to the Townshend duties and to Governor Wentworth's willingness to support them had spread throughout the province.[47]

Repeal of the duties in 1770, like the repeal of the Stamp Act four years earlier, dissipated much opposition to royal authority. But it did not eliminate all hostility, for by the late 1760s the efforts of the ministry to increase efficiency in the colonial revenue system had begun to cause Wentworth and his associates a number of problems.

Initially, few in New Hampshire complained about these efforts. The Revenue Act of 1764, which, among other things, set what the ministry thought was a reasonable tax on molasses and canceled drawbacks (repayment of taxes imposed on colonial goods shipped to England, when these goods were re-exported) had little economic impact on the province: New Hampshire contained only one small distillery, and almost no provincial exports had qualified for drawbacks. Furthermore, with James Nevin, an old friend of Benning Wentworth, in the customs office, the new administrative procedures provided in the act were probably poorly enforced. Even after passage of the Townshend duties it was possible for a writer in the *Gazette* to commend the customs service without provoking a critical response. But the arrival in Boston of the newly formed Board of Customs Commissioners in 1767 put an end to the complacency. Soon all of Portsmouth had united in condemnation of the revenue officials. Governor Wentworth himself described their conduct as "absurd, inflamatory and contumacious" and remarked that "all the paper imported since their arrival would not suffice to record their arrogance and unavailing management."[48]

Wentworth, in fact, had a number of reasons for condemning the board members. In a general sense they made his task of maintaining royal authority more difficult. As long as "the law is rendered entirely odious . . . by those that are to administer it," he told Rockingham, "what less can be expected than every art to evade its force." But the

47. Belknap Papers, 61.c.133, MHS; *New Hampshire Gazette*, July 22, Aug. 5, 1768, Apr. 15, May 11, 1770; Wentworth Letter Book no. 1, p. 351; NHSP, VII, 248–255. Langdon's quotation is from Belknap Papers, 61.c.136, MHS.

48. Belknap, *History*, III, 205; *New Hampshire Gazette*, Oct. 16, 1767 and Aug. 5, 1768; Belknap Papers, 61.c.138, MHS; Wentworth to Paul Wentworth, Nov. 15, 1768, Wentworth Letter Book no. 1, p. 152.

commissioners caused him more concrete problems. They undermined his authority as surveyor general—Wentworth accused them of publicly announcing that he and his deputies had "no lawful power" at all—and obstructed his efforts to prosecute the king's law.[49] They purged from the customs service many of his political associates, including brother-in-law John Fisher, and made it impossible for him to protect his friends' commerce. Wentworth felt they even threatened his office. He constantly noted their "disposition to injure me" and took steps to counteract the bad reports of his conduct he was certain they gave to the ministry.[50] It is entirely possible that the commissioners did influence the Board of Trade in its decision on the petition of Peter Livius.

Others in New Hampshire also had specific complaints against the reformed customs service. When James Nevin died in 1769, the board appointed George Meserve customs collector in the Portsmouth area. Already unpopular in New Hampshire—although he resigned as stamp collector, he did so with a lack of grace which alienated most of Portsmouth—Meserve quickly stirred up trouble. He seized the brig *Resolution*, owned by Samuel Cutts and other merchants, for importing unregistered molasses. Although a party had invaded the vessel, locked up its crew, and unloaded its cargo, the *Resolution* itself was condemned in the local admiralty court. Soon after this Meserve seized a second vessel, claiming it had been falsely registered by three merchants (Otis Baker, John Moffatt, and William Whipple) when the actual owner was Woodbury Langdon's brother John. John Langdon denied ownership, but both the ship and its cargo, which unquestionably did belong to him, were condemned. In both cases appeals in the Massachusetts Vice Admiralty Court failed. Since Cutts, Whipple, and Langdon later became leaders of the revolutionary movement in Portsmouth, it is not sur-

49. Wentworth to Rockingham, Nov. 13, 1768; Wentworth to Paul Wentworth, Nov. 15, 1768; Wentworth to Joshua Loring, Apr. 10, 20, May 3, 19, 1769; Wentworth to Hutchinson, Oct. 8, 20, 1769. These letters may be found in Wentworth Letter Book no. 1, pp. 149, 152, 218, 222, 236, 238, 300, 308. Wentworth to Lords of Treasury and Others, Wentworth Letter Book no. 2, p. 29. The second quotation is from the letter to Paul Wentworth.

50. Thomas C. Barrow, *Trade and Empire: The British Customs Service in Colonial America, 1660–1775* (Cambridge, Mass., 1967), 236–240; Bowdoin-Temple Papers, II, *passim*, MHS; Wentworth to Nathaniel Rogers, Jan. 13, 1769, and Wentworth to Rockingham, Feb. 16, 1769, Wentworth Letter Book no. 1, pp. 117, 203; Wentworth to Mowat, Nov. 7, 1774, Wentworth Letter Book no. 3, p. 3. The quotation is from the letter to Rogers.

prising that John Wentworth, in 1774, suggested to the Lords of Trade that Meserve's tendency to "act exclusively in his own department, without respect to . . . any other part of the provincial authority" had been a major factor in the decline of respect for royal authority.[51]

A final irritant to the colonists was the presence in North America of British regulars. Whenever troops appeared in New Hampshire, trouble arose. A recruiting party passing through Brentwood was driven from the town. Near Londonderry a group of citizens rescued some deserters being returned to Massachusetts and publicly condemned the governor's friend, Edward Lutwyche, for aiding in their capture. Even when soldiers stayed out of the province, the bitterness remained. Portsmouth passed a resolution expressing fear that "the revenues extorted from us" would be used to support a "standing army." Criticism of the Board of Customs Commissioners intensified when rumors spread that its members had recommended sending more regiments. The Boston Massacre made matters worse. "A dangerous spirit," Wentworth wrote to Rockingham that winter, is "rooting in the minds of the people, who begin to think Great Britain intends to enslave and destroy them, by mere force." The governor tried his best not to be identified with the use of such force, but in the end his efforts failed.[52]

The Stamp Act, Townshend duties, reform in the customs service, and the stationing of regular troops in the colonies all disrupted the harmony which previously had marked the relationship between the inhabitants of New Hampshire and their royal magistrates. Criticism of the home government and of provincial officials, formal resolutions condemning their policies, and even outright defiance of their authority all occurred with increasing frequency. Debates and discussions about the legitimate uses of political power accompanied these developments. The colonists had long believed that the English constitution protected them from arbitrary authority, but now

51. *New Hampshire Gazette*, July 11, 1766; Carl Ubbelohde, *Vice Admiralty Courts and the American Revolution* (Chapel Hill, 1960), 157; Mayo, *Langdon*, 38–43; Wentworth to Board of Trade, draft of intended letter, December 1774, Wentworth Papers. Documents relating to these cases are in the Langdon Papers, NHHS and HSP, and the Moffatt, Whipple, and Mason Papers, NHHS.

52. *NHSP*, VI, 640, 842; Wentworth to Gage, Feb. 2, 1769, Wentworth Letter Book no. 1, p. 182. The quotations are from *New Hampshire Gazette*, Aug. 5, 1768, and Wentworth to Rockingham, Nov. 2, 1770, Rockingham Papers.

they began to wonder. By the end of 1773 many were demanding a fundamental redefinition of imperial relationships and a thorough reform in provincial government itself.

John Wentworth, whose experience in England gave him perhaps a more profound understanding of imperial politics than anyone else in the province, was one of the most outspoken critics of the existing system. As early as 1765 he began to complain that some officials responsible for American policy operated in circumstances which inevitably produced bad results. They were misinformed, sometimes because they refused to accept what they heard and at other times because their informants were colonists on "hasty visits" to England in search of preferment and eager to please potential patrons. Moreover, these officials were under constant pressure to make colonial policy serve the needs of their immediate associates; the interests of the colonists came second. Had the ministry been properly informed of the situation and given more consideration to the colonists, Wentworth once explained, the Stamp Act might have been passed in a more acceptable form.[53]

Wentworth's frustrations as governor only sharpened his attack. Although he grudgingly accepted the necessity of colonial taxation and blamed opposition to the Townshend duties not on the taxes themselves but on those responsible for collecting them, he condemned other administrative innovations. Laws controlling colonial currency seemed to him perhaps the most absurd. In New Hampshire the economy had been seriously disrupted by lack of legislation fixing the value of bullion and coin. Pressured by the assembly, Wentworth signed such a bill and soon learned that his action had been unfavorably received in England. "In this instance," he wrote to Paul Wentworth, "I have essentially promoted His Majesty's service, preserved his province of New Hampshire from destruction, have not by any means injured either public or private interest, and extricated the service from an unreasonable dilemma," only to be condemned. How can a government that operates in such a fashion, he concluded, expect anything but censure?[54]

At another time the governor argued that the entire colonial sys-

53. Wentworth to Rindge, Nov. 29, 1765, Masonian Papers, III, 36; Wentworth to [Peirce], undated, Peirce Papers, fol. 10.
54. Wentworth to Rockingham and Wentworth to Paul Wentworth, both Sept. 17, 1769, Wentworth Letter Book no. 1, pp. 269, 276.

tem suffered from fundamental weaknesses. "It is rather to be wondered that there are not more riots," he wrote to an English friend, "when we consider the natural imbecility" of an administration "where every civil officer from the Governor to the constable are dependent on the people for annual support"; such dependence influenced personal interests and destroyed the "respect and confidence necessary to subordination." The inability of colonial governors to choose their own subordinates from among the men of natural influence in the colonies seemed equally self-defeating. Since "the other great nerve of government, reward of profit and honor, are all disposed of on your atmosphere," he continued, "what means are then left to connect and bind together the great machine which is to resist and regulate the infinite exertions of human dispositions, passions and interests?" Wentworth offered two suggestions to extricate the government from its difficulties. Home officials should "let every present commotion subside before any new measure is taken" and should "make the officers more independent—entrust them to dispense the benefits to the friends of government, hear and consider candidly their advice and information, leave them more discretionary power."[55]

Wentworth's recommendations for colonial reform developed logically from the problems he faced as governor: indeed, what in one sense he advocated was restoration of the conditions which had enabled his predecessor to rule so effectively. A few others in the province, especially the beneficiaries of family rule, might have accepted his argument had he dared to express it publicly. But there would not have been many. When Wentworth took office, the assumptions on which his logic rested—that Parliament had the right to legislate for the colonies and that Americans should accept both taxation and reform as long as they were judiciously managed—were not widely accepted. So intense had constitutional dissent become by the close of the decade that the governor told Rockingham the resistance of the colonists now rested on political principles "infinitely more likely to get rooted than all the former noise and clamor."[56] He was right.

55. Wentworth to Anthony Belham, Aug. 9, 1768, Wentworth Letter Book no. 1, pp. 130–136.
56. Wentworth to Rockingham, Sept. 17, 1769, Wentworth Letter Book no. 1, p. 266. Ideas similar to those expressed by the governor appear in the *New Hampshire Gazette,* July 17, 1767, and May 11, 1770.

Conditions in New Hampshire kept public debate on a relatively subdued and unsophisticated level. Most of those in the province with the education and literary talent to engage in constitutional controversy belonged to the governing aristocracy and sought to moderate, not accentuate, the conflict. Those who disagreed lacked the means for keeping their arguments in the limelight, for the *Mercury* folded after repeal of the Stamp Act and the publisher of the *Gazette* continued to de-emphasize imperial conflicts. Many citizens, furthermore, were anxious for New Hampshire to retain its public image of conservatism lest more authoritarian rulers be appointed in place of the Wentworths; some even hoped that good behavior might bring reversal of the boundary decision or other rewards.

What went on out of the public view, however, was a different matter. The fact that provincial inhabitants produced little polemical literature did not mean that they had no exposure to constitutional debate. Quite to the contrary. Massachusetts newspapers circulated widely in the province, especially in the Merrimack Valley. Congregational ministers, like their associates elsewhere in New England, discussed political and constitutional questions openly. After each controversial incident, no matter where it occurred, men gathered in local taverns or in individual homes and debated how best to protect their liberties. "Political inquiries were encouraged," wrote Belknap in explaining the effects of the Stamp Act, "and the eyes of the people were opened."[57]

Attention focused initially on the nature and limits of parliamentary authority. Peter Livius, who, despite his English connections, cooperated clandestinely with the Portsmouth Sons of Liberty, thought Parliament had exceeded its constitutional power in passing the Stamp Act. "Even in England where the right of taxation cannot be disputed," he wrote, "had a grant been made that in effect abolished trials by juries and gave the treasury a power of increasing the tax at will without recourse to Parliament and appointed the money raised by it to be sent out of the kingdom, all of which was the case of the Stamp Act here, could such an act be submitted to . . . while the spirit of liberty subsisted? How much less, than here

57. Clarence S. Brigham, *History and Bibliography of American Newspapers, 1690–1820* (Worcester, 1947), 470–471; *New Hampshire Gazette*, July 17, 1767, Aug. 26 and Sept. 9, 1768; Belknap, *History*, II, 334.

where the right of taxation is not so clear." Others stated more con-
cretely what Livius only suggested. "We claim a right to be governed by our own local laws, and to grant our own monies to the
King, and to be tried by our own peers for every breach of the laws,
and not by arbitrary courts of Admiralty," Samuel Langdon argued.
Parliament should only "make the most effectual provision for the
general welfare and prosperity of the whole empire, and preserve a
proper balance betwixt the national interest and that of the colonies." The Stamp Act, Townshend duties, and new customs regulations all violated these principles and thus were illegal. To be sure,
there were some who disagreed—one article in the *Gazette* signed by
"A Staunch Tory" included the statement, "Kings ought to rule and
the people are obliged to obey"—and there were others who felt less
certain where the line between imperial and local authority should be
drawn. But by the end of the sixties, the vast majority of politically
active provincial inhabitants would have agreed with Langdon.[58]

Criticism of other imperial institutions accompanied the assertion
that Parliament had no right to interfere in the internal affairs of the
colonies. Especially suspect was the ministry, which seemed intent
on burdening the colonies with officers "whose life depends upon
drawing the veins of the body politic." The officers themselves were
"designing persons" like Governor Bernard and the customs commissioners, men who spread "false and malicious accounts" of colonial conduct and who expected "to enrich themselves on the spoils
of America." And the colonists saw little chance of improvement.
"It is said publicly," Wentworth reported, "that an invariable order
is established that no man shall be employed in the revenue who was
born in America, hath been two years in the country, is married in it
or is like to be, nay further, that did not hate it." English officials,
in short, seemed engaged in a deliberate plot to prevent the inhabitants of New Hampshire and other colonies from enjoying their
just and traditional rights as Englishmen.[59]

58. Livius to Thomas Dea, Aug. 30, 1766, Livius Letter Book, 62; Belknap Papers,
61.c.112, MHS; *New Hampshire Gazette*, May 11, 1770.
59. *New Hampshire Gazette*, Aug. 5, 1768; Belknap Papers, 61.c.138, MHS; Wentworth to Belham, Aug. 9, 1768, Wentworth Letter Book no. 1, p. 130. For a more
general application of the logic presented in this and succeeding paragraphs see
Bernard Bailyn, *The Ideological Origins of the American Revolution* (Cambridge,
1967).

What could be done about it? Firm resistance to any manifestation of arbitrary authority, like the seizure of ships, was both necessary and justified—that much was clear. But even in the absence of specific grievances the colonists must be eternally vigilant lest, as a writer recommending that each anniversary of the Boston Massacre be celebrated with a lecture on government warned, citizens "grow inattentive to those concerns and designing men . . . by slow degrees invade their rights until the People are stript of all their liberties and reduced to abject slaves." Therefore, the people should double their guard when oppressions seemed least apparent. Parliament and the ministry could not be trusted.[60]

Vigilance meant keeping an eye on provincial officials too. The governor and council were subjected to the most intensive scrutiny. During the Stamp Act crisis suggestions that "our grait fokes," as one satirist writing in *Mercury* labeled the ruling oligarchy, might prove unwilling to fight for repeal appeared frequently. The refusal of Wentworth and his associates to participate in action against the Townshend duties produced more precise complaints. "Our situation is really deplorable," explained Samuel Langdon to a friend in Boston, "we have a royal government, His Excellency and his Council are appointed by the Crown and we wish their sole motives did not seem to be an implicit adherence to what they apprehend may soothe the present ministry." A few New Hampshire men carried their criticism still further, accusing the governor and council of abusing their authority as provincial magistrates. They rewarded friends and relatives with land grants, military commissions, and judicial appointments, when others were equally deserving. They corrupted the court system by appointing ignorant but politically loyal officials; in the Court of Appeals, they allowed family and class bias to affect legal decisions.[61] To some, especially among the Congregational clergy, the governor and council represented a more subtle threat to society. As political rulers they had the responsibility "to encourage piety and virtue by their good and laudable

60. *New Hampshire Gazette*, Mar. 1, 1771.
61. *Portsmouth Mercury*, Oct. 28 and Dec. 2, 1765; letter from Samuel Langdon, Belknap Papers, 61.c.136; NHSP, XVIII, 623–625; *New Hampshire Gazette*, Apr. 1, 1774; Belknap, *History*, III, 255–256. I have republished the *Mercury* article of Dec. 2 in WMQ, 3rd ser., 20 (1963), 452. Many citizens felt that John Wentworth was less guilty of these abuses than his uncle.

examples." The dancing, gambling, and other diversionary activities which the oligarchy so cherished hardly provided a proper model. "The governor . . . lives in high style," reported a young Dartmouth student traveling to Portsmouth, "and too many endeavour to imitate his mode of living."[62]

The social and political behavior of the ruling oligarchy was nothing new, of course, but it took on special and ominous meaning in the context of imperial conflict. Many colonists blamed the actions of the home government on a general moral decadence which had enabled a designing ministry to buy off Parliament and gain control of the processes of government. They feared that the same fate might lie in store for America. "This country is, by swift advance, following the British nation on the road of pleasure and dissipation," warned one New Hampshire minister. Another suggested that present American woes could be blamed on the indifference of the colonists to the sin that lay about them. No one, at least publicly, accused the Wentworths of corrupting public morals for the purpose of engrossing political power, but some apparently thought the behavior of the governor and council symptomatic of dangers which threatened all of America.[63]

The Anglicanism of the oligarchy accentuated these fears. As early as the 1750s Congregational ministers had begun to express concern over monopolization of high provincial offices by a religious minority. The Wentworths' efforts to promote their religion through the Society for the Propagation of the Gospel provided a second irritant. The Reverend Arthur Browne's advocacy of an Anglican bishopric for North America and his bitter diatribes against its opponents, especially Jonathan Mayhew, further fueled Congregationalist anxieties. Samuel Langdon, for example, firmly believed the ministry intended to establish the Anglican Church in all of America: if Browne represented the thought of his parishioners at Queen's Chapel, no resistance to such a plot could be expected from provincial rulers. John Wentworth refused to support Browne's ideas, just as he disassociated himself from the Board of Customs Commis-

62. Joseph Adams, *The Necessity and Importance of Rulers* (Portsmouth, 1769), 10–13; Samuel MacClintock, *Herodias: Or Cruelty and Revenge, the Effects of Unlawful Pleasure* (Portsmouth, 1772), 19–20; *Diary of David McClure*, ed. Franklin B. Dexter (New York, 1899), 149. The first quotation is from Adams' sermon, p. 10.
63. MacClintock, *Herodias*, 20; Adams, *Rulers*, 23.

sioners. Nevertheless, the Anglicanism of the governor and the council became increasingly distasteful to many inhabitants of New Hampshire after 1760.[64]

The gradual erosion of respect for the executive branches of government forced many of these same critics to examine the role of the legislature in provincial politics. What they discovered did not please them. Their house had remained loyal to the governor during the Stamp Act crisis while the General Court in neighboring Massachusetts not only spoke out against the measure but acted as a focal point of colonial resistance in general. The radical activity of the Bay Colony legislature after passage of the Townshend duties provided another unfavorable contrast. Moreover, individual house members seemed to have forgotten their responsibility as public servants. One writer to the *Gazette* complained that many representatives accumulated per diem while spending their time transacting private business in the capital. Another asked "whether a general appearance at the beginning of a session, and a voluntary absence the greatest part of the time afterwards" did not constitute a "matter of grievance to the people?" He also reminded his readers that each man elected should represent "the people in general, as well as the town or parish which chose him."[65]

Anxiety about the future course of imperial relationships produced a sense of urgency in those who were worried about the behavior of house members. If the ministry, aided by a corrupt Parliament and compliant colonial officials, really intended to force the colonists into submission, then the only constitutional means of resistance lay through the people's part of the legislature. Americans had both the right and the responsibility to make sure that their elected representatives did not become the dupes of royally appointed officials. Ma in New Hampshire could not be sure. The legislators, as the Walpole Sons of Liberty lamented, had "grown cold in the cause and were indifferent about it." "Probus" concluded unhappily in 1771 that the house had been "lulled into the most disagreeable indolence in

64. John Odlen to Dr. Avery, June 1753, NHHS, *Collections*, IX, 22; Ranna Cosset to Richard Hurd, Oct. 9, 1773, SPG Papers, 131; Wentworth to Joseph Harrison, Sept. 24, 1769, Wentworth Letter Book no. 1, p. 289; Carl Bridenbaugh, *Mitre and Sceptre: Transatlantic Faiths, Ideas, Personalities, and Politics, 1689–1775* (New York, 1962), 213, 228n, 244, and *passim*; William Plumer, "Plumer's Biographical Sketches," II, 500, NHHS.

65. *New Hampshire Gazette*, May 6, 13, and June 10, 1768.

the late contest for freedom," either from "ignorance" of their privileges "or from the uncertainty of them." He urged his readers not to permit a recurrence of such irresponsibility.[66]

Demands for reform in the house accompanied these criticisms. By 1767 vocal inhabitants had begun to argue that the New Hampshire Assembly should assume some of the rights exercised by the Massachusetts General Court—an argument that one moderate tried to encounter with the ineffective retort: "What will promote Liberty in one state, may destroy it in another." Before the elections of 1768 the *Gazette* published articles recommending that only candidates who promised to tend to public business and to support the people's legitimate rights be elected. Correspondents, one of whom noted that in the past "a person has been thought impertinent" who "inquired what was transacting in the House," insisted that a journal of the house be printed and that public galleries be constructed. Townsmen began to give their elected representatives written instructions. So widespread was the furor that "Americanus" could write, with obvious satisfaction: "The people being now better informed of the nature of government, can better judge of their own importance in supporting the dignity of their part of the legislature."[67]

In the months following repeal of the Townshend duties, political debate subsided. But the damage had been done. Wentworth himself warned Rockingham not to be fooled: "I fear the present calm does not proceed from content," he wrote, "alienation takes deeper root in these quieter times than when much evaporated in passion."[68] Americans, including many in New Hampshire, had begun to pass judgment on the entire system of colonial government. The beliefs and anxieties upon which they based their conclusions provided a continuing threat to the authority of all royal officials.

All of this—loss of influence in England, changing economic conditions and patterns of settlement in New Hampshire, the civil disorder and constitutional debate set off by colonial reform—made it impossible for John Wentworth to exercise the tight control of provincial political institutions which had been so pronounced in

66. *New Hampshire Gazette,* May 11, 1770, and July 12, 1771.
67. *New Hampshire Gazette,* June 19, 1767, May 6, 13, and Oct. 7, 1768.
68. Wentworth to Rockingham, July 23, 1771, Rockingham Papers.

the last fifteen years of his predecessor's regime. The new governor
had some successes, to be sure, but they stemmed as much from his
willingness to meet the demands of his subjects as from his ability
to dictate policy. His affability, political astuteness, and sensitivity
to the needs of the province could not prevent the conflict and bitterness which eventually marked his relationships with other provincial
magistrates.

In many ways the council remained devoted to the new governor's
interest. His father, Theodore Atkinson, and Daniel Warner still
held their commissions. Five other relatives—Daniel Rindge, Daniel
Peirce, Daniel Rogers, Jonathan Warner, and George Jaffrey—
received mandamuses while Rockingham and Trecothick controlled
appointments, and Paul Wentworth, although he remained in England, filled another seat.[69] John Sherburne, Thomas Waldron, and
Peter Gilman, all of whom joined in the early 1770s, had no family
connection but were personal friends of the new governor: he had
recommended them for appointment as a way of healing old political
wounds left from the struggles of 1748–1752. Under these circumstances it is not surprising that the council members supported their
chief magistrate. They accepted his recommendations for land grants
and court appointments, helped him in his battles with the House
of Representatives, sided with him when personal enemies tried
to undermine his political position, and, in general, applauded his
efforts to uphold royal authority in the face of increasing provincial
resistance.[70]

69. Wentworth to Peirce, Feb. 15, Mar. 1, 1766, Peirce Papers. The following
list, copied from Mayo, *Wentworth,* 79, suggests how completely the family dominated the council.

Councilors in 1771	Relationship to Governor
Mark H. Wentworth	Father
Theodore Atkinson	Uncle by marriage
Daniel Rindge	Uncle
Daniel Peirce	Uncle by marriage
Daniel Rogers	Uncle by marriage
Jonathan Warner	Cousin
Daniel Warner	Jonathan Warner's father
George Jaffrey	Son of George Jaffrey, whose second wife was the governor's aunt.
Peter Livius	No relationship

70. Wentworth to Board of Trade and Wentworth to Shelburne, both June 27,
1767, Wentworth to Trecothick and Apthorp, Dec. 20, 1767, Wentworth Letter
Book no. 1, pp. 3, 4, 66; *NHSP,* VII, *passim.* Benning Wentworth had made a similar

Yet relationships were not always harmonious. Wentworth, particularly after he began to build his country estate, tended to sympathize with the interests of inhabitants in the interior. He fought for the division of the province into as many as five counties, each of which would have its own court system, and sought provincial funds for the construction of roads. The council members, all seaboard residents, did not share his enthusiasm. They were willing to accept two counties and a new court at Exeter but resisted anything more. They liked the idea of roads but felt that individual towns and not the state should pay for the improvements. Only after lengthy debate could these differences be compromised.[71] The most serious source of trouble, however, was the presence of a councilor who had obtained his commission without either the knowledge or the approval of the Wentworths. Peter Livius, before he left New Hampshire in 1772, kept the government in a state of continuous disruption.

Livius had become a controversial figure during his short residence in the province. Defeated in plans to enter the masting business and afraid to engage in normal trade because of the depression and the Navigation Acts, he struck back at the royal government by cooperating with leaders of resistance to the Stamp Act and writing a pamphlet in defense of the colonists. Through his Stamp Act activities he developed friendships with a number of Portsmouth's younger and more aggressive merchants, among them John and Woodbury Langdon. Soon thereafter Livius alienated himself from the governing aristocracy (with which he was associated through his wife's family and his own wealth)[72] by refusing to pay his debts to Ports-

---

effort when in 1765 he recommended a commission be given to John Sherburne's brother Henry. Sherburne received his appointment but died soon after taking the oath of office: Benning Wentworth to Board of Trade, Oct. 5, 1765, Wentworth Papers; John Wentworth to Peirce, Feb. 15, 1766, Peirce Papers; Belknap, *History*, II, 487.

71. *NHSP*, VII, 129–276. In 1774 the council refused to accept Wentworth's recommendation that western towns be given representation in the assembly: *New Hampshire Gazette*, Mar. 18, 25, 1774.

72. Livius Letter Book, *passim*, especially Livius to Thomas Dea, Aug. 30, 1766, on p. 66; Adams, *Annals of Portsmouth*, 231. Livius obtained his council commission through the influence of his father-in-law, John Tufton Mason. While Benning Wentworth was under fire in the mid-sixties, Livius urged Mason to seek the New Hampshire governorship. Mason, however, refused even though Wentworth and Atkinson opposed his title to large land grants. See Livius to Mason, Feb. 6, 27, 1764, and Livius to O'Gara, Feb. 28, 1764, Livius Letter Book, 23–33; Brewster, *Rambles*, II, 78.

mouth merchants and, as judge of the inferior court, making decisions against royal officials. The antagonism between Livius and the governor's friends increased further after Wentworth replaced him as judge. By 1772 it was reported that "the clamor against Mr. Livius was considerably universal among what is vulgarly called the better sort of people."[73]

Livius did not hesitate to express his own hostility in council meetings. When the house demanded that the governor allow them to examine the powder money accounts and the council nonconcurred in the vote, Livius dissented and insisted that his disagreement be recorded in the official journal. When the council and the governor met as a court of appeals, Livius contested the logic and decisions of his associates. He complained about appointments, policy, and above all about the family bias reflected in almost everything the council did.[74] Not surprisingly, it was the council's action on a matter of immense importance to the Wentworth family that gave rise to Livius' most vigorous protest.

Benning Wentworth had married his housekeeper Martha Hilton in 1760. The family regretted the indiscretion but kept quiet in hope that the aging magistrate would at least have the good sense to leave most of his fortune within the family. But they were wrong, for before Wentworth died in 1770 he willed everything to his widow. "What think you of this?" gossiped John Hurd after the will had been opened, "I dare say 'twill equally surprise you with the rest of the world—our little world of Portsmouth I mean—for it engages the conversation of everybody—and doubtless chagrins many—I won't say who—but our good little governor, who best merited, bears all like a hero."[75]

John Wentworth may have maintained his public composure, but his private response was far from heroic. He sued the estate for money owed the crown by his predecessor. The following March he called the council into session and asked their opinion concerning

---

73. NHHS, *Collections*, IX, 309–363. The quotation is from a deposition in defense of John Wentworth written by Samuel Hale, NHHS, *Collections*, IX, 350.

74. NHHS, *Collections*, IX, 320–334; *NHSP*, XVIII, 599–602, 616–623, 633.

75. *New Hampshire Gazette*, Nov. 8, 1770; Hurd to Thomas Waldron, Oct. 15, 1770, New Hamp. Misc. MSS. Wentworth's first wife and all his children had died by 1760. The marriage caused adverse comment in both England and America, but Martha Hilton's ancestors were quite respectable, even by Portsmouth standards. See Nevin to Atkinson, Nov. 14, 1761, *NHSP*, XVIII 543; Shipton, *Biographical Sketches*, VI, 126.

Martha Hilton Wentworth (1737?–1805), second wife to Governor Benning Wentworth. This portrait was probably painted while Mrs. Wentworth traveled in England in the 1770s with her second husband, Michael Wentworth. Artist unknown.

the legality of land grants which the deceased governor had bestowed upon himself: after brief deliberation the council declared the grants illegal and announced that the land belonged not to Martha Wentworth but to the crown. The whole affair so infuriated Livius that he entered a violent objection to the decision, retired from the council, drafted a petition to the Board of Trade in which he accused the governor of abusing his power, gathered depositions (most of them along the Massachusetts border) to support his claims, and spent the next two years of his life trying to dislodge the Wentworths.[76] Fortunately for the political harmony of the province, his efforts carried him back to England, and quiet fell once again over the proceedings of New Hampshire's colonial council.

John Wentworth faced a different problem in dealing with his House of Representatives. His uncle had utilized his financial independence, the royal prerogative, and a system of direct personal rewards to prevent the legislature from engaging in activity which would effectively compromise either family or royal authority. But much had changed since the 1750s. The new governor was not wealthy.[77] He possessed few means of developing personal and business relationships with men of political influence in the inland communities; consequently, he hesitated to extend representation for fear that men opposed to his rule would be elected. In the towns already represented his influence on affairs was no greater. Even in Portsmouth, he once explained to Dartmouth, "gentlemen of property, experience and education" refused to run for office when he asked them because he had nothing in his power "whereby to reward such good men." The constitutional debate which began during the Stamp Act crisis further weakened his hand. Delegates long willing to tolerate executive domination of the assembly began to insist on more power. At election time the candidates who had a reputation for siding with the governor and council found themselves under pressure to change their ways; a few were not re-elected.[78]

76. Citations in n. 19 and n. 74; Wentworth to Nathaniel Peabody, Mar. 4, 1774, Wentworth Papers. Before he left, Livius asked Woodbury Langdon to gather more supporting evidence. Langdon was aided by Michael Wentworth, a retired British army officer and friend of Rockingham who later married Benning Wentworth's widow. See NHHS, *Collections*, IX, 328, and correspondence from Wentworth to Rockingham, *passim*, Rockingham Papers.

77. Wentworth was over £18,000 in debt when the revolution broke out. Most of the money he borrowed from his father, who apparently expected reimbursement from Benning Wentworth's estate. After the estate went to the widow, John Wentworth tried, at times frantically, to bolster his income. See Mayo, *Wentworth*, 99–100; Wentworth correspondence, 1771–1772, Wentworth Letter Book no. 2, pp. 10–30, and Letter Book no. 3, pp. 7, 9, 72.

78. Wentworth to Dartmouth, Aug. 29, 1774, Belknap, *History*, III, 432; *New Hampshire Gazette*, May 6, 13, and Oct. 7, 1768. Wentworth understood that any

The governor did have some leverage, however. Most representatives held land grants west of the Connecticut and fervently desired a reversal of the decision which had given their holdings to New York. During the Stamp Act crisis they had voted against sending a representative to the general congress in Philadelphia in order not to alienate the ministry; their new governor frequently reminded them that improper behavior would destroy any possibility of success in the efforts he personally was making to have the old boundary restored.[79] Moreover, John Wentworth agreed, as his uncle had not, that the province should be divided into counties. In close cooperation with assembly leaders he prepared a bill which satisfied the house and then convinced reluctant council members from Portsmouth to accept it. The house in turn promised to provide adequate judicial salaries if the division became effective. When, in the political calm following the repeal of the Townshend duties, the act of division returned from England approved, the house voted their young governor an extra £500 for his services.[80]

No such accord could be reached in matters involving resistance to imperial policy. When the house received a circular letter from the Massachusetts General Court recommending that the colonies unite to protest the Townshend duties, a majority of the representatives wanted to respond affirmatively. Wentworth opposed such cooperation and did everything in his power to prevent it. He and house Speaker Peter Gilman—Wentworth had already promised him a council appointment—wielded sufficient influence to prevent the legislature from answering the letter, but they lost control when the house received a copy of the Virginia Resolves and a formal request from the House of Burgesses to join in demands for redress of grievances. On August 27, 1768 house members approved a peti-

---

attempt by him to interfere in town politics would cause resentment against royal government: Wentworth to Peter Gilman, Nov. 25, 1767, Wentworth Letter Book no. 1, p. 57.

79. Atkinson to Trecothick and Thomlinson, Apr. 18, 1766, *NHSP*, XVIII, 569; Looney, "The King's Representative," 141; *New Hampshire Gazette*, Dec. 6, 1765, Aug. 15, Dec. 5, 1766, and Jan. 2, June 12, July 24, 1767.

80. *NHSP*, VII, 129–274; Wentworth to Shelburne, Mar. 25, 1768, Wentworth to Trecothick and Apthorp, May 23, 1768, and Wentworth to Rogers, Dec. 19, 1768, Wentworth Letter Book no. 1, pp. 104, 105, 169. The ministry, typically, admonished Wentworth for accepting the £500. He kept the money and informed his superiors it was in payment for his earlier services as provincial agent: Munroe, ed., *Acts of the Privy Council*, V, 376.

tion of protest and ordered Gilman to forward it to Trecothick and inform the burgesses of his actions.[81]

Although Wentworth and Gilman were unable to change the vote, they did prevent the petition from causing any immediate trouble. Gilman, who had been given the letters to sign and forward, simply kept them in his house at Exeter. Wentworth in the meantime made no mention of the assembly action in his correspondence to the ministry but instead emphasized the failure of the house to answer the Massachusetts letter. Some house members probably suspected their Speaker's trickery but kept silent, knowing that the planned division into counties would certainly be disallowed if the petition were sent. After the Boston Massacre the whole scheme collapsed. Exeter appointed a committee to investigate assembly behavior concerning the Townshend duties, the committee reported Gilman's negligence, and on April 14, 1770 the house again ordered their Speaker to forward the petition. This time he obeyed.[82]

The petition fiasco cost Wentworth dearly. When provincial inhabitants learned what had happened, they began to criticize their government anew. Although the governor escaped public censure, many no doubt assumed that he had had a hand in the affair. Gilman came under such attack that he lost his house seat in the next spring elections. Some men preferred to blame the entire house. The legislature, they argued, had never really wanted to petition for repeal but had been moved by public pressure; the April vote appeared "like a mighty bustle made a Saturday in the afternoon by one that has been loitering all the week before, to mend a bad week's work." In the future New Hampshire should elect representatives more devoted to the cause of liberty.[83]

At this point Wentworth could do nothing to prevent further house defiance. The Speaker who replaced Gilman (another John Wentworth but not a close relative of the governor) had long advocated provincial cooperation with other colonies. In May 1773 he received letters from Virginia and Rhode Island suggesting that

81. Wentworth to Hillsborough, June 25 and Nov. 7, 1768, Wentworth Letter Book no. 2, pp. 1, 123, 164; *NHSP*, VII, 187–192, 248–255.

82. *NHSP*, VII, 187–192, 248–255; Charles H. Bell, *History of the Town of Exeter, New Hampshire* (Exeter, 1888), 80–82; *New Hampshire Gazette*, Apr. 15, 1770.

83. *New Hampshire Gazette*, May 11, 1770; *NHSP*, VII, 286. The quotation is from the *Gazette*.

New Hampshire appoint a standing committee of correspondence to communicate with other colonies in matters of general colonial interest; after brief deliberation the house members did so. The governor had no choice but to prorogue the assembly to prevent further misbehavior.[84] For the next two years the House of Representatives continued to ignore the governor's demands that they stand aloof from intercolonial resistance to imperial policy.

John Wentworth and his friends and relatives could not dominate New Hampshire politics in the years before the revolution. They lacked sufficient influence in England to make their tenure in office secure, as well as the ability to control the behavior of elected officials and the power to prevent civil disorder. Despite the governor's personal popularity, family rule became increasingly distasteful to men of influence throughout the province; despite his flexibility as chief magistrate, his policies helped to alienate many from royal government.

The failure of Livius' scheme and the false calm in imperial affairs which followed the repeal of the Townshend duties obscured the significance of these developments. Even Wentworth, who usually manifested a keen understanding of colonial affairs, was deceived. By the summer of 1773 he had convinced himself that royal government had weathered the storm, and when a new wave of protest began later that year he blamed the disturbances on friends of Livius.[85] But the roots of his trouble lay far deeper than in the personal ambitions of a discontented placeman's supporters.

84. *NHSP*, VII, 329–336.
85. Wentworth to Eleazar Wheelock, Oct. 28, 1774, *Historical Magazine*, 15 (1869), 388; Wentworth to Rockingham, Nov. 9, 1774, *NEHGR*, 23 (July 1869), 275.

3

The Collapse

of Royal Government,

1773–1775

In late January 1774 the wealthy citizens of Portsmouth celebrated John Wentworth's exoneration in the Privy Council by giving a ball which, according to the publisher of the *Gazette*, "did in brillance and elegance far exceed anything of the kind ever seen before in this province." But conversation that evening, despite the dancing, plentiful punch, and general mood of gaiety, turned often to sobering matters. The political calm of the past two years had been shattered by passage of the Tea Act. In Boston, irate colonists had unceremoniously dumped a quantity of East India Company tea into the sea and promised to repeat the procedure should anyone attempt to import more of the unpopular commodity. Even in New Hampshire opposition to imperial policy had begun to crystallize. The Portsmouth town meeting in mid-December had approved a set of radical resolutions which Atkinson, Jaffrey, and other leading merchants opposed. Neighboring Dover, Newcastle, Exeter, and Greenland had followed suit; other towns would meet soon to discuss means of resisting the new legislation. The news from England was equally discouraging. Parliament and the ministry planned to punish any further defiance of royal authority. Livius, it had been learned, would replace Atkinson as chief justice. Earlier in January a Massachusetts paper had published a report that Woodbury Langdon would be appointed to the council and that officials at Whitehall were contemplating other changes in New Hampshire's provincial government.[1] To the men discussing these developments, the future must

1. *New Hampshire Gazette*, Dec. 10, 1773 through Feb. 11, 1774; *Essex Journal* (Newburyport), Jan. 5, 1774; Mayo, *Wentworth*, 84–85.

have looked ominous. But it is unlikely that anyone attending the ball imagined that in the next eighteen months both the power of the Wentworths and the authority of royal government in general would be totally destroyed.

The Tea Act set off a constitutional debate more bitter and intensive than even that of the late 1760s. To critics of imperial policy the new regulations were nothing more than an attempt to establish Parliament's right to tax the colonists without their consent. The amount of the tax made no difference; any such legislation, the Portsmouth resolves declared, was "unjust, arbitrary and inconsistent with the fundamental principles of the British Constitution" and violated the natural right of Englishmen "to have the power of disposing of their own property, either by themselves or their representatives." If the logic of the new measure were carried to an extreme, the colonial assemblies—which did have the right to tax—would be stripped of their powers. "We have Parliaments of our own," echoed the residents of Dover, and "we look upon our own rights too dearly bought" to admit the English Parliament "as tax masters . . . Why the King's subjects in Great Britain should frame laws for his subjects in America, rather than the reverse, we cannot well conceive."[2]

The colonists, moreover, knew precisely whom to blame for the assault on American liberties. Political discussions in the past decade had convinced an increasing number of New Hampshiremen that "designing" men in the home administration sought "by creeping in unawares to undermine us of this jewel liberty." The tea tax, explained the Hampton resolutions, not only subverted the Constitution and rendered colonial assemblies useless but introduced "that plan of arbitrary government which (to every attentive person appears) the ministry of Great Britain are artfully endeavoring to establish over the Americans." Once the tea tax was established, more would follow; eventually nothing they possessed, "whether lands, horses, chattels, money or anything else," could be called their own. "A dread of being enslaved ourselves and of transmitting

---

2. For the Portsmouth resolves see *New Hampshire Gazette*, Dec. 24, 1773, *NHSP*, VII, 333, or Adams, *Annals of Portsmouth*, 239–242. The Dover resolves are in *New Hampshire Gazette*, Jan. 14, 1774.

the chains to our posterity," the citizens of Dover declared, was the
"principle enducement" to their plan of resistance.[3]

The measures agreed upon in Dover actually were quite mild. The
town merely condemned the tax and appointed a committee of correspondence to maintain contact with other communities and keep
local citizens up-to-date on current developments. Elsewhere more
drastic steps were taken. Portsmouth, following the pattern established in Boston, promised to prevent any East India Company tea
from being landed or sold and called for a "union of all the colonies"
to obtain repeal of the act. In other towns, committees prohibited
the consumption and sale of the "noxious herb" regardless of its
origin; traders who tried to sell their remaining stock were boycotted
and their customers publicly condemned. Throughout New Hampshire energetic radicals campaigned to destroy the belief that tea
possessed medicinal powers.[4]

The success of these measures and the intensity of feeling expressed by opponents of the Tea Act soon forced New Hampshire's
more conservative inhabitants to speak out. No disagreement arose
concerning the impropriety of the tax—even Wentworth thought
the ministry foolish—but the methods adopted to oppose that tax
did disturb many. Of the thirteen men selected in town meeting
to draw up the Portsmouth resolves, six refused to sign, partly because they feared ministerial reprisals.[5] Others, questioning the sin-
cerity of the constitutional arguments employed in public resolves,
resorted to ridicule. One *Gazette* correspondent found it "truly di-
verting" to see the very people who made "such an outcry about
a farthing duty" rushing through a rainstorm to buy up remaining
tea stocks. Another thought the prohibition on tea unduly harsh to

3. The first quotation is from the Rochester resolves, *New Hampshire Gazette*,
Feb. 4, 1774. The Hampton resolutions may be found in the *Gazette*, Mar. 4, 1774,
or Hampton Town Records, Feb. 7, 1774, NHSL. For the Dover resolves see the
Gazette, Jan. 14, 1774.

4. *New Hampshire Gazette*, Dec. 24, 1773 through July 22, 1774; Bell, *History of
Exeter*, 83–87; George Wadleigh, *Notable Events in the History of Dover* (Dover,
1913), 159–161. It was reported that even the Indians in northern New Hampshire
had taken up tea burning: *New Hampshire Gazette*, Aug. 26, 1774. The quotations
are from the *Gazette*, Dec. 24, 1773, and July 22, 1774.

5. The six were Atkinson, Jaffrey, Daniel Rogers, John Parker (the sheriff of Rockingham County), Woodbury Langdon, and George King (a merchant who held
office both as deputy secretary to the council and as clerk of the superior court
and later became Atkinson's principal heir). See Portsmouth Town Records, Dec.
16, 1773, NHSL; Kenneth Scott, "Tory Associators of Portsmouth," *WMQ*, 3d ser.,
17 (1960), 513; Brewster, *Rambles*, II, 75–76.

women: if political leaders really meant what they said, why did they not stop the importation of the much more heavily taxed "wine, punch and flip"? He went on to observe that merchants who prevent the landing of East India tea and "at the same time sell their own at such an extravagant price, make it evident that it is not our interest, but their own private gain they are pursuing." Some inhabitants of western New Hampshire, already angry at eastern control of governmental offices, shared these suspicions. The town of Hinsdale, after noting that it had "become very fashionable" for New England towns to pass resolves concerning their rights and liberties, itself resolved that until people knew what rights and privileges belonged to them, they ought not to interfere in political matters. Agitation against the Tea Act had been organized "because the intended method of sale in this country by the East India Company would probably hurt the private interest of many persons who deal largely in tea." Those who declaimed most loudly in defense of their rights were parading patriotism to disguise "partial passion and private interest." Their "noisy intemperate froth of a poetical enthusiasm," concluded the townsmen, "is as far removed from a steady principle of patriotism as the dignity of solid understanding from ... poetical madness."[6]

Encouraged by these sentiments, Wentworth decided in January 1774 to risk reconvening the assembly. His hopes for legislative assistance were soon dashed. When he asked for laws to combat the "infectious and pestilential disorders being spread among the inhabitants, especially of Portsmouth," the house ignored his request. Later, when the backlog of local petitions and other noncontroversial business had been transacted, the representatives voted to write other colonial assemblies expressing New Hampshire's complete agreement with organized procedures of resistance. Wentworth immediately adjourned the assembly, then dissolved it, and with foreboding called for the new elections required by law.[7]

The spring elections of 1774 provided a fresh opportunity for inhabitants to assess provincial politics, just as the Tea Act had stimulated a new critique of Parliament and the ministry. Discussion

6. *New Hampshire Gazette*, Oct. 29, 1773, Feb. 18 and June 17, 1774; Jere R. Daniell, "Reason and Ridicule: Tea Act Resolutions in New Hampshire," *Historical New Hampshire*, 20 (Winter 1965), 23–28, contains complete versions of the last two quoted items.
7. *NHSP*, VII, 335–358. The quotation is from p. 335.

focused initially on one specific problem which had caused little trouble since the early days of Benning Wentworth's administration. Then, as a result of his victory over Waldron, the governor had been able to extend representation to every sizable community in the colony. John Wentworth, however, feared that expansion of the house would undermine his ability to influence it and restricted his recommendations for new representation to the few towns whose leading citizens were his friends. Even this proved unacceptable to the council members, who doubted the wisdom of any increase. As a result, by 1773 only 46 of New Hampshire's 147 towns and 56 per cent of its ratable polls participated in house elections; 38 per cent of provincial taxes were assessed in communities without representation, and there were only 34 house members.[8]

To a people continuously bombarded with cries of "no taxation without representation" such conditions grew intolerable. Soon after Wentworth issued writs for the elections, "Publicus" reminded *Gazette* readers that New Hampshire contained "many of His Majesty's subjects who are deprived of this inherent right of representation" yet annually pay "large sums for the support of government." Grafton County, for example, had no representatives, and neither did Nottingham and several other heavily populated eastern towns. "Publicus" went on to ridicule the idea of "virtual representation" and insisted that immediate steps be taken to give every town its constitutional rights. Such a "classical representation" would not, as some men believed, strengthen "the power of the Crown"; rather it would augment the voice of the people. "There is no drawing a line of representation," he concluded, "every freeholder in the most distant parts of the province has an equal right thereto." Other correspondents echoed his sentiments, and towns began to petition for representation.[9]

8. *New Hampshire Gazette*, Mar. 18, 25, 1774. The statistics are taken from Belknap, *History*, II, 488–490. See also George H. Evans, "The Basis of Representation in New Hampshire Previous to the Adoption of the Constitution of 1784," in James F. Colby, *Manual of the Constitution of the State of New Hampshire* (Concord, 1912), 257–267, and Jackson T. Main, "Government by the People: The American Revolution and the Democratization of the Legislatures," WMQ, 3d ser., 23 (1966), 393–394.

9. *New Hampshire Gazette*, Mar. 18, 1774; NHSP, IX, 663; fol. 774900.5, BLDC; New Ipswich Town Records, Mar. 14 and Dec. 26, 1774, NHSL. Other articles complaining about the basis of representation appear in the *Gazette*, Mar. 25, Apr. 1, and May 13, 1774.

The election produced further complaints. "Publicus" reiterated the demand for public house galleries and advocated written instructions for elected delegates. "Pro Bono Publico" criticized the council for refusing to extend representation. "Republicae Amicus" accused the government of favoritism in land grants and suggested that the "Junto of Wiseacres" in Portsmouth who opposed the candidacy of Woodbury Langdon included councilors who had no business interfering in house affairs. The election of delegates "who will withstand oppression to its face," he added, might lead to redress of such grievances as trial without jury before the Court of Appeals.[10]

Wentworth could hardly have been pleased by the election results. Langdon and two merchants (Samuel Cutts and Jacob Sheafe) who had signed the resolutions against the Tea Act won in Portsmouth. Exeter returned Nathaniel Folsom, one of the town's most outspoken radicals, in place of the governor's friend John Phillips. Nine other new delegates, seven of whom eventually served the revolutionary government, gained office. Moreover, when Wentworth called the assembly into session, the Portsmouth representatives showed up with formal instructions which promised to keep the house in turmoil. The instructions listed a dozen specific reforms needed to improve the provincial political situation; five dealt with the judicial system, one asked for an investigation of the governor's expenditure of public monies, and another demanded annual rather than triennial house elections. The remaining instructions ranged from the by-now-familiar plea for public house galleries to a previously unheard request for laws to prohibit the importation of slaves. The inhabitants of Portsmouth insisted, in addition, that the house be allowed to cooperate with other colonies in defending their constitutional rights.[11]

The session itself confirmed Wentworth's worst fears. He took, as he later explained to Dartmouth, "great pains to prevail on them not to enter into any extra-provincial measures," yet in an early meeting one of the Portsmouth delegates brought the matter up for discussion. The house decided to get routine business out of the way first, but on May 27, after a "warm debate," voted to appoint a provincial committee of correspondence. The next day it reaffirmed the decision. Wentworth in turn announced an adjournment, spent

10. *New Hampshire Gazette*, Mar. 18, 25, and Apr. 1, 1774.
11. *NHSP*, VII, 334, 359; *New Hampshire Gazette*, Apr. 22, 1774.

79

several agonizing days conferring with council members on what to do, and on June 8 dissolved the assembly for entering on matters "inconsistent with His Majesty's service and the good of this government."[12]

Tension increased rapidly during the summer. In June a tea consignment arrived in Portsmouth: only Wentworth's unwillingness to protect the shipment, the eagerness of merchants who now controlled local affairs to protect private property, and the promise of the consignee to return the tea unopened prevented the outbreak of violence.[13] Meanwhile, another source of trouble had arisen. The parliamentary legislation that closed the port of Boston until it made payment for tea destroyed the previous December stimulated a new wave of protests. In July, "Publicus" began a campaign seeking provincial assistance for the unfortunate victims of Great Britain's newest oppression. When the town clerk of Boston arrived in Portsmouth to seek help, the town first appointed a committee to accept voluntary donations and then, Wentworth reported to Dartmouth, "granted two hundred pounds proclamation money, which is near four times their province tax"; soon other towns along the seacoast and in the Merrimack Valley joined with contributions of everything from dried peas to hard cash. Two other developments followed passage of the Boston Port Act. The Portsmouth Committee of Correspondence passed a non-importation covenant, sent copies to local officials in every provincial town, and asked all patriotic citizens to affix their signatures. That same month, July, the provincial Committee of Correspondence, which had continued to meet in spite of Wentworth's dissolution of the assembly, asked each town to elect delegates to a general congress. When the delegates convened, they selected two members, John Sullivan of Durham and Nathaniel Folsom of Exeter, to attend the proposed Continental Congress.[14]

12. Wentworth to Dartmouth, June 8, 1774, NHSP, VII, 369; Wentworth to Thomas Waldron, June 8, 1774, Belknap Papers, 161.A.76; NHSP, VII, 359–369.
13. *New Hampshire Gazette*, July 1, 8, 1774; Wentworth to Dartmouth, July 4, 6, and 13, 1774, in NHSP, VII, 408–411, and in Belknap, *History*, III, 425–432; Adams, *Annals of Portsmouth*, 243–245; John Moffatt to Reynal and Coats, July 6, 1774, State Papers, 1773–1775 box, NHA. A second shipment arrived in September and received the same treatment: *New Hampshire Gazette*, Sept. 16, 1774.
14. *New Hampshire Gazette*, July 22, Sept. 23, 1774; Wentworth to Dartmouth, Aug. 29, Sept. 13, and Nov. 15, 1774, NHSP, VII, 411–418, and Belknap, *History*, III, 432–442; Joseph B. Walker, "The New Hampshire Covenant of 1774," *Granite Monthly*, 35 (1903), 188–197; NHSP, VII, 407–408.

Few provincials resisted these actions. Wentworth sat by help-lessly, lamented his "small influence," and wrote a series of increasingly pessimistic letters to England. The inhabitants who balked at the nonintercourse covenant—Belknap refused to sign because, he explained, "tyranny in one shape is as odious to me as tyranny in another"—became quiet after the Continental Congress recommended that all colonies join in a similar measure.[15] The vast majority of men considered organized protest both logical and necessary. The Port Act, the Massachusetts Government Act, the arrival of more troops in Boston, the Quebec Act—in short, the "whole train" of measures designed to punish the Bay Colony and keep Americans from further misbehavior—made it patently clear that Great Britain would not stop short of totally enslaving the colonies. Even New Hampshire, despite its previous moderation, had begun to experience direct threats to is security. John Sullivan warned in a public letter that Peter Livius had been appointed chief justice with both "a salary from the Crown and a commission during the King's pleasure to lord it over us so long as an arbitrary ministry shall be pleased with his arbitrary conduct." The Quebec Act left New Hampshire militarily exposed to Catholics and Indians whose "cursed religions" were "dangerous to the state and favorable to despotisms." The circumstances demanded total resistance. Massachusetts, as the committee from Durham which forwarded cattle and money to Boston wrote, was "standing bravely in the gap between us and slavery" and should be aided. Britain must be forced to her knees through economic sanctions. New Hampshire must cooperate with the other colonies to fix their rights on "a more firm and lasting basis." Wentworth wrote to Dartmouth in December that such "delusions" had become so great that "most people" took the recommendations of the Continental Congress "as matters of obedience, not of considerate examination."[16]

15. Wentworth to William Williams, July 22, 1774, quoted in Shipton, *Biographical Sketches*, XIII, 665; correspondence in Wentworth Letter Book no. 3, pp. 1–26; *New Hampshire Gazette*, Nov. 11, 1774 to Feb. 17, 1775. The Belknap quotation is from *Proceedings MHS*, 2d ser., 2 (1885–1886), 484.

16. Sullivan to John Langdon, Sept. 5, 1774, in Otis G. Hammond, ed., *Letters and Papers of Major-General John Sullivan* (NHHS *Collections*, XIII–XV [Concord, 1930–1939]), I, 47; Sullivan to Selectmen of Newmarket, Mar. 22, 1774, *ibid.*, I, 45; *Essex Journal*, Dec. 7, 1774; Wentworth to Dartmouth, Dec. 2, 1774, Wentworth Letter Book no. 3, p. 24. For a particularly vivid description of what the radicals believed was a ministerial plot to subvert colonial liberties, see the article by "Coloni" in the *New Hampshire Gazette*, Aug. 8, 1775.

Those who did insist on defending constituted authority found themselves on the defensive. In Salem a "notorious" and obese Tory was twice subjected to the public humiliation of a ceremony which ended with his delivery of a "monstrous foeted false conception, greatly to the joy of the beholders." Another throng forced Joshua Atherton, who tried to prevent Amherst from electing provincial congress delegates, to sign a recantation and then coerced an unpopular deputy sheriff into resigning his commission. A Walpole resident, subjected to similar treatment, signed a statement admitting that his defense of the crown had been the irrational product of an ill temper, which he promised in the future to curb. In Pembroke the number of people "engaged in the business of taking up tories" was so great that travelers could not find lodging. "Confessions and acknowledgments are becoming very common and fashionable," the publisher of the *Gazette* noted in early October; he thought the practice was productive of much good to the public.[17]

That same month an incident occurred which intensified antagonism to royal authority. General Gage, unable to hire carpenters in Massachusetts to construct barracks for his troops, asked Wentworth for help. Torn between what he considered his official duty and his knowledge that compliance would further jeopardize his already precarious authority, the governor compromised; he hired the artificers but tried to conceal his conduct by selecting men who lived near his Wolfboro estate and not telling them what they would be doing in Boston. The Portsmouth Committee of Ways and Means, a group set up to enforce community obedience to measures adopted by the Continental Congress, learned of his actions and published resolves branding him "an enemy . . . to the community." In Rochester a mob forced a public confession from the governor's unfortunate hiring agent and threatened to pillage his estate. The episode excited such "designed madness" in towns near Massachusetts, Wentworth reported to Dartmouth, that "several reprehensible violences" against royal officials resulted.[18] He commanded all officers

17. *Essex Journal*, Oct. 12, 1774; *New Hampshire Gazette*, Sept. 30 and Oct. 7, 1775; *McClure Diary*, ed. Dexter, 155; *The Diary of Matthew Patten of Bedford, New Hampshire, 1754–1788* (Concord, 1903), 330.

18. *New Hampshire Gazette*, Oct. 28 and Nov. 18, 1774; Wentworth to Henry Rust, Nov. 15, 1774, Wentworth to Matthew Thornton and others, Nov. 4, 1774, Wentworth to Corbyn Morris, Nov. 16, 1774, Wentworth Letter Book no. 3, pp. 1–15; Wentworth to Dartmouth, Nov. 15, 1774, NHSP, VII, 417. The first quotation is from the *Gazette* of Oct. 28.

in Hillsborough County, where most of the trouble occurred, to maintain civil order and warned them that it was his "incumbent duty" as chief magistrate "to be . . . a terror to evil doers." His bluster accomplished nothing. In private, Wentworth admitted he lacked "the efficient nerves of reward and punishment" which alone could quell disorder. To Rockingham he confessed: "This province, at last, has caught the infection."[19]

The seriousness of the infection became even more apparent on December 13 when Paul Revere arrived in Portsmouth bearing a message from Boston that England had banned further export of military stores to the colonies and that British troops were on their way to take possession of Castle William and Mary, the fort at Newcastle which protected both Portsmouth and Kittery. The next afternoon a crowd 400 strong assaulted the fort, took as much powder as they could carry, and sent it in small boats to nearby communities. By the morning of the 15th armed men from as far as 40 miles inland began to gather in the capital. That evening, led by Sullivan and John Langdon, they made a second attack, seized several cannon, and carried them to Portsmouth where Nathaniel Folsom stood guard until the booty could be transported up-country. Only the arrival of two men-of-war from Boston prevented further looting.[20]

Wentworth could not stop these proceedings. When the mob gathered on December 14, he tried to muster the militia, but no one obeyed. He then asked the council members and local magistrates to accompany him to the fort; some refused, others were reluctant, and, in any case, no men could be hired to put his barge in the water.

19. Wentworth to Thornton and others, Nov. 4, 1774, Wentworth to Morris, Nov. 16, 1774, Wentworth Letter Book no. 3, pp. 2 and 15; Wentworth to Rockingham, Nov. 9, 1774, *NEHGR*, 23 (1869), 275.

In Hillsborough County three special conditions tended to accentuate antagonism to royal authority. One, which Wentworth emphasized, was the county's proximity to Massachusetts. A second was the conduct of two recent royal appointees, Edward Lutwyche and John Holland. Lutwyche had been responsible for the return of British army deserters, and Holland had arranged for the escape of a prisoner indebted to him in order to place the burden of payment on county inhabitants. Racial factors provided the third. The county included a large percentage of Scotch-Irish settlers, whose ancestors earlier in the century had emigrated from Ulster to escape persecution by the British government. See Wentworth to Dartmouth, Nov. 15, 1774, *NHSP*, VII, 417; New Hampshire Loyalist Claims (transcripts), III, 1047, NHSL; Amherst Town Records, Aug. 5, 1773, NHSL. Edward L. Parker, *History of Londonderry* (Boston, 1851), 67–81 and *passim*, discusses the problem of ethnic antagonism.

20. *NHSP*, VII, 420–424; Wentworth Correspondence, Wentworth Letter Book no. 3, pp. 28–46; Elwin Page, "The King's Powder, 1774," *New England Quarterly*, 18 (1945), 83–92.

His tactics before the second attack proved equally ineffective. Two emissaries sent to disperse the massed citizens came back with a report that only a formal pardon from the governor for the previous day's activities would be successful. Wentworth refused and spent the night at home, listening to ominous movements outside. "The springs of government failed me," he explained later to Dartmouth; magistrates and militia officers who should have helped in suppressing the uproar either "joined in it" or were restrained from their duty for "fear of popular fury."[21] Royal government in Portsmouth, as elsewhere in New Hampshire, had all but collapsed.

From that point on, the governor lived in constant fear that he and his few supporters would fall victim to the public penchant for violence. He first asked for another ship and 40 or 50 marines. In mid-January he helped form an association of 59 Portsmouth residents—most of them public officials or members of the "clan"—who vowed to protect each other "from mobs, riots or any unlawful attacks whatever." But this was not enough. On the 21st he formally requested that two regiments of regulars be quartered in Portsmouth until order had been restored and the leaders of the attacks on Castle William had been punished for their crimes.[22]

Wentworth's threat forced many of Portsmouth's more moderate citizens to realize the seriousness of the events they had helped precipitate. If General Gage sent the troops and Parliament closed Piscataqua as it had Boston, the town would be in a sorry state. Merchants who had not already prepared for such eventualities—the pragmatic Woodbury Langdon had begun to retrench in December —did so now. "Candidus" lamented the "precipitate measures" and "indiscretion" of New Hampshire, predicted that "our brethren in the country will withhold every necessity to induce us to leave the

---

21. Wentworth to Gage, Dec. 17, 1774, Wentworth to Dartmouth, Dec. 20, 1774, and Wentworth to George Erving, Jan. 5, 1775, Wentworth Letter Book no. 3, pp. 33–59. Wentworth never sent the Gage letter.

22. Wentworth to Gage, Dec. 29, 1774 and Jan. 21, 1775, Wentworth to Admiral Graves, Dec. 30, 1774 and Jan. 21, 1775, Wentworth Letter Book no. 3, pp. 38–40 and 51–60; Scott, "Tory Associators," 507–515. The quotation is from page 507. The "associators" were far from popular. One colonist reported hearing that "the great ones at the bank" were almost "frightened out of their wits" because they believed "the town folks are all run mad and going to kill them because they aren't mad too." He went on to report that the associators had promised to shoot anyone who wouldn't let them "sell tea, play cards and dice the devil's device and do anything else they were amind to": *New Hampshire Gazette*, Feb. 3, 1775.

A PROCLAMATION,
BY THE GOVERNOR.

WHEREAS feveral Bodies of Men did, in the Day Time of the 14th, and in the Night of the 15th of this Inftant December, in the moft daring and rebellious Manner inveft, attack, and forcibly enter into His Majefty's Caftle William and Mary in this Province, and overpowering and confining the Captain and Garrifon, did, befides committing many treafonable Infults and Outrages, break open the Magazine of faid Caftle and plunder it of above One hundred Barrels of Gunpowder, with upwards of fixty Stand of fmall Arms, and did alfo force from the Ramparts of faid Caftle and carry off fixteen Pieces of Cannon, and other military Stores, in open Hoftility and direct Oppugnation of His Majefty's Government, and in the moft atrocious Contempt of his Crown and Dignity ;----

I Do, by Advice and Confent of His Majefty's Council, iffue this Proclamation, ordering and requiring, in his Majefty's Name, all Magiftrates and other Officers, whether Civil or Military, as they regard their Duty to the KING and the Tenor of the Oaths they have folemnly taken and fubfcribed, to exert themfelves in detecting and fecuring in fome of his Majefty's Goals in this province the faid Offenders, in Order to their being brought to condign punifhment ; And from Motives of Duty to the King and Regard to the Welfare of the good People of this Province : I do in the moft earneft and folemn Manner, exhort and injoin you, his Majefty's liege Subjects of this Government, to beware of fuffering yourfelves to be feduced by the falfe Arts or Menaces of abandoned Men, to abet, protect, or fcreen from Juftice any of the faid high handed Offenders, or to withhold or fecrete his Majefty's Munition forcibly taken from his Caftle ; but that each and every of you will ufe your utmoft Endeavours to detect and difcover the Perpetrators of thefe Crimes to the civil Magiftrate, and affift in fecuring and bringing them to Juftice, and in recovering the King's Munition; This Injunction it is my bounden Duty to lay ftrictly upon you, and to require your Obedience thereto, as you value individually your Faith and Allegiance to his Majefty, as you wifh to preferve that Reputation to the Province in general ; and as you would avert the dreadful but moft certain Confequences of a contrary Conduct to yourfelves and Pofterity.

GIVEN at the Council-Chamber in Portfmouth, the 26th Day of December, in the 15th Year of the Reign of our Sovereign Lord GEORGE the Third, by the Grace of GOD, of Great-Britain, France and Ireland, KING, Defender of the Faith, &c. and in the Year of our Lord CHRIST, 1774.

By His EXCELLENCY's Command, with Advice of Council.

J. WENTWORTH.

Theodore Atkinfon, Sec^ry.

G O D SAVE THE K I N G.

Proclamation issued by Governor John Wentworth soon after the attack on Castle William and Mary.

town, the better to thereby show a resentment to the quartering of such troops," and called for restoration of the fort at public expense. "Bystander" took advantage of the situation to condemn those who met to villify their neighbors, "putting the mark of *Cain* on one, and stigmatizing another . . . Oh my countrymen," he asked, "this is liberty?" Even the members of the Committee on Ways and Means, who refused either to apologize or retreat, organized nightly patrols to discourage further disorder.[23]

No such reaction occurred outside Portsmouth. Wentworth's actions since the attacks on the fort meant that he, too, intended to take part in the ministerial plot to destroy colonial liberties. And if this were true, then the people of New Hampshire must strike. Royal officials who still supported their governor found themselves subjected to new and more dangerous intimidations; some left the countryside for Portsmouth or Boston. Sullivan, whom Wentworth had dismissed from the militia, urged his fellow officers to resign en masse and organized weekly military drills in Durham and neighboring towns. When a captain in Newton refused to muster the local militia, the regiment appointed new officers, began to train, and publicized their efforts as an example for others to follow. To many inhabitants the advice must have seemed gratuitous, for by then dozens of towns had begun preparations to defend their rights by force of arms.[24]

Meanwhile Wentworth, hoping desperately to restore some semblance of constitutional authority, decided once again to convene the assembly. This time he took steps to prevent a repetition of the previous spring's fiasco: he added three small Connecticut Valley towns, where personal friends supposedly dominated local politics, to the list of those eligible for representation; he timed the elections to coincide with the expected arrival of British troops; and he laid plans to arrest any successful candidates who had instigated or par-

23. Langdon to Eastman and Webster, Dec. 17, 1774, *NEHGR*, 22 (1868), 337; *New Hampshire Gazette*, Feb. 17 and 24, 1775; on the patrols see Wentworth to Dartmouth, May 17, 1775, Wentworth Letter Book no. 3, p. 97.

24. Wentworth to Dartmouth, Mar. 10 and 16, 1775, Wentworth Letter Book no. 3, pp. 67–70; *New Hampshire Gazette*, Mar. 10, 17, and 31, 1775; Hammond, ed., *Sullivan Papers*, I, 53–58; State Papers, 1620–1789, 1775 folder, NHA. See also individual town records for February and March 1775: NHSL has, on microfilm, most town records up to 1800. Earlier, Sullivan had written an elaborate justification for military preparedness: Hammond, ed., *Sullivan Papers*, I, 50–53.

ticipated in the attack on Castle William.[25] But his maneuvering backfired.

In the first place, the election results were not what Wentworth expected. Both of the Langdons, Folsom, and many of "their connections" gained seats—so many that they composed, Wentworth reported, at least a third of the house. To make matters worse, General Gage decided soon after the elections that he could not spare his regiments. Quickly Wentworth requested other assistance which would make the planned arrests possible and just as quickly postponed the first assembly meeting until early May. This, too, caused trouble. "Spectator" condemned the adjournment as the latest in a series of arbitrary measures which had "deprived the people from any share in their own government for near twelve months" and reduced them "to the sad necessity of being governed by the Crown, or its immediate servants, or of being reduced to a state of anarchy." Such conduct, he concluded, had helped destroy the "much deluded" chief magistrate's popularity and power.[26]

Wentworth's attempt to pack the house exacerbated his difficulties. Political discussions the previous year had convinced many colonists that every town should have the right to vote in assembly elections and that representation should be roughly proportional to population. Since the new precepts covered only three towns, and those three—Plymouth, Orford, and Lyme—contained far fewer inhabitants than dozens of other unrepresented communities, the governor had violated both principles.[27] Furthermore, he and the council had issued the precepts without consulting anyone in the house. Benning Wentworth had been able to get away with an identical intrusion on house privileges, but now things were different. "There is no legal authority vested in any separate branch or

25. Wentworth to Dartmouth, Mar. 10, 1775, Wentworth Letter Book no. 3, p. 67; *NHSP*, VII, 371. Wentworth constantly overestimated the amount of support he could muster. In part this stemmed from his feeling that if a few "indefatigable incendiaries"—he undoubtedly had Sullivan, Folsom, and John Langdon in mind—could be controlled, the whole movement would collapse. See especially Wentworth to Paul Wentworth, June 29, 1775, Wentworth Letter Book no. 3, p. 119.

26. Wentworth to Dartmouth, Mar. 10, 1775, Wentworth Letter Book no. 3, p. 67; *NHSP*, VII, 370–371; *New Hampshire Gazette*, Mar. 17, 1775. The *Gazette* article is republished in Peter Force, comp., *American Archives*, 4th ser., II, 159.

27. Butters, "Meshech Weare," 144, estimates that there were 45 larger but unrepresented towns. Some contained as many as 1500 inhabitants; the total population of the three Grafton County communities was 856.

branches of the legislature . . . to issue such writs," read a petition asking that the new members not be seated and signed by 59 residents of Portsmouth. "We apprehend the exercise of such authority therefore not only unwarranted by the British Constitution or the laws of this province, but in its consequences subversive of both and pregnant with many alarming evils." "Spectator" accused Wentworth of sending precepts only to towns where "placemen," "pensioners," and people dependent on land grants abounded. The election by Plymouth of John Fenton, a close friend of the governor, reinforced the growing conviction that Wentworth must be thwarted in his efforts.[28]

Before the assembly met, most of New Hampshire was already in total rebellion against royal authority. The failure of Gage to send troops had cost the government much of its authority; the fighting at Lexington and Concord completed the process. In troublesome Hillsborough and Cheshire counties mobs prevented the courts from convening and drove officials still loyal to the crown from their homes. John Hurd reported from Grafton County, which until now had been relatively quiet, that the impassioned settlers "burned" to be among their victimized countrymen, "to assist, and if possible, to revenge the innocent blood." He and other royal officials—Hurd held office both as a justice of the peace and as collector of quitrents —began to resign their commissions. In the Portsmouth area, the situation was hardly more peaceful. Although the town, in a last gesture of respect, voted to protect Wentworth against "any insult being offered to his person and dignity," bodies of armed men roamed outside the capital, disarming known loyalists and threatening to seize the governor and other royal officials. One such group actually entered Portsmouth, but the local Committee of Ways and Means kept them under control.[29]

The assembly session dashed Wentworth's last hope of moderating lawlessness. In an emotional introductory speech he reminded

28. *NHSP*, IX, 714; Langdon Papers, 103, HSP; *New Hampshire Gazette*, Feb. 10, 1775. Fenton, a retired British army captain, was clerk of the Court of Common Pleas and judge of probate in Grafton County and a colonel in the provincial militia: Scott, "Tory Associators," 512.

29. Loyalist Claims, III, 1047 and 1160, NHSL; *New Hampshire Gazette*, May 5 and 19, June 2, 1775; Belknap, *History*, II, 394; Hurd to Joshua Brackett, May 6, 1775, *Proceedings MHS*, 1st ser., 5 (1860–1862), 2–3; "John Hurd" in Shipton, *Biographical Sketches*, XII, 164–171; Adams, *Annals of Portsmouth*, 251; Wentworth to Dartmouth, May 17, 1775, Wentworth Letter Book no. 3, p. 96.

the assemblymen that the "strongest ties of kinship, religion, duty and interest" bound them to the parent state and pleaded with them to consider measures which would "lead to a restoration of the public tranquillity" and "an affectionate reconciliation with our mother country." But the house members could not be moved. They first appointed a committee to report on the "sundry" petitions complaining about representatives returned in an "unconstitutional manner," then asked for an adjournment to consult their constituents. Wentworth at first refused—he knew that many of the representatives planned to attend an illegal congress of town delegates—but when it became evident the house would break up anyway he granted their request. The representatives gathered again in June, by an overwhelming majority refused to seat the new delegates, and told the governor they were "entirely at a loss" to know what measures they might take to re-establish the "much desired reconciliation." Wentworth immediately announced a second adjournment, this time without being asked.[30]

That evening John Fenton, who had disrupted the house meetings by advocating acceptance of Lord North's conciliatory proposals, visited Wentworth. While the men dined, the governor's wife Frances wrote a long letter to Lady Rockingham. Since Lexington, she explained, it had been necessary for someone in the house to stand watch, lest they be surprised in their sleep and taken. The long vigil and tumultuous events in the province had been particularly hard on her husband: once "as popular as his heart could wish," he now faced an "enraged multitude" which would be satisfied with nothing less than his appearing in arms against the king. Every time "his office duty" required him to act contrary to popular wishes, his life and the lives of his friends and relatives were threatened. "The governor is so distressed at the times," she burst out at one point, "it preys on him—he has lost a great deal of flesh—and all his spirits I tell him—but he don't own it." Soon after she finished the letter she learned that a crowd demanding Fenton's arrest had gathered outside. Fenton at first refused to appear, but when the mob brought up a cannon and started beating on the house with clubs, he surrendered. That night Wentworth, his wife, and their five-month-old

---

30. The quotations are from *NHSP*, VII, 370–380. *New Hampshire Gazette*, May 6 and June 14, 1775; Wentworth to Dartmouth, May 12 and June 15, 1775, Wentworth Letter Book no. 3, pp. 94, 115.

Frances Deering Wentworth (1745–1813). Portrait painted by John Singleton Copley in 1765 when Frances was the wife of Theodore Atkinson, Jr.

child moved to the fort, where they would be protected by the guns
of His Majesty's Ship *Scarborough*.[31]

Wentworth's flight completed the disintegration of family and
royal government. Atkinson tried to keep up appearances in Ports-

31. Frances Wentworth to Lady Rockingham, June 13 and June 26, 1775, Rockingham Letters, Ramsden Papers, Sheepscar Library, Leeds, England; Belknap, *History*, II, 385.

mouth but possessed no effective authority. Wentworth himself could do nothing but issue orders through Atkinson and hope that General Gage would send troops. Life at the fort was both dangerous and boring—"among the infinite vexations of such disquieted time," the governor wrote in one letter, is "that social reciprocations are interrupted and those hours intended for society are condemned to solitude"—so when the *Scarborough*, cut off from all supplies by the Portsmouth Committee of Ways and Means, left for Boston, Wentworth and his family were aboard. In September he hired a sloop, sailed to an offshore island, and prorogued the assembly. After this pathetic voyage, New Hampshire's last royal governor never returned to his native province.[32]

32. *New Hampshire Gazette*, Aug. 15, Sept. 26, 1775; *NHSP*, VII, 381–390; Wentworth Correspondence in Wentworth Letter Book no. 3, pp. 116–152; David McClure to Eleazar Wheelock, Aug. 15, 1775, fol. 775465.1, BLDC. The quotation is from Wentworth to Tristan Dalton, July 31, 1775, Wentworth Letter Book no. 3, p. 128.

Part II
Republicanism Established:
The War Years

4

Political Authority in
the Revolutionary Crisis,
1774–1776

In some localities attacks on royal government threatened further social and political chaos. The men who gathered to silence suspected Tories often enjoyed their work so much that magistrates trying to preserve order could not as one Portsmouth official explained, "persuade them to disperse until they exceed the bounds of reason." Individuals took revenge on personal enemies by accusing them of disloyalty. Local officials, especially those holding royal commissions, found their authority weakened and their right to perform normal governmental functions challenged. After the courts closed, debtors refused to fulfill contracts and ordinary crime went unpunished. By the summer of 1775 influential men throughout New Hampshire, including many who had been outspoken in their criticism of Parliament and the ministry, worried lest the entire fabric of civil authority be torn apart.[1]

The disruptions, however, were limited in scope and of short duration. Even before Governor Wentworth fled Portsmouth, concerned citizens had constructed a network of local organizations to guarantee the maintenance of peace and good order, and the provincial congress had begun to assume responsibilities that were legally in the hands of the governor and assembly. The movement toward setting up a revolutionary government gained momentum after Wentworth left New Hampshire. The congress handled general matters

1. Belknap, *History*, II, 394; *New Hampshire Gazette,* June 27, Aug. 29, 1775. The quotation is from *NHSP*, VII, 502.

while the towns authorized individuals and groups to exercise power previously wielded by royally appointed officials. In January 1776 the congress declared itself the new House of Representatives and adopted a written constitution to legitimize its authority. Some opposition to these measures arose, but by spring the vast majority of residents had given full allegiance to the new government.

The transition in authority from royal to revolutionary government involved a dramatic reshaping of provincial politics. The institutional structure emerged in a form which reflected criticisms generated in the constitutional debate of the sixties and early seventies. New Hampshire's new political leaders represented economic interests and shared ideological assumptions different from those of their colonial counterparts. For nearly two decades the revolutionists continued to experiment with political and constitutional reform, but none of their subsequent efforts altered the pattern of power as decisively as did events between 1774 and 1776.

INSTITUTIONS

Royal authority, even at the peak of Benning Wentworth's power, was never deeply rooted at the town level. The political activity in which the Wentworths, Waldrons, Sherburnes, Gilmans, and other gentlemen engaged affected ordinary inhabitants little. Royally appointed local officials—justices of the peace, militia officers, and, after 1771, county magistrates—customarily were men whose economic and social status made them natural community leaders; their influence stemmed as much from this as from their royal commissions. Even in Portsmouth, where the bulk of the provincial oligarchy lived, men whose "interest" with the Wentworths was at best marginal managed local affairs. Furthermore, royal government had almost no direct influence on political matters of primary interest to the average male citizen. Ministerial salaries, road and bridge building, the use of common lands, and care of the town poor were all discussed and voted on in town meetings. Officials elected at these gatherings—selectmen, constables, tithingmen, hogreves, and many others—exercised power locally. They collected taxes, including those assessed by the colonial assembly, enforced or chose not to enforce provincial laws, settled disputes, and in general saw to the maintenance of civil order. Controversies which could not be settled by town government sometimes reached the General Court, but there, too, locally elected men, either house representatives or specially selected agents, played major decision-making roles.[2]

As a result, when royal authority began to collapse, local authority remained intact. Many royal officials continued to enforce the law although their commissions had become worthless. Locally elected officials did the same; in Hillsborough County, for example, the grand jury instructed a constable, who had been criticized for invoking the authority of the crown to break up a fight, to keep enforcing the law but to avoid mentioning His Majesty's name. Only for a brief period in June 1775 did any significant general challenge to existing community government arise. The provincial congress responded quickly by recommending "that with regard to all those who have been in the usual reasonable manner chosen into any office in towns, they should as formerly be considered as the proper officers," and instructing "selectmen, constables and other officers" to "proceed in the usual manner" in fulfilling their traditional responsibilities. Magistrates were aided by what Belknap later described as "habits of decency, family government, and the good examples of influential persons." These, he felt, "contributed more to maintain order than any other authority."[3]

Even the militia, which more than any other locally based colonial organization was under the ruling oligarchy's influence, survived the disintegration of royal government. Colonial law required every male citizen between sixteen and sixty to provide himself with musket, powder, and other necessary military equipment, and imperial instructions obligated the governor to organize a militia and keep it in a state of readiness. John Wentworth had tried to obey his instructions. Military appointments afforded an opportunity to reward his friends and to obligate those who were not his friends; besides, the young governor found the pageantry of muster days much to his liking. By 1774 the militia was better organized than at any other time since the end of the war.[4]

2. Wentworth to Dartmouth, Aug. 29, 1774, in Belknap, *History*, III, 435. There is no good discussion of the relationship between town and provincial government in colonial New Hampshire. My analysis is based on a study of town-meeting records and town petitions to the assembly published in *NHSP*, IX, XI–XIII. The best treatment of political life in an eighteenth-century colonial New England community is Charles S. Grant, *Democracy in the Connecticut Frontier Town of Kent* (New York, 1961).
3. *New Hampshire Gazette*, Feb. 10, June 27, 1775; Belknap, *History*, II, 394.
4. Batchellor and Metcalf, eds., *Laws of New Hamp.*, IV, 39–57; Mayo, *Wentworth*, 45–46.

That fall Wentworth discovered that the effectiveness of his efforts had done nothing to bolster royal authority. Militiamen ignored his plea to protect Castle William from attack. When he revoked the commissions of officers who took part in the assault, they continued to assert their leadership and to train their men. Regimental commanders who remained loyal to the governor lost their authority; men more "patriotic" in sentiment were elected by the rank and file to replace them. Indeed, the fact that an officer had once possessed "interest" with the Wentworths made him suspect. The militia consequently provided a ready-made instrument for revolutionary leaders to exploit. Entire regiments hurried down to Massachusetts in the dead of night after messengers brought news of the fighting at Lexington and Concord. Afterward local and provincial officials built a reasonably effective military establishment on the foundations so carefully constructed by their royal predecessors.[5]

The revolutionists found existing civil institutions equally useful in the political crisis. Town meetings served a variety of purposes. They voted funds and supplies to support the militia, passed resolves against the Tea Act, provided help to the victims of the Boston Port Bill, lent support to measures adopted in the Continental Congress, and in general were instrumental in articulating the logic which justified resistance to imperial legislation. They responded readily when asked to elect members to provincial congresses and passed resolutions to implement the recommendations of the emerging state government. At the same time they assumed responsibility for preventing breakdown of community discipline. In the fall of 1774 when groups of men roamed the countryside looking for Tories, Francestown resolved to "show our disapprobation of all unlawful proceedings of unjust men congregating together as they pretend to maintain their liberties," and other communities passed similar votes. A year later the citizens of Keene explained in a public resolution that since English law had ceased to be effective, "disorderly" people threatened "to abuse and destroy the persons and property of many of the good and wholesome inhabitants of the land," and since

5. See citations in n. 21 and n. 24, chap. iii. The most famous militia officer victimized for past associations with Wentworth was Benjamin Thompson (later Count Rumford, an important British physicist and statesman): Joseph B. Walker, "Life of Honorable Timothy Walker," typescript, 1903, 62–64, NHHS. For a discussion of revolutionary military organization see Richard F. Upton, *Revolutionary New Hampshire* (Hanover, 1936), 88–105.

neither the Continental Congress nor the provincial congress had "as yet found out or published any method or system of government," it was necessary for them to take decisive action. They outlawed swearing, loitering, tippling, fighting, and name-calling, set up a three-man committee to enforce these regulations, and promised to have published in the *Gazette* the names of all who refused to accept its decisions. Peace and good order soon reigned in Keene.[6]

The device of creating special committees to execute the general will as expressed in town meetings became a favorite of revolutionists. During the Stamp Act crisis Exeter and Portsmouth had appointed groups of men to prevent rioting and to protect the stamp collector from personal injury. Committees of correspondence were organized in many towns to implement provincial resistance to the Tea Act. After Portsmouth learned that a local merchant who had bought tea from the East India Company would soon receive his first consignment, the town meeting chose a committee to deal with him and assigned a watch of twenty-five to guard the shipment once it had been landed. At the same time it appointed a general committee of inspection to prevent further imports; when the committee—on its way to inspect a ship rumored to have tea aboard—saved a boy from drowning, one *Gazette* correspondent declared that even "the most determined enemy of the country must allow that Providence makes use of and approves of such men." Dozens of other communities organized similar groups to implement the nonimportation agreement passed by the Continental Congress.[7]

The collapse of royal government in the winter and spring of 1775 placed additional burdens on local authority. Most communities responded by appointing a committee of safety (in some places called the Committee of Ways and Means) charged with the general responsibility of doing whatever seemed necessary to protect the colonists and to maintain community discipline. Portsmouth acted first, and with a good deal of success. The committee members, as-

6. New Hampshire Town Records, NHSL, *passim*; *New Hampshire Gazette*, Nov. 18, 1774, Feb. 10, 1775. The quotations are from *NHSP*, VII, 417, and *The Repertory*, 1 (April 1925), 241–244. Samuel T. Worcester, "Hollis, New Hampshire, in the War of the Revolution," *NEHGR*, 30 (1876), 288–298, provides a thorough description of activities in one town. For events in Keene read Abner Sanger, "Ye Journal of Abner Sanger," *The Repertory*, 1 (1924–1925), *passim*.

7. Belknap, *History*, II, 328, 336; *New Hampshire Gazette*, June 27, July 22, 1774; New Hampshire Town Records, *passim*. The quotation is from the *Gazette*, July 22, 1774.

sisted by Governor Wentworth, made a series of agreements with the
Scarborough's captain which effectively neutralized danger from that
quarter and eventually forced the man-of-war to leave the harbor
altogether. The problem of internal order proved more serious. Portsmouth, as the committee chairman explained, labored under "pecu-
liar" difficulties. The stagnation of trade and the return of much
shipping left a large number of people who "for want of employment" readily fell into disorder. At times the populace got out of
hand: one citizen complained in August that "scarcely a week" went
by "but either men in arms or in liquor, sometimes in both," disturbed the peace and "reduced the interest of inhabitants . . . to a
tottering, precarious condition," but for the most part the committee
members kept matters under control. They arranged for nightly
patrols, dealt with refugees seeking asylum, and provided a forum in
which potentially explosive personal disputes could be settled in an
orderly fashion.[8] Committees of safety proved equally effective elsewhere.

The stability and continuity of local government made possible
the creation of political organizations which assumed authority to
act for more than the individual community. A few of these formed
at the county level. Before the revolution the Court of General
Sessions, attended by specially delegated justices of the peace, conducted much of the important county business. These courts provided a ready-made instrument for intercommunity action once royal
government began to weaken. In November 1774, court members in
Hillsborough County helped organize a congress where locally
elected representatives gathered to discuss the critical state of affairs.
Although little came out of this meeting, a second congress, which
was called the following March, did produce results. Wentworth
labeled the session "illegal" and those attending guilty of "high
treason," but the warning accomplished nothing. The convened
delegates passed a resolution condemning "licentious attacks" on
persons and property, recommended disciplined military training in
all communities, and attempted to strengthen the county judicial
system. A few weeks later they reconvened, declaring that measures
were needed "for the better security . . . of the county, to prevent

8. Wentworth correspondence, Wentworth Letter Book, no. 3, pp. 97–109; *NHSP*,
VII, 375–389. The quotations are from *NHSP*, VII, 502, and *New Hampshire Gazette*, Aug. 29, 1775.

declining into a state of nature," and formed a committee of safety which for a brief period assumed authority to punish ordinary criminals as well as suspected Tories. A congress of delegates from towns in Cheshire County also met and issued resolutions similar to those of the Hillsborough gathering.[9]

The movement toward strengthening county governments, however, never spread throughout the province. Local officials in the older eastern communities kept matters well enough in hand to prevent the development of any serious disorder. In the more recently settled western areas, town organizations proved less effective, but still they could move with greater efficiency than their regional counterparts. The one group which did attempt to enforce county authority, the Hillsborough Committee of Safety, frequently met with local opposition which made implementation of its decisions impossible.[10] By the summer of 1775 the county organizations had begun to outlive their usefulness. Their main function—to provide a mechanism for intercommunity cooperation—had been taken over by the emerging provincial government.

The Committee of Correspondence appointed by the House of Representatives in May 1774 provided the initial stimulus in forming New Hampshire's revolutionary government. When Wentworth dissolved the assembly in an attempt to keep the committee from meeting, its members refused to disperse; instead, they issued a summons for the representatives to reconvene. Enough of the legislators obeyed to convince the governor he had a serious rebellion on his hands. After the delegates had gathered in the assembly room, he entered, solemnly warned them that their behavior was both illegal and unwarranted, and had the local sheriff read a proclamation ordering them to keep the king's peace. The convention members were sufficiently impressed by his performance to leave the room, but they met at a local tavern. By nightfall they had agreed to ask each town in the province to elect members for a general congress at

9. Edward D. Boylston, *The Hillsborough County Congresses, 1774 and 1775* (Amherst, 1884); Wentworth to Benjamin Whiting, Mar. 30, 1775, Wentworth Letter Book no. 3, 74; "Revolution" folio, box II, Tolford-Patten Papers, NHSL; Jaffrey Town Records, Jan. 18, 1775, NHSL. The last two quotations are from *NHSP*, VII, 447–451.

10. *NHSP*, VII, 450; Josiah Brown to Sullivan, Sept. 16, 1775, in Hammond, ed., *Sullivan Papers*, I, 88; Samuel T. Worcester, *History of the Town of Hollis* (Boston, 1879), 144–145.

Exeter. Those who gathered at Exeter would, in turn, select delegates for the proposed Continental Congress. The towns were also asked to collect funds to pay these delegates and to observe the fourteenth of July as a day of fasting and prayer. Wentworth had few illusions about what would happen next. "It is as yet uncertain how far these requisitions will be complied with," he wrote to Dartmouth, "but I am apt to believe the spirit of enthusiasm, which generally prevails through the colonies, will create an obedience that reason or religion would fail to procure."[11] He was right.

New Hampshire's first provincial congress gave the protest movement an organized stature it previously had lacked. Eighty-five delegates, mostly from the seaboard area, responded to the call. In a hurried session they not only chose Sullivan and Folsom to attend the Continental Congress but appointed a treasurer to receive the £200 contributed by the towns to defray their expenses, formed a committee to instruct them, and in a final gesture recommended that all communities in New Hampshire send aid to the victims of the Boston Port Act. No significant opposition to any of these votes arose.[12]

The Committee of Correspondence, which during the summer had encouraged towns to enter into nonimportation agreements, called a second provincial congress for January 1775; again the declared aim of the meeting was to select and finance delegates for the Continental Congress. But by the time the congress convened, affairs in New Hampshire had become so chaotic that many thought more should be done. After Sullivan and John Langdon had been appointed to go to Philadelphia, the two men, supported by Folsom, tried to obtain a petition asking Wentworth to reconvene the assembly with the promise he would not dissolve it. Meshech Weare and several other delegates opposed the motion. The congress, they argued, had been called for specific purposes, and to exceed these purposes would be illegal. Sullivan replied that since the whole meeting was unlawful it might do anything it pleased. Although the proposed petition apparently was never authorized, Sullivan's logic prevailed. Before adjourning, the congress appointed its own Com-

11. *NHSP*, VII, 399–401, 411; Wentworth to Dartmouth, July 13, 1774, Belknap, *History*, III, 431.
12. *NHSP*, VII, 407–408. Joseph B. Walker, *New Hampshire's Five Provincial Congresses, July 21, 1774–January 5, 1776* (Concord, 1905), summarizes proceedings in this and subsequent provincial congresses.

mittee of Correspondence and issued a set of recommendations which Governor Wentworth labeled an attempt to assume "uncontrolled dictatorial power."[13]

These recommendations reflected the same concerns expressed by the town and county organizations. Alarmed at the past months' disorders, the congress asked that "all trespasses and injuries against individuals and their property" be terminated, that provincial law be supported, and that "due obedience" be accorded all magistrates. Yet "due obedience" should not be interpreted to imply any reduction in efforts to resist the oppressive measures adopted by the British ministry. All the recommendations of the Continental Congress should be implemented. The inhabitants of New Hampshire should "encourage and support" the "several committees of correspondence and inspection in discharging the very important trust . . . reposed in them." Since a well-disciplined militia would provide excellent defense if America were "invaded by his Majesty's enemies," all citizens should arm and train themselves. The congress also advised the practice of "economy and industry," the avoidance of lawsuits, and frequent recourse to prayers for the restoration of peace and tranquility.[14] It is impossible to measure the impact of these resolutions, but there can be no doubt that the men who met at Exeter played an important role in the general hardening of provincial attitudes which took place in February and March.

Neither can it be questioned that Wentworth considered the congress a major threat to his authority. He complained to one councilor that the delegates, in sacrificing "their reason and constituents to their fears and to their popularity," had left no ground for amnesty. There was little hope of repairing the damage—"peace," he wrote, "has by unwise men been driven out; they know not what they do"—but he must try. Shortly thereafter, Wentworth issued writs for the election of members to what became New Hampshire's last colonial assembly.[15]

The drift of power to the provincial congresses continued despite this assembly. Even before the governor convened the representatives, a third congress met in the emergency created by the bloodshed

---

13. *NHSP*, VII, 442–444; Wentworth to Thomas Waldron, Jan. 27, 1775, *Belknap Papers, MHS Collections*, 6th ser., IV, 73.

14. *NHSP*, VII, 443–444.

15. Wentworth to Waldron, Jan. 27, 1775, *Belknap Papers, MHS Collections*, 6th ser., IV, 73.

at Lexington and Concord and, after pledging themselves to secrecy, appointed Folsom commander of New Hampshire's troops in Massachusetts and ordered him to purchase necessary supplies. When the assembly did meet, its behavior confirmed Wentworth's worst fears. The same man (the other John Wentworth) who had been chairman of the first three congresses was elected Speaker of the house. He and the five house members who were on the Congressional Committee of Correspondence immediately requested a recess to confer with their constituents about the seating of members from the newly represented towns. Wentworth complied, even though he knew a fourth provincial congress had been called into session. Early in June this congress resolved that new house members should not be seated. The old house members, thirteen of whom were members of the congress, encountered no difficulty making certain the resolution was not violated; "the voice of the convention," Belknap later noted, "was regarded by the House as the voice of their constituents."[16]

The fourth provincial congress, however, had more pressing business than dictating policy to the virtually defunct colonial assembly. Already requests for military supplies had been received from Folsom and his fellow officers. The Portsmouth committee asked for instructions concerning disposition of mast trees afloat in the Piscataqua. Frontiersmen, frightened by rumors of an impending attack from Canada, sought aid in bolstering their defenses, as did seacoast inhabitants alarmed by reports that armed cutters had been seen leaving Boston. The Massachusetts provincial congress requested more military assistance and approbation for their assumption of authority. Congress members at Exeter took up each specific problem as it arose, but they spent most of their energy establishing general procedures and mechanisms for implementing the power they now wielded. They voted to raise 2,000 soldiers, appropriated £10,500 to support them, and created committees of safety and supply to handle the details. Instructions for the handling of suspected Tories, ordinary criminals, and deserters from the army were sent to each town and parish. The colonial records and the £1,500 of public money held by Treasurer George Jaffrey were confiscated and moved from Portsmouth to Exeter. The Congress set up a post-office system,

16. *NHSP*, VII, 359–386, 452–467, 506–507; Belknap, *History*, II, 385.

authorized bounties for the manufacture of saltpeter, and asked creditors to treat debtors, especially those in the army, with leniency. When the congress adjourned on July 8, President Meshech Weare reported that New Hampshire was "wholly governed by this congress and the committees of the respective towns." A few days later Governor Wentworth told Dartmouth the same thing.[17]

The members of the fourth provincial congress continued to exercise authority until mid-December. They reconvened in mid-August and again in late October, each time sitting for about two weeks, and charged the Committee of Safety with broad powers of public responsibility while the full convention was in recess. Both congress and committee cooperated closely with local organizations. When the local committee in Mason captured two thieves, the congress authorized it to administer appropriate justice. After it was reported that some towns had refused to punish violations of the nonintercourse agreements, the congress voted to have the committees of safety in neighboring towns enforce the regulations. The provincial Committee of Safety scolded the inhabitants of Newton for failing to follow the congressional recommendation to create a committee for apprehending deserters and asked the selectmen to correct the omission. To be sure, some confusion resulted—military leaders, for example, were not certain what specific powers the Committee of Safety had, and a few local committees took action in the name of provincial authority which provincial officials later felt obliged to condemn—but for the most part the arrangement worked smoothly and to the satisfaction of those involved.[18]

One crucial political question faced New Hampshire's new governmental leaders: how far should they go toward assuming the full powers exercised by their predecessors? Although as early as May some delegates advocated looking "to our whole political affairs," a majority in the congress refused to take action which might suggest a general assumption of civil authority. Instead of making laws, they passed recommendations and resolves. They voted to print money but would not assert the power of taxation. When the courts closed, no effort was made either to reopen them or to appoint new judicial

17. *NHSP*, VII, 468–554; Weare to Continental Congress, July 8, 1775, *NHSP*, VII, 561; Wentworth to Dartmouth, July 17 and 20, 1775, Wentworth Letter Book no. 3, 136–142.
18. *NHSP*, 511–664; *New Hampshire Gazette*, June 9–July 4, 1775; Committee of Safety to Sullivan, Sept. 28, 1775, in Hammond, ed., *Sullivan Papers*, I, 92.

officers. In August, after discussing the constitutional implications of its earlier decision, the congress rescinded a vote providing travel pay for those who had attended the two previous Houses of Representatives. The congress, its leaders felt, had been organized to resist the threat of British tyranny. They would not consider "taking up government" unless specifically authorized to do so.[19]

Wentworth's flight from Portsmouth, evidence of internal disorder, and the battle of Bunker Hill, which shocked those still hoping for a general reconciliation, led the congress to seek such authorization. Initially they turned to the Continental Congress. The Committee of Safety members informed Langdon and Sullivan that they were "anxious to know the results of your deliberations in order to conduct the affairs of this colony, which at this time is in some confusion." The president of the Exeter convention was more insistent. "We greatly desire some other regulations," he wrote to the Continental Congress in July, "as our present situation is attended with many difficulties." He promised, however, that nothing "of that kind" would be attempted "without direction."[20]

The request came at an opportune time. Early in June, John Adams had delivered a speech before the Continental Congress in which he pointed out the necessity for individual provinces to set up their own governments. The idea had seemed far too radical to most members, but Sullivan (who in the second provincial congress had argued for the assumption of unlimited powers) and Langdon were impressed. Prompted by the letters from Exeter, they entered into a series of private consultations which were so encouraging that early in October Langdon and Bartlett—Sullivan had been appointed a general in the Continental army—informed the provincial congress it should submit a formal "petition for government." The congress never drew up the petition, but it made no difference. Langdon and Bartlett announced they had received appropriate instructions and moved that since New Hampshire possessed no charter and its governor had fled, the province be asked to take up civil government. On November 3, 1775 the Continental Congress passed a resolve to that effect.[21]

19. *NHSP*, VII, 483, 561, 575–578.
20. William Whipple to Sullivan and Langdon, July 8, 1775, and Weare to Continental Congress, July 8, 1775, *NHSP*, VII, 559, 561.
21. *Diary and Autobiography of John Adams*, ed. Butterfield, III, 310, 317, 352–356; Bartlett and Langdon to Thornton, Oct. 2 and Nov. 3, 1775, *NHSP*, VII, 615,

While the provincial congress awaited news from Philadelphia, it began to consider related constitutional problems. The matter of representation loomed most important. By 1775 most colonists resented the exclusion of over half New Hampshire's towns and nearly half its voters from participating in assembly elections. Each provincial town, as a result, had been invited to send delegates to the various provincial congresses, and most had responded; the fourth congress included 153 members representing 113 communities, nearly 80 per cent of those officially incorporated.[22] But provincial leaders felt that the system of representation needed to be regularized. If the present arrangement continued, the number of delgates, already too large, might continue to grow. Moreover, failure to specify the number of representatives each town was permitted to elect had produced inequities which might in the future become a serious source of conflict.

Although the delegates agreed on the necessity of formal apportionment, deciding on its details proved a thorny undertaking. One committee appointed to handle the problem found its recommendations rejected by the convention as a whole, and another was unable to agree on any plan. The congress passed a motion made from the floor setting general guidelines for representation but later rescinded its vote. There were, however, many areas of agreement. No one questioned the assumption that towns provided the basic units of representation, and few disputed the argument that in order to reduce the size of future conventions small towns should be grouped in "classes" containing approximately 100 voters, each class to elect one delegate. Nor did anyone challenge the idea that large towns should have more than one representative. How many more, however, was a question not easily answered. Many delegates, including those from Portsmouth, insisted that representation should be directly proportional to population and that every town should be permitted to send one member for each one hundred voters it contained. Others rejected these conclusions. Such an arrangement, they feared, would permit the seaboard communities which had domi-

641. Adams specifically mentions Sullivan as one of the delegates who listened to his ideas "with apparent pleasure." For details of maneuvering in the Continental Congress before the resolution to take up government, see Herbert J. Henderson, "Political Factions in the Continental Congress," unpub. diss. Columbia University, 1962, 74–80.

22. *NHSP*, VII, 665–669; Belknap, *History*, II, 488–490.

nated the colonial assembly to gain control of the new government. In the end this second group won. The final plan allowed five different towns two delegates and Portsmouth three. The total number to attend the next congress was set at 89.[23]

The fourth provincial congress enacted one additional constitutional reform. Colonial law provided that only town inhabitants possessing £50 of ratable estate could vote for assemblymen and that the men selected should be worth at least £300. To those who had become convinced that government controlled primarily by the very wealthy sometimes failed to protect the people's liberties, the law seemed arbitrary. They did not reject the idea of rule by men of property—the congress at one point voted to keep the £300 qualification and in the end only reduced it by one third—nor did they feel that town residents had been prevented from electing men who were willing to serve local interests; their dissatisfaction stemmed more from the implication that only £50 freeholders had sufficient wisdom to determine which among the local elite should serve in the people's part of the legislature. The congress first reduced the figure to £20, then voted simply that for the purpose of electing provincial representatives "every legal inhabitant paying taxes shall be a voter."[24]

Agreement on constitutional reform and the reports from Philadelphia helped dissipate the reluctance of New Hampshire's revolutionary leaders to assume full civil authority. One unrelated event provided a further stimulus for taking up government. Early in November the British navy bombarded and largely destroyed Falmouth, a seaport less than fifty miles north of Portsmouth. Panic gripped the seaboard area of New Hampshire. The wealthy retreated en masse, and even royalists like George Jaffrey helped to erect hasty defenses against expected depredations. One ardent revolutionist gleefully informed Langdon that "the unheard-of cruelties of the enemy had so effectually united us, that I believe there are not four persons now in Portsmouth who do not justify the measures pursued in opposition to the tyranny of Great Britain." The congress, still in session, provided 800 additional soldiers to defend the Piscataqua area and hurriedly completed its remaining business so that members could

23. NHSP, VII, 584, 606, 644, 655–660; Colby, *Manual of the Constitution*, 262–263.
24. NHSP, VII, 644, 657–660.

return to help organize local military preparations. On November 15, after issuing precepts for a fifth convention and specifying that it might, with permission of the Continental Congress (news of the authorization had yet to arrive), resolve itself into a house of representatives, New Hampshire's fourth provincial congress voted to disband.[25]

The members of the fifth provincial congress, which convened in mid-December, moved quickly to establish civil government. In doing so they had the benefit of much outside advice. The formal recommendation of the Continental Congress included one important restriction which guided their thinking: whatever the form of the new government it should hold power only for the duration of the present conflict. Langdon and Bartlett regretted the limitation —it had been included, they wrote home, "to ease the minds of some few persons who were fearful of independence; we thought it advisable not to oppose that part too much, for once we had taken any sort of government nothing but negotiation with Great Britain can alter it"—but they urged provincial leaders to exercise similar caution. Instead of erecting a full government, New Hampshire, like Massachusetts, should create a house of representatives whose members would choose a council of about fifteen, "these two branches to act in all cases whatever." The province at present, they argued, "should not proceed so far as a governor," though the door might be left open for that purpose.[26]

John Sullivan offered more detailed and somewhat different counsel in a letter to Meshech Weare from his military encampment near Boston. Sullivan assumed that since New Hampshire possessed no charter it would be necessary for the provincial congress to write a formal constitution, and that the opportunity should be used to create as ideal a form of government as possible. "All government," he argued, "is or ought to be instituted for the good of the people . . ." The only way to protect the people from abuse was to give them control over their rulers. All representatives, councilors, and the governor should be elected directly by provincial voters and at frequent enough intervals—preferably one year but in no case more

25. *New Hampshire Gazette*, Nov. 2 to Dec. 5, 1775; Sullivan to Committee of Safety, Nov. 30, 1775, in Hammond, ed., *Sullivan Papers*, I, 129; Whipple to Langdon, Nov. 12, 1775, Langdon Correspondence, 590, NYPL; *NHSP*, VII, 647–664.
26. Bartlett and Langdon to Assembly, Nov. 3, 1775, *NHSP*, VII, 641–642.

than three years—"to operate as a check upon their conduct." Laws should be passed to prevent bribery and corruption during elections. The governor should not have the right to negate the house choice of Speaker, nor should he be allowed an absolute veto. The house and council should have all the powers held by the colonial assembly. In addition they should participate in the appointment of all civil officers. If the New Hampshire convention followed his suggestions, Sullivan concluded, it might produce a constitution better even than the "happiest" one he knew, the colonial charter of Connecticut.[27]

The members of the provincial congress carefully considered the recommendations of their former and present delegates to the Continental Congress. Weare had copies of Sullivan's letter distributed. He and the other representatives appointed to "draw up a plan for the government of this colony" recommended that the congress formally vote to resolve itself into a house of representatives and, as Langdon and Bartlett had suggested, appoint a council. The congress did this and then selected a second committee, which also included Weare, specifically for the purpose of drafting "a new constitution." This group, in turn, produced a document which on January 5, they presented for adoption.[28]

The proposed constitution began with a lengthy apologia for taking up government. New Hampshire did not wish "to throw off" its "dependence" on Great Britain, but present circumstances gave it no other choice. Ships and lading owned by "honest and industrious inhabitants" had been seized arbitrarily. The departure of the governor and many of his council had left the province "destitute of legislation," without the means of punishing criminal offenders, and its citizens "liable to the machinations and evil designs of wicked men." Further, the constitution now proposed would continue only for the duration of "the present, unhappy and unnatural contest" with the mother country. The government, in accordance with the resolve already passed, would be composed of a council and house, the former to be chosen by the latter. Five councilors would be from Rockingham County, two each from Strafford, Cheshire, and Hillsborough, and one from Grafton County. The General Court or

27. Sullivan to Weare, Dec. 12, 1775, in *NHSP*, VII, 685–688 and Hammond, ed., *Sullivan Papers*, I, 141–148.
28. *NHSP*, VII, 690–709, and VIII, 2–4. Copies of Sullivan's letter may be found in "Revolution" folio, box II, Tolford-Patten Papers, NHSL, and in New Hamp. Misc. MSS.

Assembly—both terms were used to describe the government— would remain in power one year. If the contest lasted longer, there would be a new election; and in this the councilors, as Sullivan's logic indicated, would be chosen by voters in the individual counties. There would be a Speaker of the house and a president of the council, but neither would wield any special powers; all acts, resolves, and appointments would be made with the approval of a majority in both branches of the legislature. The right to select many minor officials, military as well as civil, was given directly to the people.[29]

By now, serious opposition to all these proceedings had developed. A few delegates disapproved of the proposed institutional arrangement.[30] Many more had begun to have second thoughts about the whole idea of New Hampshire becoming the first province to adopt a formal constitution. Such action, they argued, would play into the hands of English officials who had long justified their oppressive measures by claiming that Americans sought nothing less than total independence. If the people of Great Britain supported the colonists in their quest for redress of grievances and, as reports from London indicated, the present ministry was in deep political trouble, then the congress should be more patient.[31] Besides, the Continental Congress had not instructed New Hampshire to take up government; it had merely given permission should the Congress think such action necessary. The new government already possessed full authority. What more could be gained by adopting a formal constitution? Even after the constitution was adopted on January 5 by a two-to-one majority, the reluctants refused to give in. The Portsmouth delegates, who had been instructed to oppose taking up government and who probably led the opposition in congress, returned home and helped call a town meeting which voted unanimously to petition for a reconsideration and to send circular letters urging other towns to "remonstrate likewise." Twelve representatives, most of them from

29. NHSP, VIII, 2–4.
30. Weare to Continental Congress, Feb. 10, 1776, NHSP, VIII, 66. Unfortunately, I have been unable to locate any records indicating what alternatives to the house-council arrangement were considered. Sullivan's letter provides the only extended discussion of constitutional principles written by a New Hampshire resident in the period before the congress took up government.
31. New Hampshire Gazette, April 14, Aug. 8, and Dec. 26, 1775; NHSP, VII, 701, and VIII, 66. Those who articulated this logic misread the English political situation completely. By late 1775 the advocates of strong reprisals were in firm control at Whitehall: Bernard Donoughue, British Politics and the American Revolution: The Path to War, 1773–1775 (New York, 1965), 231–291.

the Piscataqua area, presented a written protest; by the end of the month eleven different towns had submitted similar petitions.[32]

But the opponents of the constitution gained little by their efforts. The house tabled most of the petitions and dismissed the others. When the *Gazette* published a lengthy condemnation of the decision made on January 5, the representatives labeled the piece "ignominious, scurrilous and scandalous" and ordered the printer to appear at Exeter to explain his unpatriotic behavior. The one gesture of compromise the house did make—it agreed to submit the controversy to the Continental Congress—only served to emphasize the isolation of the reluctants. Bartlett and William Whipple, who had replaced Langdon in Philadelphia, considered the squabble so petty they refused to bring the matter to the attention of their associates. Instead they accused the assemblymen of backsliding. By springtime, most of the protesters had grudgingly accepted their defeat.[33]

Meanwhile the new government had begun to solidify its authority. The house chose twelve of its members to become councilors and ordered elections to fill the resulting vacancies. Both branches of the legislature then adopted rules to govern their internal deliberations. A joint committee was established to recommend revisions in the legal code; for the present, laws passed by the colonial legislatures, with a few obvious exceptions, were to remain in effect. Before adjourning late in January the assembly began to fill the local, county, and provincial offices left vacant by the collapse of royal government, and it authorized judicial officers to handle all cases except those involving debt. It also passed a £20,000 tax bill, made the necessary military appropriations, and created a committee of safety to handle affairs while it remained recessed.[34] In short, the house and council members assumed full responsibility for the conduct of provincial affairs. They continued to do so for the seven years New Hampshire's first written constitution remained in effect.

32. *NHSP*, VIII, 12–17, 33, 65–66; *PCSM*, XIX: *Transactions* (1916–1917), 295–296; *A Journal for the Years 1739–1803 by Samuel Lane of Stratham, New Hampshire*, ed. Charles L. Hanson (Concord, 1937), 10–11; State Papers, 1776 Box, NHA; Ebenezer Thompson to Bartlett, Jan. 29, 1776, Bartlett Papers, I, fol. 776129, BLDC. The quotation is from *NHSP*, VIII, 12.

33. *NHSP*, VIII, 12–27, 66; *New Hampshire Gazette*, Jan. 9, 1776; Bartlett to Langdon, Mar. 5, 1776, Langdon Correspondence, NYPL; Eleazar Russell to Thomas Waldron, Mar. 16, 1776, New Hamp. Misc. MSS.

34. *NHSP*, VIII, 4–114.

Colony of New-Hampſhire.

By *the* COUNCIL *and* ASSEMBLY,

A PROCLAMATION.

WHEREAS the CONGRESS of this Colony have, agreeable to a Recommendation from the Honorable CONTINENTAL CONGRESS, reſolved on, and form'd themſelves upon a PLAN of GOVERNMENT by a COUNCIL and Houſe of REPRESENTATIVES ; which Plan has been publiſhed, and diſperſed through the Colony, and is to be in Force during the preſent Diſpute with Great-Britain, unleſs otherwiſe advis'd by the Continental Congreſs :---conformable to which ſaid Plan of Government, the Council and Aſſembly have choſen, and appointed the proper Officers for the Adminiſtration of Juſtice, in the ſeveral Counties, who are to be ſworn to the faithful diſcharge of their ſeveral Truſts ;--It is therefore expeċted, that no Perſon or Perſons, claim, or exerciſe any civil Authority, but ſuch as are, or may be appointed as aforeſaid, on the Penalty of being deemed inimical to their Country.

Provided nevertheleſs, and this PROCLAMATION is intended not to interfere with the Power of the neceſſary Committees of Inſpection, or Safety, choſen in the ſeveral Towns through the Colony, by Virtue, and in Conſequence of, any Recommendation or Reſolves of the Continental Congreſs,---Whereof all Perſons concerned, are to take due Notice, and govern themſelves accordingly.

And at the ſame Time it is earneſtly recommended, that in this diſtreſſing Day of public Calamity, when our Enemies are watching all Opportunities to enſnare and divide us, every one would ſtrive to prevent, and if poſſible, to quell all Appearance of party Spirit, to cultivate and promote Peace, Union and good Order, and by all Means in their Power, to diſcourage Profaneſs, Immorality, and Injuſtice.

By Order of the Council and Aſſembly at Exeter,
the 19th Day of March, Anno Domini 1776.

M. WEARE, Preſident of the Council.

E. THOMPSON, Secretary.

GOD SAVE THE PEOPLE.

PORTSMOUTH, Printed by DANIEL FOWLE.

Broadside printed for the revolutionary government soon after the constitution of 1776 had gone into effect.

MEN AND IDEAS

These institutional innovations, capped by the recasting of provincial government in a form expected to prevent the executive and judicial "abuses" which had marked colonial politics, were paralleled by equally significant changes in the composition of New Hampshire's political leadership. The two patterns had much in common. Just as the traditional institutions of local authority remained intact, so most of the men who before 1774 had ruled at the community level retained their influence after the collapse of royal authority. More displacement occurred at the county level, mainly in those areas where distrust of Wentworth's appointees had been intense and consequently county organizations assumed responsibility for maintaining social and political order. The provincial government experienced the most dramatic turnover. There the revolution brought into power a group of men who had exercised little control over decisions made by the Wentworths and their friends in the assembly, and whose political beliefs differed in essential details from those of their predecessors.

Several factors contributed to the continuity of local leadership. In the first place, the ideology expressed to justify rebellion channeled resentment against Parliament, the ministry, and to a lesser extent the ruling oligarchy, but not against local political elites; indeed, town leaders were largely responsible for articulating the colonists' grievances. Secondly, the revolutionists had few complaints about the way colonial community authority had been exercised. Elected officers had proved responsive to popular needs and effective in promoting local interests, and most royally appointed officers acted in a similar fashion. As a result there was a general feeling, as one writer noted, that inasmuch as towns had been allowed to handle their own affairs "their business had been managed to great advantage." Thirdly, many royal officers had become so infuriated at imperial policy—Wentworth at one point wrote that some magistrates "of worth and independence" could "scarcely [be] restrained from becoming private men" because they felt obliged to "vindicate their right to decency with their swords"—that they relinquished their commissions early in the conflict. Under such circumstances the revolutionists had no reason to displace local magistrates. Townsmen continued to elect the same officers, and the House of Repre-

114

sentatives appointed as justices of the peace many of the same men who had held office under royal government. The new justices were also selected from among citizens with experience in local government.[35]

Community leaders who refused to participate in revolutionary proceedings did suffer, of course, but even here conditions tended to prevent a total loss of power. Most inhabitants continued to respect all men with wealth and education. The advice of reluctants was sometimes sought in solving community problems which had nothing to do with the imperial conflict. After the Declaration of Independence, Tories who had been restricted to their farms or otherwise punished were allowed to move freely. A few communities even left town affairs in the hands of men who openly questioned the wisdom of the rebellion.[36]

There was more change at the county level. The constitution provided that, except for three minor offices, all county magistrates would be appointed by the house and council. Provincial leaders naturally selected men whose qualifications included a strong commitment to the revolution; this, just as naturally, excluded many of Wentworth's former appointees. A clean sweep occurred in Hillsborough County: of the nine newly chosen magistrates—the judge and registrar of probate, four justices of the Inferior Court of Common Pleas, the recorder of deeds, the treasurer, and the sheriff—not one had held office in 1773. Six of the nine were new in Rockingham and Cheshire counties, five in Grafton County, and three in Strafford County. The courts of general sessions, made up of county justices of peace and the quorum, experienced similar but less pronounced modification.[37]

The men who had dominated political affairs in the provincial

35. The first quotation is from *Freeman's Journal* (Portsmouth), June 29, 1776; the second is in Wentworth to Belham, Aug. 9, 1768, Wentworth Letter Book, no. 1, 130. The generalizations about continuity of officeholding at the local level are based on selective reading in town records and a comparison of justice-of-peace listings in the *New Hampshire Register* (Portsmouth, 1772); in NHSP, VIII, 61–64, 174–175, and XVIII, 680–684; and in Boylston, *Hillsborough County Congresses*, 51–53.
36. See "John Phillips" and "Paine Wingate," *Biographical Sketches*, IX, 564–565, and XIV, 539–540; NHSP, XI, 181–182, 365–366, and XXII, 856; Otis F. R. Waite, *History of the Town of Claremont* (Manchester, 1895), 219–230; James O. Lyford, *History of the Town of Canterbury* (Concord, 1912), 107–124; Hinsdale Town Records, NHSL; Arthur Livermore, Memoranda of Samuel Livermore, Livermore Papers, NHHS.
37. Belknap, *History* (Dover, 1831 edition), 419–421; NHSP, VIII, 61–64.

government lost power completely. Disintegration of imperial relationships separated the ruling oligarchy from their source of authority. John Wentworth, who fought for the British army before going to England, where his interest with Rockingham later gained him the lieutenant governorship of Nova Scotia, never returned to New Hampshire. Some of his close associates also left the province. Others chose to remain in New Hampshire but lived out their days without trying to reassert their political influence. Of the prerevolutionary councilors, only two held office in the spring of 1776: Jonathan Warner retained his justice-of-the-peace commission, and Thomas Westbrook Waldron filled two posts in Strafford County. Two of the four justices of the superior court, the local admiralty officials, the provincial secretary, treasurer, attorney general, surveyor of lands, collector of customs, comptroller, naval officer, postmaster, and the two militia generals all lost their offices. It is little wonder that in July one Portsmouth resident observed the "disconsolate" appearance of "some broken councilors" and their friends.[38]

Lesser participants in New Hampshire's colonial politics lost influence too. Most of the displaced county magistrates had gained office by cooperating with the governor, usually as elected members of the colonial House of Representatives. Many other members of the assembly hesitated to get involved in revolutionary activities: distaste for illegality, the political handicaps of past cooperation with the governor, and in some cases old age all contributed to their reluctance. Of the thirty-four house delegates returned in 1771, only twelve held provincial office in 1776, and four of these retired soon. Although the contrast is somewhat exaggerated—at least one of the old representatives had died, and another was with the army in Massachusetts—the point is still valid: the revolution resulted in a general withdrawal from the political arena of the wealthy assemblymen and county magistrates who had helped John Wentworth run provincial affairs.[39]

The transition in authority, furthermore, bypassed many of John Wentworth's most outspoken political enemies. Woodbury Lang-

38. Mayo, *Wentworth*, 157–195; Belknap, *History* (1831 ed.), 419–421; *NHSP*, VIII, 61–64; letter from Pierce Long, July 29, 1776, State Papers, 1776 Box (source of quotation).

39. *NHSP*, VII, 286–287, 690–693, and VIII, 61–64; Main, "Government by the People," *WMQ*, 3d ser., 23 (1966), 398–399, has arrived at the same conclusion.

don left for England to collect his debts and remained there until 1777. George Boyd, who returned to New Hampshire with council mandamus in hand, surveyed the situation and sailed back across the Atlantic. John Sherburne, John Wendell, and Joshua Wentworth sat tight, hoping for a reconciliation which would permit restoration of the trade on which their personal fortunes rested, and eventually led the movement against taking up government. Sherburne lost his post as judge of probate in Rockingham County, and Wendell was thwarted in efforts to gain a nomination for office. Even John Langdon, despite his early election as a delegate to the Continental Congress and subsequent appointment as continental marine agent for New Hampshire, found himself frustrated by his lack of interest at Exeter.[40]

Those who emerged as the most powerful political leaders did so in part because of their consistent and effective service in the provincial congresses. Six men, all of whom were rewarded with council appointments, stand out. Council President Meshech Weare had been on almost every important committee in all five congresses, acted as president pro tem in two of them, became the most active member in the powerful Committee of Safety, and probably wrote the final draft of the constitution. The record of Matthew Thornton is equally impressive: he became president of the last two conventions, helped coordinate the political activities in which Massachusetts and New Hampshire were mutually concerned, and like Weare accepted various committee responsibilities. Nathaniel Folsom managed to keep his political influence even after his appointment as general in charge of all New Hampshire troops in Massachusetts, served as a Committee of Safety member, and provided liaison between Thornton and the Bay Colony leaders. Josiah Bartlett and his close friend William Whipple both filled a series of important posts before being appointed delegates to the Continental Congress. The final member of the inner circle was Ebenezer Thompson, secretary in the third, fourth, and fifth congresses as well as the council, a

40. Mayo, *Langdon*, 82–90; Wentworth to Dartmouth, Aug. 3, 1775, Wentworth Letter Book no. 3, 141; New Hampshire Loyalist Claims (transcripts from the Public Record Office, London), I, 165–166, NHSL; State Papers, 1776 Box; Wendell to Weare, June 29, 1778, Weare Papers, I, MHS; Langdon to Bartlett, June 3, 1776, John Langdon Papers, box 3, NHHS.

Matthew Thornton (1714–1803), president of the fourth and fifth provincial congresses. Portrait by N. B. Onthank from an engraving of unknown origin.

functionary on most key committees, and the main arbiter in disputes over the distribution of civil and military commissions.[41]

41. *NHSP*, VII, 407–710, and VIII, 6. Biographical information on these men used here and in succeeding paragraphs may be found in the following publications: "Meshech Weare" in Shipton, *Biographical Sketches*, IX, 590–603; Butters, "Public Career of Meshech Weare"; Charles T. Adams, *Matthew Thornton of New Hampshire* (Philadelphia, 1903); Henry M. Baker, "General Nathaniel Folsom," NHHS *Proceedings*, 4 (1899–1905), 253–267; Elwin L. Page, "Rider for Freedom: Josiah Bartlett, 1729–1795," MS, NHHS; Fred M. Colby, "Moffatt-Whipple Mansion," *Granite Monthly*, 13 (1890), 219–227; William Plumer, "Ebenezer Thompson," in *NHSP*, XXII, 852–854.

Several others held less influential positions. The Speaker of the last two colonial houses, John Wentworth, acted as chairman of the first three congresses before ill health forced him into temporary retirement. He, Samuel Ashley, Benjamin Giles, and Wyseman Claggett all were active on convention committees, accepted important judicial appointments (as did Weare, Thornton, Bartlett, and Folsom), and joined the new council. Samuel Cutts rendered important political services although primarily engaged in commissary operations. Timothy Walker, Jr., son of the Concord minister who had fought against the Wentworths in the Rumford-Bow controversy, helped write the constitution and gained the respect of his fellow legislators. John Langdon kept in contact with the new leaders when his activities brought him close to home.[42]

These revolutionary leaders represented economic and social interests in sharp contrast with those of their colonial counterparts. Of the thirteen men mentioned, all, unlike their Anglican predecessors, were either Congregationalist or Presbyterian. Only Whipple, Cutts, and Langdon had been active in overseas commerce, and none of these three had been involved in either the masting business or trade with the Wentworth's English associates.[43] Thornton, Bartlett, and Thompson were doctors, Claggett and John Wentworth lawyers, Ashley, Giles, and Weare all properous farmers. The sectional distribution of power had shifted too. Men from Portsmouth and to a lesser degree other communities in the Piscataqua watershed had dominated political affairs before 1774. Many of the new rulers came from that area, but they found themselves in a minority. Weare lived in Hampton, Thornton in Londonderry, Bartlett in Kingston; Claggett, Ashley, Walker, and Giles resided west of the Merrimack River. Towns within ten miles of Portsmouth had pro-

42. NHSP, VII, 407–710, and VIII, 6, 61–64. See the following for biographical data: Bell, *Bench and Bar*. 30–31 (John Wentworth); Charles B. Spofford, "Samuel Ashley," *Granite Monthly*, 14 (1892), 141–147; Walker, *Five Provincial Congresses*, 49–54 (Claggett, Cutts, and Giles); Walker, "Hon. Timothy Walker"; Mayo, *Langdon*.

43. They were also less wealthy than their more moderate fellow merchants, as these excerpts from the 1774 Portsmouth Tax Records, City Hall, Portsmouth, indicate. (Figures have been rounded to the nearest pound.)

Family Members	Tax	Reluctants	Tax	Radicals	Tax
Theodore Atkinson	£21	George Boyd	£68	Samuel Cutts	£10
Mark H. Wentworth	£27	Woodbury Langdon	£27	John Langdon	£ 9
Jonathan Warner	£28	Joshua Wentworth	£27	William Whipple	£ 9
George Jaffrey	£15				

vided two thirds of the colonial assembly membership. They sent only one fourth of the revolutionary representatives.

The men who ran the new government also represented different political interests. The authority of prerevolutionary provincial rulers rested ultimately on their imperial connections. It is true that Benning Wentworth and Atkinson launched their political careers by gaining election to both town offices and the assembly, and to a certain extent their provincial power depended on their ability to maintain contact with the voters. But others among the elite, particularly those appointed after 1760, served no such apprenticeship. John Wentworth was without governmental experience when he left for England in 1763. Most of the colonial councilors and many of the county magistrates held few community offices, either before or after receiving their commissions. Peter Livius obtained a mandamus before setting foot on New Hampshire soil. The authority of revolutionary leaders, on the other hand, depended entirely on their ability to satisfy local interests; indeed, they had been elected to the provincial congresses in part because of their past community services. Virtually every new legislator had previously served in several local elective offices. Of the seventy-plus delegates who attended the fifth provincial congress, over thirty were former justices of the peace and sixteen had been elected to the provincial House of Representatives. The twelve councilors included nine justices of the peace and nine men with assembly experience, two of them former house Speakers. Even the legislators who had gained favor under the Wentworths—the new council contained five colonial militia colonels, four inferior court justices, and one superior court justice, Meshech Weare—were distinguished by their willingness to assume town responsibilities.[44] Before the revolution an ambitious and able local politician might, especially if he lived in a town represented in the assembly, rise far enough to benefit directly from family rule and to participate in the provincial deliberations affecting his own locality. In 1775 and 1776 the same man found himself making decisions an matters of fundamental importance to the whole colony.

Weare, Bartlett, Whipple, Thornton, and their associates in the congresses, however, did not consider themselves primarily representatives of any special economic, social, sectional, or local interests.

44. See n. 35, n. 37, and n. 39 above for sources from which the statistics and generalizations have been drawn.

Their sense of common purpose—and for that matter the unity of the revolutionary movement as a whole—stemmed more from the set of political beliefs and assumptions which they shared. Most of them accepted the idea that rulers in Great Britain were engaged in a systematic effort to subvert their natural liberties: "Such are the measures adopted by the British ministry for enslaving you," read a public address issued by the second provincial congress, "and with such incessant vigilance has their plan been prosecuted, that tyranny already begins to wave its banners in your borders and to threaten these once happy regions with infamous and detestable slavery." Initially there was disagreement over the methods most likely to gain redress from felt grievances—Weare in particular tried to bridle the radical tendencies of his fellow malcontents—but by the summer of 1775 this had disappeared.[45] The flight of Governor Wentworth, evidence that the British would use force to put down protest, and their mutual fear of social and political disorder convinced them that the congress should assume full provincial authority and write a new constitution based on what they considered fundamental principles of good government.

Good government meant a number of different things to New Hampshire's revolutionary leaders. Consistent with their common political experience at the county and community level, they shared a deep faith in local institutions of authority and the ability of locally elected officials to handle the administration of government. Indeed, their anxiety about the ultimate goal of Parliament, the ministry, and even New Hampshire's own colonial rulers was in part a product of this faith. The British seemed intent on grasping powers traditionally wielded by the people's part of the provincial government; the Massachusetts Government Act meant that even town governments could be made powerless if imperial oppression were carried to its logical end. The argument that "the people" provided the only source of legitimate political authority made sense when measured by past successes at the local level and the uneven record of centrally appointed officials. Diffusion of power, moreover, would prevent inefficiency and waste. "Small bodies," noted one

45. The quotation is from *NHSP*, VII, 443; see also Wentworth to Waldron, Jan. 27, 1775, and Paine Wingate to Timothy Pickering, Apr. 28, 1775, both in Wingate, *Paine Wingate*, I, 152–162. At first, Weare refused to participate in the fourth provincial congress but he changed his mind after Bunker Hill and the governor's flight from Portsmouth.

commentator who praised town and county governments, "manage affairs much easier and [more] cheaply than large ones."[46]

But rule by elected officials within a decentralized institutional framework did not guarantee future justice. Steps had to be taken to protect the system from those who might corrupt it. In England ambitious men had learned to purchase votes, either with money or liquor; the provincial congress provided that "no person be allowed a seat in Congress" who attempted to treat electors "with an apparent view of gaining their votes." Most important, the people must guard themselves against the luxurious and dissipated behavior which had become so common under royal government. Early in the conflict the citizens of Exeter, Brentwood, Epsom, and several other communities passed resolves condemning traders who tempted "women, girls and boys with their unnecessary fineries." The Portsmouth Committee of Inspection threatened to publish the names of men caught wagering, and a mob broke into the house of Moses Woodward to smash his billiard table. Provincial leaders refused to condone such violence, but they approved of the sentiment which produced it. The congress condemned gambling, drunkenness, and disorder, specifically recommended less drinking "upon the publication of commissions and other military occasions," and asked all citizens to exercise "laudable moderation and economy" in their daily lives.[47]

By the summer of 1776 some of the revolutionary leaders had begun to view the various elements of their political ideology as an integrated commitment to what classical scholars had labeled "republicanism." The formal definition of the term—government in which political power emanated from the people ruling through elected representatives—fitted with what they had established in the constitution and what they had found satisfactory in their colonial experience. Republicanism was thought by Montesquieu and others to work best in small political units where the people could keep a close check on those in power. What could be more "republican" than a system based on local autonomy operating in an area as re-

46. *Freeman's Journal*, June 29, 1776.
47. Sullivan to Weare, Dec. 12, 1775, in Hammond, ed., *Sullivan Papers*, 141–148; *NHSP*, VII, 425–445, 477, 499, 605, 657, and VIII, 361. The quotations are from *NHSP*, VII, 657, 425, and 605. Edmund Morgan, "The Puritan Ethic and the American Revolution," *WMQ*, 3d ser. 24 (1967), 3–43, finds this same moralism present throughout the colonies.

stricted as New Hampshire? One further convergence of contemporary belief with traditional assumptions about republicanism cemented the association. Republics could succeed only if the people practiced frugality, industry, and temperance, and their elected representatives remained disinterested and self-sacrificing. "Virtue," explained a patriot minister to Whipple, "is the basis of a republic." Without it "we shall soon become corrupt . . . anarchy and confusion will take place and we shall be in a worse state than if we had remained as we were." The revolutionary leaders could not be certain that their efforts to purify society would be successful—Whipple, after hearing reports of profit-seeking among the legislators, observed that it was "much more difficult to reduce a society of men who had drunk deep in the waters of corruption to the true principles of virtue than to bring a society from the state of nature to the same meridian"—but they were eager to try.[48] Their mutual commitment helped carry them through the difficult years ahead.

48. The quotations are from Samuel McClintock to Whipple, Aug. 2, 1776, Whipple Papers, 189, LC, and from Whipple to Joshua Brackett, July 29, 1776, *Proceedings MHS*, 5 (1860), 6. For general discussion of republican ideology in the early years of the American Revolution, see Cecelia M. Kenyon, "Republicanism and Radicalism in the American Revolution: An Old-Fashioned Interpretation," WMQ, 3d ser., 19 (1962), 165–168, and Gordon S. Wood, "The Creation of an American Polity in the Revolutionary Era," unpub. diss. Harvard University, 1964, 32–96.

5

Problems of Power:
State Government,
1776–1784

Governing New Hampshire proved far more difficult than the revolutionary leaders expected. Inadequacies in the constitution, the inexperience of delegates, and disagreements over policy all hampered efforts to turn the General Court into an efficient ruling body. Inflation, which could not be controlled, kept the state on the verge of bankruptcy. Inhabitants disobeyed laws which compromised their personal interests. Citizens in the Portsmouth area bombarded the legislature with criticism, while towns in Grafton County tried to become part of neighboring Vermont. Some of the rulers became distressed at the complexity and seeming insolubility of their problems. "Where is the spirit that actuated us in the beginning?" asked councilor Josiah Bartlett in the spring of 1779. "Gone, alas! I fear forever!" A few weeks later he wrote: "I have no doubt that our cause is as just as any the Israelites were ever engaged in, and am sorry to find that like them we are a crooked and perverse generation, longing for the fineries and follies of those Egyptian task masters from whom we have so lately freed ourselves." John Langdon complained about the rise of a "levelling spirit" which threatened to destroy all political discipline.[1]

Gradually, however, the situation improved. Meshech Weare (who served as council president, a member of the Committee of Safety, and chief justice of the superior court as long as the war lasted), Bartlett, and their political allies provided the state with

1. Bartlett to Whipple, April 24 and May 29, 1779, Bartlett Papers, photostats, NHHS; John Langdon to Bartlett, June 24, 1776, *Historical Magazine*, 6 (1862), 240.

imaginative, flexible, and effective leadership. By 1784 the legislature had resolved its internal troubles, restored fiscal order, calmed many of its critics, and convinced the citizens of Grafton County to accept its authority. New Hampshire enjoyed the "peace, union, and good order"[2] the revolutionists thought necessary to the success of their experiment in republicanism.

Although the members of the fifth provincial congress adopted the temporary constitution fully confident it would provide New Hampshire with an adequate framework for the determination and administration of public policy, they soon had reason to question their optimism. To begin with, the behavior of the House of Representatives left much to be desired. The first Speaker, a man whose previous political experience in state politics had been limited to organizing back-country support for Peter Livius, gave delegates such free rein that, according to John Langdon, they did little but appoint each other to office and spent the rest of the time "punning" and "laughing." Langdon may have exaggerated—he had been disappointed in his own efforts to obtain a military commission—but his accusations were not entirely unjustified. The house made several appointments which the council felt obliged to negate. Policy decisions made one day were reversed the next. Members insisted that matters which could have been handled more efficiently in committee be determined in full session: meetings, as a result, often became lengthy and boring. William Whipple, who initially blamed the "wild steerage" on inexperience and hoped for quick improvement, complained late in 1776 that the representatives went on "in the same old way, spending much time about trifles."[3] Others made similar observations.

Time did not improve the situation. Langdon, who sought and gained election as Speaker, insisted on more decorous behavior and obtained votes formalizing legislative procedures, but he could not keep members from spending what he considered an excessive amount of energy discussing appointments and the punishment of suspected loyalists. Moreover, Langdon himself proved undepend-

2. The phrase is from a house resolution printed in *NHSP*, VII, 103.
3. Langdon to Bartlett, June 24, 1776, *Historical Magazine*, 6 (1862), 240; Langdon to Whipple, Aug. 5, 1776, John Langdon Papers; *NHSP*, VIII, 3–68; Whipple to Brackett, July 29, 1776, *Proceedings MHS*, 5 (1860), 6; Whipple to Bartlett, Sept. 10, 1776, Bartlett Papers, I, fol. 776510, BLDC.

able. He missed meetings without warning, left correspondence unanswered, and once lost a petition sent to him by a local committee of safety.[4] John Dudley, a farmer from Raymond who became the regular Speaker pro tem, was a better administrator, yet he too experienced difficulties. Once the basic job of establishing the government had been completed and provincial offices distributed, many state legislators began to lose interest in their jobs. Often they found it inconvenient to travel to Exeter, and when they did go they found the town ill equipped to house the state government: inns were few and crowded, the community had neither forage yard nor post office, and after 1780 no newspaper. Experience in the house further dulled their eagerness to serve the state in a legislative capacity, for much time spent in sessions seemed wasted and the pay was inadequate. After 1777 the average annual turnover among representatives rose to more than 50 per cent. Attendance became so poor quorums were difficult to obtain. One of Bartlett's friends described a typical session when he reported: "The General Court met the twelfth instant and set about two weeks, but few of the members attending and did very little business."[5]

Lack of coordination between the house and the council added to the general inefficiency. The constitution-makers had not charged any single individual or group with responsibility for organizing the General Court: undoubtedly they assumed the council president and house speaker would share the task. But the arrangement did not work well. Langdon's lackadaisical attitude toward administration affected his dealings with the council, and the fact that he handled some matters and Dudley others added to the confusion. President Weare understood precisely what was wrong—he once wrote Bartlett that because no one had authority "to lay matters before the General Court" some letters were "forgot and no persons appointed to return any answers about them"—but refused to take up the

4. NHSP, VIII, 580, and *passim;* Weare to Bartlett, Aug. 8, 1778, *Historical Magazine,* 4 (1860), 332; Committee of Chesterfield to Committee of Safety, New Hampshire Council Correspondence, 1777, LC.

5. Noah Emery, Jr., to Peabody, Aug. 12, 1780, NHSP, XVII, 403; Brigham, *American Newspapers,* I, 451–457; NHSP, VIII, 874, 919; Samuel Philbrick to Bartlett, Aug. 26, 1778, Bartlett Papers, BLDC. Statistics on membership may be found in John K. Gemmill, "The Problems of Power: New Hampshire Government during the Revolution," *Historical New Hampshire,* 222 (Summer 1967), 35n. NHSP, XXI, 794–798, contains a brief biography of Dudley written by William Plumer.

slack lest he "be thought assuming." The results were apparent to everyone familiar with the internal operations of the General Court. Business requiring approval of both branches was sometimes delayed for months. Joint committees that were assigned special jobs never completed them. On one particularly embarrassing occasion, the government never replied to a request sent by the president of the Continental Congress.[6]

The incident helped convince state leaders something had to be done to rationalize assembly procedures. Weare knew he was the logical person to serve as coordinator and was willing to accept the job if the court asked him to. One obvious way to get the "particular direction" he considered necessary was to seek constitutional reform. The task, however, proved more difficult than he imagined. A convention of town delegates called in the summer of 1778 refused to recommend the creation of an independent executive. Moreover, public response to the convention made it clear New Hampshire's governmental structure would not be changed at all for some time.[7] Weare and his associates had to adopt a different tactic to compensate for what they considered the inadequacies of the constitution.

They knew what to do. If the house and council were too cumbersome to handle the everyday affairs of government, the Committee of Safety offered more promise. In the first place, it was small. The General Court, which appointed the committee annually, limited membership to about a dozen. An even smaller number did most of the work: meetings were so frequent that often only Weare, Bartlett, Dudley—all three served continuously after 1776—and one or two others who lived near Exeter found it possible to attend. Secondly, the legislators appeared willing to let the committee take on additional responsibilities; they already had asked it to keep meeting during assembly sessions and had given it the authority to try and imprison men suspected of disloyalty. Finally, the fact that the committee's most influential and experienced members were highly respected—one observer wrote in 1779 that Weare had "acquired so much popularity his countrymen expected salvation from his

6. Weare to Bartlett, July 3 and Aug. 8, 1778, *Historical Magazine*, 4 (1860), 299 and 332; *NHSP*, VIII, *passim*.

7. Weare to Bartlett, Aug. 8, 1778, *Historical Magazine*, 4 (1860), 332; [Samuel Philbrick to Bartlett], June 10, 1778, Bartlett Papers, I, BLDC. For further details on the convention see chap. vi.

wisdom or arm alone"—meant that serious opposition to their serv-ing as a quasi executive probably would not arise.[8]

New Hampshire's Committee of Safety virtually ran the govern-ment after the summer of 1779. It controlled the militia, settled claims against the state, issued permits to privateers, regulated trade, administered tax collection, and once on its own initiative appointed a delegate to the Continental Congress. When the General Court met, committee members continued to exercise their influence, espe-cially after Dudley replaced Langdon as Speaker. Adjustments were made in house procedures: matters not easily handled on the floor were given to the committee for action, debate was limited, and the quorum reduced from about fifty to thirty. Since Weare and Dudley worked well together, business requiring both council and house action was easily expedited. The state government's organizational problems had been solved.[9]

New Hampshire's revolutionary leaders did not expect serious economic disturbances to follow independence. Most people would farm, as they had in the past. The abrupt cessation of overseas trade might mean temporary commodity shortages and ruin a few merchants, but it also would have beneficial effects: money would no longer be wasted on luxuries, home manufacturing would be stimu-lated, and the state as a whole would become more self-sufficient. The war itself could be financed through currency emissions to be redeemed by future taxes. The presence of paper money—which had been outlawed by the imperial government—would facilitate busi-ness transactions. Furthermore, the legislators thought they could effectively regulate the economy should trouble arise. Public appeals, price and wage controls, trade restrictions, bounties, legal-tender laws, taxes—any combination of these could be used to promote economic prosperity and stability.[10]

In some ways experience during the war corresponded with this set of assumptions. The revolution brought New Hampshire un-

8. NHHS, *Collections*, VII (1863), 1–340; *NHSP*, VIII, 592–593, and *passim*; Butters, "Weare," 159; *New Hampshire Gazette*, Feb. 9, 1779.

9. Butters, "Weare," 156–159; Agnes Hunt, *Provincial Committees of Safety of the American Revolution* (Cleveland, 1904), 180; Plumer, "John Calfe," *NHSP*, XXI, 786–787; NHHS, *Collections*, VII (1863), 1–340; *NHSP*, VIII, 919, and X, 503–602.

10. Belknap, *History*, II, 425; E. James Ferguson, *The Power of the Purse* (Chapel Hill, 1961), 3–24.

precedented economic opportunities. Although the mast trade virtually disappeared and lumber exports declined, military operations in nearby states created a heavy demand for grain and livestock. Agricultural prosperity in conjunction with the continued expansion of the state's population triggered a land boom. Privateering offered the possibility of immediate and perhaps great wealth. The government, moreover, could justly credit itself for helping inhabitants take advantage of these opportunities. It bought commodities, issued privateering permits to all who applied, sold land which might otherwise have been unavailable for use, and provided much of the circulating medium necessary to support the raised level of economic activity. In 1782 a traveling French nobleman, the Marquis of Chastellux, observed that the people were happy with their experiment in republicanism and that the country presented "a very flourishing appearance"; the two phenomena were not unconnected.[11]

But in other ways experience proved inconsistent with expectations. The legislators could not prevent inflation. They emitted over £80,000 in 1776, imagining, as Belknap wrote later, "that the justice of [their] cause and the united ardor and patriotism of the people" would prevent deterioration in money values. With state, continental, and counterfeit currencies circulating, goods in heavy demand, and trade with Britain cut off, prices began to soar. The General Court at first simply asked local officials to take appropriate action. When complaints were received that merchants and traders who controlled town committees of inspection were themselves marking up goods, Weare, Bartlett, and their associates changed their policy. Statewide price and wage scales were established, sometimes in cooperation with authorities in neighboring governments. To bolster public faith in the currency, the assembly passed a law making paper money legal tender for all debts and canceling debts when creditors demanded payment in specie; then the courts were opened to civil cases. Another law prohibited the sale of goods for specie if the seller had previously been unwilling to accept state or continental currency. The legislators tried to stabilize prices and pro-

11. Upton, *Revolutionary New Hampshire,* 106–175; *Freeman's Journal,* Jan. 7, 1777; Marquis de Chastellux, *Travels in North America in the Years 1780, 1781, and 1782,* trans. Howard C. Rice, Jr. (Chapel Hill, 1963), II, 488. No thorough analysis of economic change in revolutionary New Hampshire has been made.

tect the value of the state's treasury notes through two additional enactments: public auctions were outlawed, and the punishment for counterfeiting was increased. But nothing stopped inflation; by the end of 1777, £100 in paper money was worth £30 in silver.[12]

The court members also encountered difficulties trying to finance the war. Money printed in 1776 soon ran out, as did the £70,000 voted the following year. Further emissions, it was felt, would be inconsistent with the campaign to stabilize prices; yet cash had to be obtained somewhere. Admitting they were "greatly perplexed," the representatives told the treasurer to borrow from individuals. The £10,000 he raised—only half of what had been authorized—soon was spent on war supplies and enlistment bounties. When orders came in the summer of 1778 to send troops south to Rhode Island where invasion threatened, the treasury stood empty. In desperation the state pleaded with town selectmen to lend them money from local treasuries, drafted troops to avoid payment of bounties, and warned that towns not filling their assigned quota would be taxed.[13] But these were emergency measures with limitations state leaders understood. By now almost everyone in the legislature agreed that drastic changes would have to be made in fiscal policies.

The solution to the financial problem of New Hampshire—indeed, of all America—seemed simple to some: state and continental governments should drain off the excess money supply through heavy taxation, simultaneously halting inflation and providing authorities with funds to fight the war. Langdon and Bartlett had urged such a policy as early as the fall of 1775, before prices began to rise. As time passed, they gained more supporters. Congress delegate William Whipple wrote from Philadelphia late in 1776 that "the people certainly were never so able to pay a large tax as at this time." Nicholas Gilman, an influential council member from Exeter who also served as state treasurer, wanted to do anything which could ease the burdens of his job. Weare became convinced

12. Belknap, *History*, II, 425–427; *NHSP*, VII, 606, 638, VIII, *passim*, and XVII, 56, 121–123. NHHS, *Collections*, II (1827), 58–68, and IX (1889), 245–303; Batchellor and Metcalf, eds., *Laws of New Hamp.*, IV, *passim*.

13. Upton, *Revolutionary New Hampshire*, 132–147; *NHSP*, VIII, 588. The quotation is from Weare to Bartlett, August 1778, Weare Papers, I, MHS. *New Hampshire Gazette*, July 21, 1778; Weare to Sullivan, May 29 and July 28, 1778, in Hammond, ed., *Sullivan Papers*, II, 71, 131.

and helped overcome the reluctance of legislators who feared taxation might undermine prosperity. The first sizable assessment—minor taxes had been imposed earlier—passed late in 1777. Continued inflation and complaints from constituents did not weaken the assembly's resolve. An emission of £40,000 early in 1778 was the last. New general taxes were voted that year, in part to cover the initial Continental Congress requisition. By 1780 congressional and state assessments together reached over £2,000,000, several times the amount voted in 1777 even if depreciation is taken into account.[14]

New Hampshire's unimproved lands provided another potential source of revenue. From time to time colonial legislatures had attempted to tax such land but had been thwarted by the governor and councilors, who owned large tracts in the colony. At the outset of revolution the legislators—most of whom themselves possessed some unimproved property—saw no need for land taxes. But conditions had changed. Money had to be acquired somewhere; besides, many of the largest landholders were Portsmouth merchants, who if not active loyalists obviously were not ardent patriots. In 1777 the court imposed a tax of one half of 1 per cent annually on the real value of unimproved lands. Towns containing land for which taxes could not be collected were empowered to sell part of the property for payment.[15]

State income could be increased in one other manner: by confiscation and sale of royalist estates. Originally many opposed such a measure, some from fear of British reprisals and others out of respect for property and the men who owned it. But increasingly their arguments fell on deaf ears, for during 1777 anti-loyalist sentiment in the colony was fueled by rumors of a plot in Cheshire County to aid Burgoyne and by discovery of active counterfeiting in many parts of the state. Fearing internal conspiracy, a group of militia officers petitioned the General Court to punish disloyalty; others asked permission to secure the property of Tories to defray the expenses of jailing them. In November 1777 the Continental Congress

14. Bartlett and Langdon to Matthew Thornton, Oct. 2, 1775, *NHSP*, VII, 615; Whipple to Bartlett, Dec. 23, 1776, Bartlett Papers, NHHS; Upton, *Revolutionary New Hampshire*, 134–136.
15. *NHSP*, VI, 341–472; Batchellor and Metcalf, eds., *Laws of New Hamp.*, IV, 131.

recommended that individual states confiscate and sell Tory estates.[16]

Even before the recommendation reached Exeter the legislature began to prepare for confiscation. Loyalists were encouraged to leave New Hampshire and were prohibited from transferring their property before flight; it was to be held in trust by local selectmen. When the confiscation act came up for house consideration, debate was intense. Would all who fled lose their property, or only those who took up arms against the revolutionists? Who would be responsible for the sale of confiscated estates? How would the families of loyalists be treated? In November 1778, after the action of other colonies had been studied, differences were compromised and two separate acts passed. A proscription act exiled seventy-eight men who had left the state, thirty-three of them former Portsmouth inhabitants. In the act for confiscating estates, twenty-five men who had fought against the revolution were listed and county committees appointed to seize their property, sell it at public auction, and remit proceeds to the treasurer.[17]

One additional step was taken to solve New Hampshire's financial problems. The legislators were confident taxation and confiscation would give the government an adequate income, but they were not at all certain whether inflation would stop. Perhaps the court should once again try to set price and wage levels. Or, better still, why not let the people themselves take responsibility for protecting the value of their money? In the summer of 1779 Langdon and a few other representatives helped organize a campaign for voluntary controls. First they convinced a group of Portsmouth merchants and traders to hold prices for a month and to promise that if other towns in the state adopted similar measures, prices would be lowered. The failure of this effort—only Exeter responded—forced the legislators to take another tack. A convention to create a plan for appreciating the currency met that fall in Concord and published a list of recommended limits. Two weeks later the Portsmouth group announced it was selling all goods at a 5 per cent discount. Meanwhile a congressional letter, praising paper currency as "the only kind of money

16. Otis G. Hammond, *Tories of New Hampshire* (Concord, 1917), 12–24; Bartlett to Whipple, Exeter, Mar. 15; and Kingstown, April 21 and May 9, 1777, Bartlett Papers, photostats, NHHS; Proceedings of a militia meeting, 1777, Weare Papers, LC; *NHSP*, VIII, 499–593, 728–730, and XVIII, 138.

17. Hammond, *Tories*, 20–24; Batchellor and Metcalf, eds., *Laws of New Hamp.*, IV, 71, 79, 128; *NHSP*, VIII, 603, 721, 808–814.

which could not make itself wings and fly away," was printed and circulated.[18]

The short-term impact of these new policies offered the court members some encouragement. Throughout 1779 and 1780 Gilman had enough cash to meet current expenses. The amount of state currency in circulation declined as notes issued early in the war were received as tax payments, retired, and burned. Inflation began to abate, especially after the Continental Congress voted to exchange one dollar in new bills for each forty of the old. For a brief period near the end of 1780 it seemed as though the struggle against financial disorder had been won. "Paper money," a farmer named Samuel Lane recorded in his journal, "is again (by reason of exceeding high taxes) in very good credit . . . and nobody can get enough of it."[19]

But taxation, confiscation, and renewed appeals for citizens to hold the line against inflation did not provide a permanent solution to New Hampshire's fiscal problems. To begin with, the state received less income than its political leaders had hoped. Towns in Grafton County refused to pay any general taxes, and local officials elsewhere made only partial returns; by 1781 nearly £400,000 remained uncollected. Taxes on unimproved lands did not live up to expectations. Confiscated estates proved an even poorer revenue source. Local committees appointed to administer sales were so inefficient the legislature asked probate judges to appoint trustees "for bringing the net produce of such estates into the treasury of this state as soon as may be." The trustees were just as independent. They let friends make exaggerated claims against loyalists, did little to prevent looting, ignored depreciation tables, and in a few cases actually embezzled. Weare's neighbor, Paine Wingate, later declared he had "always heard that the confiscations . . . were a considerable expense to the state. Nobody reaped any profit by themselves unless the trustees, who had the opportunity of paying themselves very well for their services."[20]

Secondly, the tax on unimproved lands could not be administered

18. *New Hampshire Gazette,* July 6, Aug. 3, Sept. 28, Oct. 5, and Nov. 16, 1779; Weare Papers, VII, 49, NHA; the quotation is from Belknap, *History,* II, 428.

19. *Journal of Samuel Lane,* ed. Hanson, 86.

20. New Hampshire Tax Book, 1775–1781, NHA; Batchellor and Metcalf, eds., *Laws of New Hamp.,* IV, 198, 216 (source of quotation), 498; New Hamp. Loyalist Claims, I, 99–104; Weare Papers, V, 133, NHA; *NHSP,* X, 537; Wingate to Belknap, Mar. 6, 1790, *Belknap Papers, MHS Collections,* 6th ser., IV (1891), 463.

properly. Town magistrates often rigged public auctions of land seized for delinquency so that they and their friends benefited. Although the legislature created a central agency to collect non-resident taxes in response to complaints about "the conduct of the constables," local officials continued to consider any absentee proprietor fair game. Huge plots were sold for small sums, until the state prohibited sale of more land than was needed for immediate tax payments. In 1780 the court repealed all previous laws and established entirely new procedures to protect proprietors and soldiers from having land seized. But the new laws were circumvented as easily as the old. The abuses became so notorious that when General John Stark left the state, he begged the Committee of Safety to protect his property while he remained in public service.[21]

Finally, prices began to rise again. Those who had accumulated paper money for speculative purposes or to pay taxes hastened to get rid of it, recalling, perhaps, that in the three years before 1780, £100 in state bills had been reduced in value to £3 6s. Creditors and traders demanded specie payments, in part because the legislature had repealed its laws concerning contracted debts. Within six months the currency had completely collapsed. Samuel Lane reported a "sudden unexpected total dissolution of our emission money which . . . nobody would take for anything" and added that the new continental bills "passeth but little better." Weare wrote to one of New Hampshire's congressional delegates, "The present situation of our currency makes me shudder."[22]

The legislators had no choice but to change their fiscal policies once again. Paper money had become useless, so they withdrew it from circulation by collecting taxes in continental currency and specie, which they used to redeem state bills. Next, a law making gold and silver legal tender for all debts was passed. Weare and his associates also devised several new techniques for financing governmental operations. In 1781 an excise tax on liquors went into effect. The continental requisitions of 1780 and 1781 had been collected in

21. Batchellor and Metcalf, eds., *Laws of New Hamp.*, IV, 131, 163, 202, 265; Philbrick to Bartlett, May 29, 1778, Bartlett Papers, I, BLDC; Maurice H. Robinson, *A History of Taxation in New Hampshire* (New York, 1903), 153–157; *New Hampshire Gazette*, Aug. 23, 1783; Chester B. Jordan, "Colonel Joseph Whipple," NHHS, *Proceedings*, 2 (1888–1895), 310.

22. NHSP, VIII, 858; Upton, *Revolutionary New Hampshire*, 132–147; *Journal of Samuel Lane*, ed. Hanson, 87–88; Weare to Samuel Livermore, July 9, 1781, Weare Papers, II, MHS.

beef and rum, and the system worked so well the court decided to try the same approach. In 1782 they assessed a general town tax payable in specie, state loan certificates, rum, beef, leather shoes, cloth, yarn, hose, wheat flour, felt hats, or blankets. The goods were then sold or used as military supplies. In its final two years of operation New Hampshire's revolutionary government collected most of its taxes in gold and silver.[23]

The new arrangement worked better than any tried previously. For the first time since the spring of 1775 citizens and their political representatives did not have to worry about inflation. Trade continued—albeit at a reduced level—with specie or personal notes serving as currency; in some areas bartering became the normal means of exchange. Although the government itself went through a brief period of insolvency which forced the Committee of Safety to call a special assembly session, the crisis had passed by the summer of 1782. External circumstances, of course, were partly responsible for these developments. The resumption of overseas trade which followed Washington's victory at Yorktown brought specie into the state; the presence of gold and silver, in turn, helped fill the need for a circulating medium and facilitated tax collection. Furthermore, the government's expenses declined as the continental army dispersed and the militia returned to a peacetime status. But the revolutionary leaders wasted little energy on such analysis. They congratulated one another on what appeared to be the success of their fiscal reforms and, perhaps, wondered why they had not adopted similar policies earlier.[24]

New Hampshire's political leaders wrestled with a third type of problem. They had warned soon after the controversy over taking up government that any further evidence of "party spirit" would encourage "enemies" of the rebellion and that no republic divided against itself could long endure.[25] But influential citizens in two sections of the state—Piscataqua and the upper Connecticut River valley—ignored the warning. They questioned the legitimacy of the government, criticized its policies, disrupted its proceedings, and

23. Upton, *Revolutionary New Hampshire*, 132–147.
24. Weare to Livermore, Exeter, Feb. 23, 1782, NHSP, X, 578; Belknap, *History*, II, 432; Upton, *Revolutionary New Hampshire*, 142–143.
25. NHSP, VII, 103. For another attack on political dissent see Sullivan to Weare, Dec. 12, 1775, NHSP, VII, 685–688.

challenged its authority. The war was nearly finished before the malcontents could be quieted.

Loss of political influence helps explain why inhabitants of Portsmouth and surrounding communities in the Great Bay area complained about the General Court. The fifth provincial congress —controlled by representatives from the interior—adopted a constitution which made merchant domination of house and council proceedings impossible. One result of this shift in power was the rejection of demands for reconsideration of the decision to take up government. The revolutionary legislature, furthermore, turned a deaf ear to recommendations that revolutionary merchants be given important civil and military appointments. John Wendell found the office he sought given to Wyseman Claggett, a councilor from Litchfield. Wendell, Joshua Wentworth, and other wealthy and well-educated Portsmouth men were bypassed when the revolutionary judiciary was formed; instead, appointments went to Weare, Thornton, Bartlett, Folsom, and their friends. Even Langdon bemoaned his fate. After telling Bartlett that his "ambitions for [the] military" were great, he complained that he knew of "no commission which our gentlemen would compliment me with . . . I do not expect," he added, "to be honored any way here, nor . . . do I desire it now, as I would not accept any of their dirty laps after every dog has lapped." So many others felt similarly slighted that Ebenezer Thompson, who as secretary of the assembly was in a position to know, considered the whole controversy over independency a product of their "disappointment" over not being "chosen to such offices as they desired."[26]

Portsmouth residents also disapproved of the way the government dealt with political dissent. A majority in the assembly felt that all citizens unwilling to support the revolution should be identified and punished. For the most part, local committees of safety cooperated fully with the effort to stamp out disloyalty, especially when the discovery of counterfeiting rings or the presence of British troops in nearby states heightened anxieties about the dangers of internal con-

26. Wendell to Weare, June 29, 1778, Weare Papers, I, MHS; *NHSP*, VIII, 61–64; Langdon to Bartlett, June 3, 1776, John Langdon Papers; Thompson to Bartlett, Jan. 29, 1776, Bartlett Papers, I, fol. 776129, BLDC. See also Peirce Long to Bartlett, July 2, 1776, *Historical Magazine*, 7 (1863), 48.

spiracy against the revolution.[27] But officials in the Piscataqua area sometimes refused to cooperate. A few of them still hoped for reconciliation with the British. Others, although supporting independence, argued that only those openly engaged in loyalist activities should be restricted and that the assembly's preoccupation with loyalty oaths and what John Langdon labeled "tory matters" seemed a bit paranoid. The merchant-dominated Portsmouth Committee of Inspection proved so lax that at one point John Sullivan, who was in charge of constructing local defenses, complained to Washington that the "infernal crew of tories, who have laughed at the Congress, despised the friends of liberty, and endeavored to prevent the fortifying of this harbor . . . walk the street here with impunity and . . . with a sneer, tell the people in the streets their liberty poles will soon be converted into gallows." In the spring of 1776 the few outspoken loyalists who had been arrested following the shelling of Falmouth were set free. The *Gazette* continued to publish articles defending the right of Mark Hunking Wentworth, Atkinson, Jaffrey, and the forty-odd other men who refused to sign the loyalty oath to live unmolested. The Portsmouth Committee of Inspection obstructed efforts by state authorities to apprehend suspected loyalists, and at least once the local sheriff openly allowed a captured Tory to escape.[28]

Economic developments accentuated the alienation still further. Portsmouth and the surrounding area did not share in the general prosperity of revolutionary New Hampshire. The town reported in 1779 that of the twelve thousand tons of shipping owned by local citizens before the Tea Act, only eight hundred remained. With money scarce, provisions expensive, and jobs hard to find, "multitudes" in the "once flourishing" community had been "reduced from easy circumstances to want and beggary." So many people had left that the alarm list was dangerously reduced; annual expenses for

27. Hammond, *Tories, passim.* Fear of internal conspiracy grew particularly strong during Burgoyne's campaign in 1777 and in 1779; see especially the Bartlett-Whipple correspondence in Bartlett Papers, photostats, NHHS. There was a good deal of counterfeiting: Kenneth. Scott, "New Hampshire Counterfeiters Operating from New York City," *New York Historical Society Quarterly,* 34 (1950), 31–57.
28. Langdon to Bartlett, June 24, 1776, *Historical Magazine,* 6 (1862), 239; Sullivan to Washington, Oct. 29, 1775, in Hammond, ed., *Sullivan Papers,* I, 119; *NHSP,* VII, 636, 652, 662, and VIII, 266–270, 577; Hammond, *Tories,* 29; *New Hampshire Gazette,* Sept. 21 and 28, 1776, and Feb. 18, 1777.

supporting the poor had reached £30,000. The report may have been exaggerated, for Portsmouth was seeking a tax reduction, but other observations confirm the tales of woe. Samuel Lane noted in his journal the shortage of food in seaports. When Whipple returned from the Continental Congress, he found trade at a standstill and the population fearful of starvation. Newcastle, a community completely dependent on trade, announced early in the 1780s it could no longer afford to send a delegate to the General Court.[29]

The merchant community was particularly hard hit. Old aristocrats attempted to live off their incomes, but inflation made living intolerably expensive, and taxes on unimproved lands stripped them of cash until most were forced to leave their holdings at the mercy of local officers conducting auctions for unpaid taxes. In 1786 John Peirce told former Governor Wentworth that "absentees had not the least idea how much the friends of government who remained have suffered in their estates, I mean all those who did no business which were generally the case with those whose property could maintain them . . . Your uncle Hunking, for instance, died as poor as a beggar, and Doctor Rogers whose property was so clear is greatly reduced . . . Your father . . . lost his whole stock in trade." Many patriots were similarly affected. Peirce acknowledged that "by far the greatest part of the town" had fared no differently from the friends and relatives of the governor. Peirce Long and Supply Clap, two of Portsmouth's most influential leaders, claimed to have lost money during the war. Samuel Cutts later informed his British agent, "I was particularly unfortunate during the war by losing all my navigation, and not being concerned in privateering (which I could not make consonant to my own feelings) I was left at the peace without any trading stock."[30] Only merchants with greater agility and fewer scruples than Cutts managed to increase their wealth. John Langdon, for example, used his influence in Philadelphia to gain the lucrative office of Continental agent for Piscataqua and obtain contracts for building Continental ships; in addition he engaged in

29. *NHSP*, XII, 695, and XIII, 286–287; *Journal of Samuel Lane*, ed. Hanson 87–88; letter from Whipple, Nov. 22, 1779, Langdon Papers, 147, HSP; *Freeman's Journal*, Jan. 7, 1777.

30. Peirce to [Madam Wentworth], Oct. 15, 1786, and Peirce to John Wentworth, Mar. 9, 1787, Masonian Papers, III, NHA; Long to Bartlett, Sept., 15, 1778, Bartlett Papers, I, BLDC; *NHSP*, XVII, 446; Cutts to Lane, Son, and Fraser, Aug. 10, 1785, Miscellaneous Manuscripts, 146, NHHS.

Portsmouth Harbor about 1778 as seen from Kittery. Strawberry Bank, where many well-to-do merchants lived, is in the center of the print. The church closest to the viewer is Queen's Chapel.

several successful privateering ventures, built ships of his own—with government funds, if the accusations of John Paul Jones are correct—supplied masts to the French navy, and speculated with Robert Morris in "prize goods." John Wendell, John Penhallow, and Joshua Wentworth were successful enough in obtaining goods needed by the Committee of Supplies and later the Board of War—of which Penhallow and Wentworth were members—to add to their personal fortunes. But even these men, despite their excellent political connections, struggled to prevent financial reverses.[31]

Given the circumstances, it is not surprising Portsmouth merchants and their sympathizers found fault with many of the government's economic policies. They approved of price fixing but accused the legislature of setting country produce at full value and undervaluing stock-in-trade. Before 1777 the state would not let them collect past debts; after passage of the legal tender law they had to accept depreciated currency. Inflation, triggered by what the merchants considered irresponsible fiscal policies, greatly complicated their everyday life. Taxes on unimproved lands made it risky for them to purchase new country properties and, in some cases, endangered their present holdings. Confiscation threatened the security of credits in England, while the state's periodic embargoes on overseas trade deprived them of the opportunity to obtain credits elsewhere[32] Moreover, cooperation with revolutionary authorities brought few rewards. Payment for goods sold to the government came in the form of paper currency or not at all. The Committee of Safety borrowed £1000 from Wendell in 1779 with the promise that the debt would take precedence over other state obligations, but five years later it had not been paid. In 1782 Supply Clap resigned his post as victualler for troops because the slowness of state payments promised to "reduce" him "to beggary." To be sure, many of the merchants sympathized with the difficulties faced by Weare and his associates and,

---

31. Mayo, *Langdon*, 115–139, 174–178; "John Wendell" in Shipton, *Biographical Sketches*, XII, 592–597; business correspondence of Joshua Wentworth, Larkin Papers. Evidence of Langdon's widespread activities may be found in Charles O. Paullin, ed., *Outletters of the Continental Marine Committee and Board of Admiralty* (New York, 1914), I and II; Langdon Correspondence and Langdon Papers, HSP; John Langdon Papers, NHHS. Governor Wentworth reported Langdon most assiduous in pursuing the rebellion because it made him rich: Wentworth to Lord Germain, Jan. 6, 1777, Wentworth Letter Book no. 3, 177.

32. *New Hampshire Gazette* and the *Freeman's Journal*, both published in Portsmouth, are filled with these complaints.

as committed revolutionists, were willing to work for small profit; but they still found the legislators unnecessarily unsympathetic to their needs. As one writer put it after the state issued a new list of recommended prices: "What encouragement has the merchant to hazard his interest when his merchandise is fixed at a price by gentlemen who are mostly unacquainted with the hazard and expense of trade?"[33]

Nor is it surprising the frustrated merchants and their friends sought political power: how else could they protect their personal and community interests? Langdon ran successfully for the house in December 1776, as did John Pickering, another strong critic of the government and one of the state's leading lawyers. At the same time George King, heir apparent to the aging Theodore Atkinson and a man Governor John Wentworth had once described as "unexceptionably the best man I know in America," gained election to the council on the strength of his support in the Piscataqua area. When Langdon's brother Woodbury returned from England in 1778, he joined in, first as a house member and later as King's successor on the council.[34]

Of these, John Langdon was in the best position to affect state policies. A recognized hero of the attacks on Fort William and Mary and an outspoken radical in early provincial congresses, he enjoyed an added advantage as one of the wealthiest and most articulate members of the house. After replacing the first Speaker, Langdon did his best to prevent the excesses which inexperience and anti-merchant sentiment might produce. He helped Weare and Bartlett engineer the fiscal retrenchment which began in the winter of 1777 and ended in 1782 with repeal of the tender laws and passage of an act making gold and silver the only legal money. He urged the formation of a permanent Board of War to replace the temporary and undependable Committee of Supplies, and after the assembly ac-

33. William Gardner to J. T. Gilman and Nathaniel Rogers, Nov. 12, 1792, New Hamp. Misc. MSS; Wendell to Committee of Safety, Weare Papers, XII, 85, NHA; *NHSP*, VIII, 500, and XVII, 446 (source of first quotation). The second quotation is from *Freeman's Journal*, Feb. 25, 1777.

34. For biographical data on Pickering and King, see William Plumer, "John Pickering" and "George Atkinson," *NHSP*, XXII, 839–843 and 824; and Mayo, *Langdon, passim.* The quotation is from Wentworth to William Reeve, Sept. 17, 1769, Wentworth Letter Book no. 1. Earlier King had refused appointment to the Rockingham County Inferior Court: Whipple to Brackett, July 23, 1776, *Proceedings MHS*, 5 (1860), 5.

cepted the recommendation he obtained board appointments for two of his merchant friends. He gained government support for the two price-fixing conventions which he and other traders in the state convened during 1779. Once the Speaker even badgered the assembly into holding a session in Portsmouth, much to the glee of his constituents.[35]

One of Langdon's most substantial victories involved state policy toward those who had fled New Hampshire because of the revolution. The Speaker, albeit reluctantly, had gone along with the mild confiscation and proscription acts passed in 1778, but when pressures mounted for the seizure of real property owned by all absentees, he balked.[36] Since a majority of the assembly seemed intent on passing the stronger measure, the two Langdons resorted to subterfuge: they first convinced their fellow house members that the act should cover all British property, including private debts, then turned around and launched a campaign to defeat the proposal. Woodbury Langdon, King, and their fellow supporters in Portsmouth called a town meeting which quickly adopted a petition against the proposed act. Additional confiscation, the petitioners argued, would benefit neither the state nor its inhabitants because proceeds would be liable to embezzlement, and British retaliation would deprive many worthy citizens of their personal property. More important, it was unjust to condemn absentees unheard: to confiscate their holdings without trial smacked of the very arbitrariness which as good republicans the revolutionists should avoid. Meanwhile John Langdon worked on the council, which eventually rejected the entire act even though its advocates in a last ditch effort had softened many of its provisions.[37]

Langdon's maneuvering, however, brought him into open conflict with other state leaders. The trouble began when the Committee of Safety rejected the Speaker's request that an imprisoned Tory be exchanged for his brother, who at the time was held prisoner behind British lines in New York. Soon thereafter Langdon accused the

35. *NHSP*, VIII, 428–579, 606, and 770–816 *passim*.
36. The proscription act exiled seventy-eight men who had left the state, thirty-three of them former Portsmouth residents. Only twenty-five of those proscribed had their estates confiscated. Langdon signed the proscription act but Dudley the confiscation act: *NHSP*, VIII, 810–814.
37. *NHSP*, VIII, 821–826; *New Hampshire Gazette*, Mar. 30, Apr, 6, 13, and 20, 1779; Adams, *Annals*, 268.

committee of faulty accounting methods and tried unsuccessfully to have Bartlett removed as a delegate to the Continental Congress. Woodbury Langdon's return to Portsmouth—the details of his "escape" remain unknown—and his entry into state politics made further confrontation inevitable.[38]

Most members of the legislature distrusted Woodbury Langdon and, for that matter, anyone else who had failed to support the radical steps taken by the revolutionists between 1774 and 1776. Bartlett doubtless had the new house member in mind when he wrote in February 1779 that "we have more to fear from . . . late conversions" than from rank Tories and expressed both a wish that they would not "designedly introduce themselves to important stations" and a fear that "there may be a collusion between them and some of our enemies." Weare, Dudley, Whipple, and others in what Portsmouth men had begun to call the "Exeter Party" shared his suspicions.[39] In addition, recent developments had made these same men question John Langdon's dependability. The Speaker's economic ambitions had become so apparent that Whipple felt obliged to remind him that "true republicanism knows no interest in the least degree incompatible with that of the public weal. May I presume so far in your friendship," he added, "to recommend the study of republicanism? This will have a tendency to abate your anxiety for the acquirement of wealth and prepare the mind to meet adversity with a smile."[40] And even though Langdon's credentials as a patriot seemed impeccable, his cooperation with men of doubtful commitment made some legislators wonder.

Woodbury Langdon's appointment to replace Whipple in the Continental Congress, which his brother engineered, precipitated a crisis. The Committee of Safety quickly asked Whipple to remain in

38. Mayo, *Langdon*, 166–168; NHHS, *Collections*, VII, 117; *NHSP*, VIII, 768, 783.

39. Bartlett to Whipple, Feb. 20, 1779, Bartlett Papers, photostats, NHHS. In revolutionary America "party" still had negative connotations; it meant a group of men who sought political power in order to serve their own special interests rather than the interests of society as a whole. Thus politicians would never admit to "party" identification even though they cooperated year after year with the same men. For a general discussion of the problem of political factionalism during the revolution see William N. Chambers, *Political Parties in a New Nation: The American Experience, 1776–1809* (New York, 1963), 17–33.

40. Peabody to Bartlett, Oct. 18, 1779, in Edmund C. Burnett, ed., *Letters of the Members of the Continental Congress* (Washington, 1921–1936), IV, 491; Whipple to Langdon, June 21, 1779, Langdon Papers, HSP.

Philadelphia and ordered the new delegate not to go. When Langdon ignored the order, his political enemies took a different tack. George Gains, a Portsmouth house delegate and Committee of Safety member who liked late converts no better than did Bartlett, arranged a town meeting in which Whipple was elected to replace Woodbury Langdon in the house. Meanwhile, Weare, Bartlett, and Dudley convinced the assembly to retract its recent vote and make Nathaniel Folsom of Exeter the new congressional delegate. By the spring of 1780, Woodbury Langdon was without office.[41]

The challenge did not go uncontested. Furious, John Langdon attacked both the men who had thwarted him and the institution through which they held power. "A certain gentleman," reported Bartlett of the house Speaker, "who was displeased with the members of the Committee of Safety last summer for desiring his brother not to proceed to Congress, took every means in his power to injure them, finding fault with everything they did and taking advantage of the new members to insinuate things much to the disadvantage of many of the Committee and carried matters so far that the Court reduced the Committee to five and took from them almost all the powers they formerly had." Although Bartlett exaggerated—the most serious restrictions prohibited the committee from settling accounts with local officers or drawing money from the treasury without specific authorization from the General Court—the committee did find its effectiveness temporarily impaired. That summer one state resident refused Weare's request to return as a special delegate to Congress until appointed by the assembly. And the new restrictions made it more difficult for Weare and his colleagues to manage the state's confused financial affairs.[42]

After 1780, however, Langdon's influence declined. His obvious favoritism toward his brother alienated representatives who had condemned colonial magistrates for similar practices. The legislature soon discovered it could not operate effectively without a strong Committee of Safety; as a result the restrictions were forgotten and the man who introduced them lost face. The Speaker's antagonists,

41. *New Hampshire Gazette*, Nov. 23 and 30, 1779; Woodbury Langdon to Peabody, Dec. 5 and 28, 1779, Woodbury Langdon Papers, NHHS. Further details on the confrontation between the committee and the Langdons may be found in Page, "Bartlett," 577–582 (app. B).

42. Bartlett to Folsom, Mar. 11, 1780, Bartlett Papers, photostats, NHHS; Weare Papers, VII, 101, NHA; Livermore to Weare, July 3, 1780, Livermore Papers.

on the other hand, gained complete control of the government. Dudley, Bartlett, and four close political allies were the only delegates to serve on the Committee of Safety after 1781. Together they successfully sponsored a bill confiscating the estates of all absentees; another law required all citizens to take an oath of allegiance before voting in town and state elections. Langdon, who had opposed both measures and was not one to waste his energy on lost causes, retired in the fall of 1782. Harmony once again prevailed in the General Court.[43]

Outside criticism of the government also became less intense. Many seaboard inhabitants felt that the assembly had shown sensitivity to their needs by adopting fiscal reforms, repealing the legal tender act, and establishing a central agency for the collection of nonresident taxes. Others were so busy taking advantage of opportunities opened by the resumption of overseas trade they became indifferent to politics. General conditions in the early eighties tended to make men forget past animosities; the fighting had stopped and independence seemed assured. Even those who still considered the state authorities inept and unjust had something to be optimistic about. A convention to write a permanent constitution had been convened, and Portsmouth's delegates controlled it; surely the recommended reforms would provide New Hampshire with government more sympathetic to their interests. Under these circumstances it really didn't make much difference what the men who ruled at Exeter did. They soon would be replaced.[44]

The state government faced a different type of opposition in the upper Connecticut River valley. By the end of 1776 many area residents had convinced themselves the legislature had no right to rule over them. They remained in open rebellion for several years.

The westerners' dissatisfaction lay deeply rooted in past experiences. Hanover, Lebanon, and the two towns opposite them on the western bank of the river—Norwich and Hartford—had been settled by an associated body of petitioners from the same general area in eastern Connecticut. Many residents of Plainfield, Lyme, and Enfield—all named for Connecticut towns from which their original settlers came—had similar backgrounds. Their emigration to New

43. *NHSP*, VIII, 887–985.
44. See chap. vi.

Hampshire after the end of the French and Indian Wars did not mean the end of association with one another or with their families and friends to the south. The need for cooperative defense against Indian attacks, continued intermarriage, and the Presbyterian organization of their churches all tended to strengthen a sense of community derived from the pattern of settlement. The obvious advantages of river trade with Connecticut further reinforced old ties.[45]

In New Hampshire these settlers were subjects of an unfamiliar government. Connecticut had no royal governor and few royal officials. Local inhabitants ran their own affairs and felt estranged from the system of family domination which characterized New Hampshire's political structure. Fortunately, authorities in their adopted province left them alone. The awkwardness of communications between the river valley and Portsmouth would have made imposition of royal authority on the new settlers difficult at best. In any case, Governor John Wentworth had no desire to alienate his western subjects. He appointed as justices of the peace men who already commanded the respect of their fellow émigrées, like Eleazar Wheelock and his son-in-law Bezaleel Woodward in Hanover and Israel Morey of Orford. Furthermore, the Portsmouth aristocracy provided much financial support for Dartmouth College, which many settlers looked upon as visible evidence of the civilization they were creating in the wilderness. After Wentworth had been driven from the province, the inhabitants of Grafton County, like others in the province, were quick to condemn the oppressive constitution under which they existed; but at the same time they acknowledged that "the goodness of the ruler" who exercised authority under that constitution had prevented them from feeling the "whole weight" of British tyranny.[46]

Community leaders in Grafton County naturally watched the proceedings at Exeter carefully. What they witnessed bothered them. After Wheelock, the president of Dartmouth, looked at the plan of representation voted in the fourth provincial congress, he complained

45. Chase, *Dartmouth*, 156–215, and *passim*; Rice, "Dartmouth and New Connecticut," *Papers and Proceedings of the Connecticut Valley Historical Society*, 1 (1876–1881), 157–161; Charles A. Downs, *History of Lebanon, New Hampshire* (Concord, 1908), 1–66; John Wheelock to Colonel Chase, July 18, 1775, fol. 775418, BLDC.

46. Oscar Zeichner, *Connecticut's Years of Controversy, 1750–1776* (Chapel Hill, 1949), 4–5, and *passim*; Chase, *Dartmouth*, 90–156, 217–318; NHSP, XVIII, 656, 684, and X, 230 (source of quotation).

to the governor of Connecticut that the "melancholy situation" in New Hampshire could not be repaired because state leaders were "not of the greatest abilities." Experience with the revolutionary government confirmed their worries that independence would do nothing to improve their political status. The new seat of government was no less remote than the old. Town delegates from the county found themselves isolated and ignored during the first session of the assembly. But most important, the westerners felt that the constitution perpetuated control by eastern seaboard interests. "It appears from the whole face of the thing," inhabitants of eleven towns in Grafton County complained in a printed address to other towns in the state, "that monopolizing and aggrandizement are the principal objects in view; and that this mode of government is a little horn, growing up in the place where the other was broken off; for by this plan the majority of the Council are to be chosen out of a part of the colony; perhaps not more than one-fourth part of the extention of the inhabited territory in the colony . . . Pray where is the difference between this establishment and the former one, so much complained of, except that the Governor had the power in the former, and a number of persons in the latter."[47]

The author of this address, probably Bezaleel Woodward, knew the constitution could easily be defended by those who adopted it. Had not Weare and his associates eliminated the evils of the old system by instituting proportional representation in both the house and council and giving general political authority to the assembly? No, the address declared. The system of classifying towns into units of one hundred voters for purposes of representation had prostituted the very political liberties it intended to protect. Legitimate representation could not be based on population alone, for "every body politic incorporated with the same powers and privileges, whether large or small, are legally the same . . . no person or body corporate can be deprived of any natural or acquired right without forfeiture or voluntary surrender . . ." "We think it of utmost importance," concluded the westerners, "that every inhabited town have the liberty, if they please, of electing one member at least to make up the legislative body." The argument made sense to the inhabitants of

47. Wheelock to Trumbull, December 1775, *Historical Magazine*, 16 (1869), 241; *NHSP*, XI, 440, and X, 233 (source of the quotation). Most of the important documents dealing with the rebellion are published in *NHSP*, X, 228–500.

Bezaleel Woodward (1745–1804), Dartmouth College faculty member and publicist for the western rebellion. Copy by U. D. Tenney from a Richard Jennys portrait ca. 1785.

Grafton County, just as did their claim that councilors should be elected at large; both practices had been considered of fundamental constitutional importance in Connecticut.[48]

The address went further: regardless of its formal content, the constitution should be considered illegitimate because of its manner of adoption. The provincial congress had not been authorized "to institute a lasting plan of civil government," nor its members empowered to engross the general authority they now claimed as legislators. The assembly was therefore an illegal body, and petitions such as those made by Portsmouth and other towns in protest of taking up government had been "absurd." "The true state of the case," announced the western towns, "is that we have no legal power

48. The quotations are from *NHSP*, X, 231–233; see also Zeichner, *Connecticut*, 4–5.

subsisting in the colony." Only the addressees, "the inhabitants of the several towns in the colony of New Hampshire," could legally create a government. They should "exercise their rights and privileges . . . to erect a supreme legislative court for the colony, in order to lay a foundation and plan of government in this critical juncture of affairs."[49]

The arguments presented by the westerners received support from a second pamphlet, "The People the Best Governors," printed, as the address had been, in Connecticut. "The People" manifested the same concerns as had the earlier appeal. It insisted that each town have at least one representative and that senators be elected at large. But the pamphlet did something the address had not: it proposed "a concise plan" of government, founded on what the westerners considered just principles of law.[50]

The plan would eliminate much of what the "college party"— as the leaders of the rebellion were soon labeled—found unacceptable in the state constitution. To limit the power of a legislature which would be dominated by eastern interests even if each town sent one representative, it proposed a popularly elected governor, "without any concern in the legislature," and a council of twelve elected at large to advise the assembly. County officials, including justices of the peace and inferior court judges, would be elected by county inhabitants instead of being appointed by the assembly. No person would be allowed to hold more than one public office, or any office at all unless he possessed a belief in "one only invisible God . . . and that the Bible is his revealed word; and that he be also an honest moral man." Since "social virtue and knowledge" was the "only qualification" for officeholding, there would be no property requirements for assembly membership.[51]

The inhabitants of Grafton County took these arguments seri-

49. *NHSP*, X, 230, 234–235.

50. "The People" is printed in Chase, *Dartmouth*, 654–663. Much has been made of "The People" by those seeking to identify the revolution with such radical ideas as universal manhood suffrage and the elimination of property qualifications for officeholding: see Elisha P. Douglass, *Rebels and Democrats* (Chapel Hill, 1955), 15–16, 116; and Harry A. Cushing, "The People the Best Governors," *American Historical Review*, 1 (1896), 284–287. These ideas are presented almost as afterthoughts in the document; the main emphasis is on town representation and limitation of assembly power. The writer of "The People" has for the most part claimed universal validity for political practices generally accepted in Connecticut before the revolution.

51. Chase, *Dartmouth*, 654–663. The quotations may be found on pages 660, 661, and 659.

ously. Woodward, Payne, and John Wheelock organized regular correspondence among town committees of safety and created a group called the United Committees, of which Woodward was appointed clerk. Hanover had refused to send a delegate to the fifth provincial congress, and when elections for the next assembly were announced in the winter of 1776 at least thirteen other communities joined the boycott, justifying their action in now familiar terms. All protested the system of representation; Hanover demanded elimination of property qualifications; Alstead proclaimed that such qualifications only served "to discourage virtue and promote vice." They also noted their dislike of the newly appointed county sheriff.[52]

The behavior of the westerners worried the state legislators. Grafton County, although distant from the seat of government, was important for the conduct of the war. Early in 1776 the house had asked Wheelock to exercise his influence over the Indians to prevent depredations. Frontier towns had been provided with powder and arms and were considered the first line of defense against attack from Canada. And although the rebels were professed and ardent patriots and many in the Connecticut Valley still supported state government, their rebellion obviously interfered with military efficiency.[53] For example, when the Haverhill and Newberry Committees of Safety found Asa Porter, a wealthy Anglican and former royal official in Haverhill, guilty of dealing with the British, he convinced committee members that he should not be turned over to state authorities whose legitimacy the committee members disavowed. Though Porter was finally taken to Exeter to stand trial before the assembly, the problem remained.[54] Political disorder in the west could not be ignored.

"At the first breaking out of the disease," Weare wrote later, "it was thought lenitives would cure it." Acting on this hope the assembly quickly resolved that as towns grew in size their representation

52. Chase, *Dartmouth*, 424–426; NHSP, VIII, 78–80, 421–426, XI, 2, 23 (source of quotation), 329, and XII, 163, 509, 573.
53. Chase, *Dartmouth*, 318–422; NHSP, VIII, 307, and XVII, 369; Moses Dow to Weare, Mar. 17, 1777, Weare Papers, IV, 28, NHA; John Hurd to Joseph Whipple, Nov. 19, 1776, *Proceedings MHS*, 5 (1860), 6.
54. NHSP, XXV, 659, and VIII, 324–330, 413. Porter defended himself before the assembly by claiming that the people had not delegated judicial or executive authority to the General Court, nor given it the right to deprive him of trial by jury. Disturbed by Porter's accusations, the house appointed a committee to consider where "supreme executive authority" lay. The committee only recommended a change in the treason law: NHSP, VIII, 452, 459.

would correspondingly increase. Wheelock and Woodward were appointed justices of the peace and Woodward an associate justice in the Grafton County Inferior Court; later another leading rebel, Elisha Payne, was offered the post of chief justice, with Woodward his senior associate. When such peace offerings seemed ineffectual, the assembly determined to send Weare and other councilors to the area to work out a plan of reconciliation. Meanwhile Weare pondered ways to refute the constitutional propositions put forth in the address to the inhabitants of New Hampshire.[55]

The president of New Hampshire admitted that the state constitution was far from perfect. But formation of a permanent government, he felt, would require much more time and deliberation than the present situation allowed. Furthermore, the constitution had not been thrust arbitrarily upon the people of New Hampshire but adopted by representatives specifically authorized to form themselves into a house of representatives. The members from Grafton County who had sat in the convention which adopted the constitution had not uttered one word against it.[56]

More important, Weare considered the theory of representation presented by the western rebels ridiculous. "Will anyone in his senses," he argued, "say that the people are equally represented when a town that has but five electors in it is to have an equal voice in all legislative matters with one that has five hundred?" It was from such unequal representation that the independency of Parliament had been destroyed and that "venality and corruption" had been introduced. New Hampshire had perhaps two hundred townships, more than half of them without settlers. "How easily might a man of large fortune and ambitious views purchase a right or two in each of these towns," warned Weare, "and put on settlers for his purpose where there is none and bribe voters in those where there are only a few inhabitants and those chiefly of the lower sort and thereby have the General Assembly at his beck." Nothing could be more dangerous to republican liberties. "It gives me singular concern," he added, "that such logic and such politics should be taught in any seminary of

55. Weare to [Benjamin Giles], Exeter, Feb. 13, 1781, Weare Papers, II, MHS. *NHSP*, VIII, 344, 450, 826; Chase, *Dartmouth*, 428–429, 479; Woodward to Weare, Exeter, June 25, 1779, Weare Papers, I, MHS.
56. Weare never published his arguments, but two different drafts of a response to the address of the Grafton County towns have been preserved in his handwriting; see Weare Papers, XII, 107, NHA, and Misc. MSS, 1778, MHS.

learning. I trust it is not in more than one throughout all the United States." Ready to defend the state government, Weare set off for Grafton County with Bartlett, John Wentworth, and Benjamin Giles, who represented neighboring Cheshire County in the council.[57]

On February 13, 1777, the councilors met with twenty-eight representatives of the United Committees. The rebels held their ground: "No one of us," they reported, "is as yet in any degree convinced of the justice or equity" of the assembly plan of representation. Moreover, the councilors discovered that matters were even worse than they had imagined. Settlers across the river in the New Hampshire grants had just formed themselves into a state they called New Connecticut, and many in New Hampshire seemed inclined to join them. And apparently the Continental Congress remained unconcerned. Through the influence of the Connecticut delegates, it was rumored, a Continental regiment was to be raised and stationed in the river valley under the command of Colonel Timothy Bedel, among the busiest and most officious of the malcontents.[58] The discouraged councilors had no alternative but to return to Exeter, their problems still unsolved.

That summer and fall, hope for compromise gradually rose. In June the United Committees affirmed their desire to become part of New Hampshire if a new constitution were written giving each town the option of selecting at least one representative and if the "seat of government" were fixed "as near the center of the state as conveniently as may be." Western towns cooperated with state officials in the military preparations designed to protect New Hampshire from Burgoyne's troops. When the assembly met soon after the victory at Saratoga, Payne and Woodward delivered the June petition and met with an assembly committee, which recommended that a constitutional convention be convened as soon as the circumstances

57. Weare Papers, XII, 107, NHA; Misc. MSS, 1778, MHS; *NHSP*, VIII, 450, 463.

58. *NHSP*, XIII, 761 (source of quotation); Chase, *Dartmouth*, 450; Bartlett to [Whipple], Mar. 1, 1777, Langdon Correspondence, HSP; Weare Papers, IV, 21, NHA. Bedel was given command of a valley regiment and made John Wheelock his lieutenant colonel. State leaders accused Bedel of using Continental funds to further the rebellion and urged that his regiment be disbanded; in 1779 it was. See Chase, *Dartmouth*, 390–396, and Edgar Aldrich, "The Affair of the Cedars and the Service of Colonel Timothy Bedel in the War of the Revolution," NHHS, *Proceedings*, 3 (1895–1899), 223–225.

of war would permit. Soon thereafter the house acted positively on the recommendation.[59]

The willingness of state authorities to consider a constitutional convention with all towns represented presented the college leaders with a dilemma. From the beginning of the rebellion they had been motivated as much by a desire to prevent political separation from their friends to the west of the river as by their intellectual commitment to the constitutional ideas expressed by Woodward. Their reluctance to accept the political authority of New Hampshire had been reinforced by the failure of the state to support Dartmouth College once Wentworth had departed. Furthermore, even if a new constitution were to be adopted they could hardly hope to influence state affairs significantly. In such circumstances their commitment shifted; political independence from New Hampshire rather than reform of the existing constitution would best satisfy their aims. Although they had demanded a constitutional convention, they now realized such a convention might destroy any chance for this independence.[60]

Before the convention was called, Woodward and his colleagues worked out a plan of action. The rebellious towns in New Hampshire would join the new state in the grants, which by now had adopted the name Vermont and a constitution guaranteeing each town at least one representative. Once accepted, the representatives from east of the river would join with their valley friends across the Connecticut to control the new government. Hanover—or Dresden, as the rebels called the college part of the community—might well become the state capital. If the plan worked, the state government of New Hampshire and the illegal constitution under which it operated could safely be ignored.[61]

To implement this bold scheme the western leaders again resorted to the press. "Republican," in a public letter to the inhabitants of the grants, argued that neither New York—which in 1764

---

59. *NHSP*, VIII, 758, 774–776, XIII, 762–764 (quotation from 763); Page, "Bartlett," 309.

60. Samuel Tenny to Belknap, Mar. 10, 1791, Belknap Papers, IV, 161.D.81, MHS; *NHSP*, X, 267, and XI, 440.

61. Eliakim P. Walton, ed., *Records of the Council of Safety and Governor and Council of the State of Vermont* (Montpelier, 1873–1880), I, 81–103; the constitution of Vermont was modeled on that of Pennsylvania. For the history and background of the Vermont movement, see Matt B. Jones, *Vermont in the Making*, and Chilton Williamson, *Vermont in Quandary* (Montpelier, 1949), 1–90.

had been awarded jurisdiction over lands west of the Connecticut—
nor New Hampshire could legally claim authority over any towns
in the grants, and that the grants included all towns in New Hampshire beyond the bounds of the original Masonian patent. He reas-
oned that British authority, having been exercised only through
coercion, became "null and void" after the Declaration of Independence. "There being no compact or agreement of the people whereby
they become united with either" New Hampshire or New York, the
inhabitants of the grants "reverted to a state of nature as to government, and stand entirely unconnected with them." In this state of
nature no new "power of jurisdiction" could arise except "from the
people who are to be the subjects of this government." Only "their
mutual compact and agreement" could give "any body of men power
or right to exercise government in and over themselves." The implication could not have been more obvious: inhabitants of the grants
to the west of the Connecticut had acted in accordance with their
fundamental rights when they formed the state of Vermont, and
inhabitants east of the river would assert the same rights if they
joined the new government.[62]

As soon as the house voted to ask the people of New Hampshire
whether a constitutional convention would be called, the rebel leaders hurried into action. "Republican," whose letter was not yet
printed, added a postscript warning those east of the Connecticut
that if they took part in any convention, "once the plan is formed
and settled, be it what it will, like it or not like it, they are as effectually bound by it as if they had made it altogether themselves."
The United Committees met January 28 and again on February 12.
One month later, sixteen New Hampshire towns petitioned the
Vermont Assembly for admission to the new state.[63]

Throughout the summer of 1778 everything proceeded according
to plan. As expected, the Vermont Assembly—controlled by the
Allen brothers and others whose interests lay to the west of the
Green Mountains and who were well aware of the plot to take over
the state they had created for their own purposes—hesitated to accept the proposal. But when eastern Vermont towns threatened to
secede unless the New Hampshire towns were admitted, the Bennington party, as Allen and his associates were called, agreed to sub-

62. *NHSP*, X, 259–266 (quotations from 264 and 265).
63. *NHSP*, X, 266, 267 (source of quotation), and 276.

mit the matter to the vote of towns already in Vermont. A majority, in part influenced by the "Observations" of "Republican," responded favorably. The sixteen New Hampshire towns were formally admitted despite the Allens' protest. By the end of June, Dartmouth College had been taken under the protection of Vermont, and before October most Grafton towns and a few communities in Cheshire declared themselves confederated with Vermont.[64]

Success, however, was brief. Encouraged by opposition to the secession among New Hampshire leaders, Ethan Allen proceeded to Philadelphia and there extracted from Bartlett a promise to support congressional recognition of Vermont if, in return, Allen used his influence to detach New Hampshire towns from the new state. He then hurried back to Vermont and convinced a majority of the assembly that Congress would not extend recognition to Vermont unless the new towns were ejected. Thwarted, the Grafton County delegates withdrew with delegates from ten towns west of the river. Next the entire group met, dispatched John Wheelock to Philadelphia to prevent the recognition of Vermont, and called a convention to meet at Cornish early in December. Woodward, Payne, and their most prominent associate west of the river, Jacob Bayley, then wrote a "Public Defense of the right of the New Hampshire Grants . . . on both sides of the Connecticut River to associate together and form themselves into an independent state." Before the Cornish convention the pamphlet had been printed by a press recently set up in Dresden to implement political maneuvers of the college party.[65]

The "Public Defense" summarized the basic constitutional argument of the western rebels: the Declaration of Independence had severed all political ties except those of incorporated townships whose original charters "were not held at the pleasure of the King . . . but were perpetual": towns were therefore free to form themselves into a government for the mutual benefit of all concerned. But after justifying their behavior in legal language, the writers of the "Public Defense" abandoned their constitutional arguments, which by now even they seemed to consider weak. They argued that

64. *NHSP*, X, 272–295; and fols. 778354 and 778365, BLDC. The part played by the Allen brothers in the western rebellion is described by Williamson, *Quandary*, 24–127.
65. *NHSP*, X, 283–335; Elisha Payne to Roger Sherman, Oct. 28, 1778, fol. 778578, BLDC; Chase, *Dartmouth*, 467–469.

grants on both sides of the river should be erected into an independent state because "their local situation" demanded it. Cut off from New York and New Hampshire by mountains and distant from the seat of government in both states, the inhabitants of the valley were tied together through "connections and commerce" so tightly "it would be very disadvantageous to be in two different jurisdicions." Since most valley dwellers had emigrated from Connecticut, "their manners, customs and habits" were "conformable to each other, and their principles and sentiments the same in regard to religion and civil government." Under such circumstances, inevitable disputes would arise from combination with either New York or New Hampshire, where different sentiments predominated. Moreover, if "Dr. Wheelock's charity school" were to fall under New Hampshire jurisdiction (Wheelock had failed in his efforts to move the college to the confiscated estate of the former Indian Commissioner, Sir William Johnson, in upstate New York), it would "be in a state which has heretofore . . . shown a very cool disposition toward it." Having concluded their arguments, the writers expressed determination to remain together and suggested that if neither the states nor the Congress would allow them to become an independent state they would consider uniting with New Hampshire, providing a form of government could be agreed upon.[66]

It soon became evident that, should the valley remain intact, it would be under New Hampshire's jurisdiction. The convention at Cornish attended by delegates from eight Vermont and fourteen New Hampshire towns plotted to regain control of Vermont but, acknowledging the probability of failure, agreed to negotiate with New Hampshire should the Bennington party be victorious. When it was, Bayley set out for Exeter with an associate to negotiate terms for a reunion with New Hampshire.[67]

Most New Hampshire legislators responded to recent developments in the west with exasperation. Weare, who had taken seriously the original constitutional arguments of the rebels, soon became scornful: at first, he wrote, "we are entertained with publica-

66. *NHSP*, X, 296–324 (quotations from 312, 320, 321, 322). For Wheelock's attempt to move Dartmouth to New York, see fols. 777168.1, 777168.2, 777177, and 777213, BLDC.
67. *NHSP*, X, 325–336.

tions about the connection between an incorporation and representation that would puzzle all the logicians on earth . . . then we were turned over to a state of nature . . . and the world was to begin anew, every man or body of men had a right to go where they pleased . . . When it was found this would not do, then another new discovery was made." The whole mess, concluded Weare, had been caused by the "art and cunning of some designing men who wish for nothing more than to bring everything into confusion, neglect the common cause and sacrifice that by getting into heats and parties about things comparatively of no importance." Timothy Walker, a councilor who as "Pacificus" answered the "Observations" of "Republican," blamed the feud on "the disappointments of a small junto of aspiring, avaricious men in their endeavors to raise themselves and their connections to a degree of importance in the state far, very far, beyond what their numbers or estates gave them any pretence to." Others agreed. A writer to the *Exeter Journal* excoriated the malcontents and labeled "their whole fraternity . . . admirers of *Payne*, misery, confusion and disorder."[68]

Despite their exasperation Weare and his colleagues did not want to confront the rebels with force. Civil war, they felt, might do irreparable damage to their precarious experiment in republicanism. Furthermore, the westerners had some support in the east—one legislator received an anonymous letter labeling the people in the grants "hewers of wood and drawers of water" who as true republicans possessed the right to determine their own government—and they continued to support the revolution unequivocally: even when they refused to collect taxes for the state government, the malcontents taxed themselves, deposited the money in local treasuries, and employed it in defending the frontiers. Time and the Continental Congress would eventually resolve the dispute satisfactorily.[69] Under these circumstances, Bayley's proposals seemed worth listening to. Why shouldn't New Hampshire have jurisdiction over the area which until 1764 their royal governors had assumed belonged to

68. Weare to [Benjamin Giles], Feb. 13, 1781, Weare Papers, II, MHS; *NHSP*, X, 268–271 (Walker's quotation from 271); *New Hampshire Gazette*, Aug. 5, 1778, and May 25, 1779; *Exeter Journal*, May 18, 1779.

69. State Papers, 1779–1780 box, NHA (source of quotation); fols. 779413 and 780120, BLDC; Chase, *Dartmouth*, 471; Weare to Congressional Delegates, Aug. 19, 1778, *Historical Magazine*, 4 (1860), 333.

the province? The two councilors from Cheshire County, Samuel Ashley and Benjamin Bellows, had originated the idea, and Whipple had written from Philadelphia the previous December recommending such a claim. Accordingly, after considering the matter six months, the assembly agreed to claim jurisdiction over the whole grants. At the same time it authorized Congress to decide whether the grants west of the river should be permitted to continue as a separate state.[70]

The assembly recommendation healed the wounds of rebellion temporarily. The New Hampshire delegates to Philadelphia, Woodbury Langdon and Nathaniel Peabody (who was secretly purchasing the old Benning Wentworth grants west of the river), eagerly supported the claim.[71] By January the house had appointed Samuel Livermore—a former royal official who had retired to Holderness in eastern Grafton County at the start of the war, later joined the House of Representatives, and commanded the respect of both Weare and the leaders of the rebellion—a special delegate to Congress; in March 1780 Livermore reported that the prospect of success looked "better and better"[72] Settlers in the valley did what they could. Woodward and Peter Olcutt of Norwich proceeded to Philadelphia with a message to Congress which stated that "the people in these parts . . . will cheerfully acquiesce on anything Congress may judge proper, but ardently wish a union of the two sides of the river. New Hampshire will be their choice, if a new state be not admitted, which they have generally done expecting." The Cornish committee called a convention to meet at Hanover and plan an attack on Canada, a patriotic gesture which could not help gaining the approval of a Congress already disturbed by rumors—later substantiated—that the Allens were negotiating with the British for recognition as an independent country. Congress, however, when

70. Page, "Bartlett," 330–332; Whipple to Weare, Dec. 8, 14, 1778, in Burnett, ed., *Letters*, III, 522, 534; *NHSP*, X, 336–351; Bartlett to Whipple, Apr. 3 and June 25, 1779, Bartlett Papers, photostats, NHHS.
71. *Dresden Mercury*, July 13, 1779; *NHSP*, X, 355–358; Peabody to Weare, in Burnett, ed., *Letters*, IV, 498.
72. Livermore to Weare, Mar. 24, 1780, in Burnett, ed., *Letters*, V, 73. On Livermore see William Plumer, "Samuel Livermore," *NHSP*, XXI, 816–818, and Arthur Livermore, Memoranda, Livermore Papers. A graduate of Princeton, Livermore had served as New Hampshire's attorney general before the war and had married a daughter of the Reverend Arthur Browne.

confronted with conflicting claims from New York and New Hampshire, as well as the boycott of Vermont agents who denied the Congress had any authority to act in the matter, refused to make any decision.[73]

The inaction of Congress did not displease everyone in New Hampshire. By the summer of 1780 many in the state had begun to have qualms about absorbing the grants, for union would mean not only an immediate increase in the state's population and taxable land but also the eventual removal of political power from the southeastern section of the state.[74] One who shared such concern was John Sullivan, recently returned to New Hampshire after resigning his Continental commission. Sullivan, who temporarily replaced Livermore in Philadelphia, let it be known that as long as towns east of the Connecticut remained in New Hampshire's jurisdiction he would not oppose an independent Vermont. When Livermore returned to Congress the following summer, he found sentiment "vastly changed . . . I have been told in Congress," he informed Weare, that "in insisting to have the Grants wholly annexed to New Hampshire . . . I did not speak the wish or voice of my state. My business now is if possible to secure the Grants east of the river."[75]

Sullivan's attitude was only one of many factors leading to the failure of Congress to support New Hampshire's claim to the grants. As Livermore acknowledged, congressional fear of civil war should the land west of the Green Mountains be attached to New Hampshire, apprehension lest Vermont join the British, and the unwillingness of New York and Massachusetts to surrender their claims to the land all played important roles. But to the inhabitants of the valley, the performance of the Exeter government seemed inexcusable. Sullivan was accused of accepting huge amounts of land in

73. Joseph Marsh *et al.* to Congress, July 20, 1780, *NHSP*, X, 364 (source of quotation); Moses Hazen to Sullivan, Sept. 13, 1780, in Hammond, ed., *Sullivan Papers*, III, 185. For a discussion of the British negotiations see Williamson, *Quandary*, 90–127.

74. Paine Wingate to Belknap, Mar. 6, 1790, *Belknap Papers, MHS Collections*, 6th ser., IV (1891), 461; Hammond, ed., *Sullivan Papers*, III, 628; Livermore to Weare, June 26, 1781, in Burnett, ed., *Letters*, VI, 130; *NHSP*, X, 375, 389.

75. *NHSP*, XVIII, 765; Livermore to Weare, July 3, 1780, Livermore Papers; Livermore to Weare, Aug. 7, 1781, in Burnett, ed., *Letters*, VI, 172. Livermore had refused to return to Philadelphia because the Committee of Safety, not the General Court as a whole, had appointed him.

Vermont and a promise of its governorship in return for support of Vermont independency. Those who believed the general to be "a man of too much honor" to deceive them accused the Committee of Safety of giving him "private direction" and forcing him to undermine congressional support of New Hampshire's claims. With sentiment running high against both the Exeter government and the Continental Congress, the college leaders again took matters into their hands and called for a convention to meet at Charleston, New Hampshire, early in 1781.[76]

The delegates who met represented forty-three towns, all in the valley area. Among them were eleven members of the Exeter government from Cheshire County, prepared to convince their fellow delegates that the state still sought jurisdiction over all the grants. At first they succeeded, and by a large majority the convention voted that New Hampshire undertake such an extension. But the victory was short-lived. Ira Allen arrived shortly after the vote had been taken and, seeing his hopes of an independent Vermont threatened, offered to cooperate with Woodward and other convention leaders and promised that the Vermont Assembly would readmit the New Hampshire towns it had previously rejected. The prospect of a union with Vermont excited convention members; they still distrusted the Exeter government and disliked its constitution. Despite the protest of Cheshire County members, union with Vermont was approved. By the following October the Vermont legislature had admitted thirty-five New Hampshire representatives, erected counties, established courts, and organized the militia east of the river. Elisha Payne had been elected lieutenant governor; Payne and Woodward both had been chosen justices of the Vermont Supreme Court.[77]

The second union with Vermont brought matters quickly to a head. Many in the New Hampshire towns which had joined Vermont refused to obey Vermont officials. Citizens loyal to the New

76. Livermore to Weare, Aug. 14, 1781, in Burnett, ed., *Letters*, VI, 184; Sullivan to Weare, Dec. 11, 1780, Feb. 5, July 10, 1781, and Sullivan to John Wendell, Jan. 21, 1781, all in Hammond, ed., *Sullivan Papers*, III, 240, 268, 282, 334; *NHSP*, XIII, 765, and X, 375–380; Benjamin Giles to Weare, Jan. 22, 1781, Weare Papers, II, MHS (source of quotations).
77. Chase, *Dartmouth*, 490–494; *NHSP*, X, 381–398; Giles to Weare, Jan. 22, 1781, and General Bellows to Weare, Feb. 1781, Weare Papers, II, MHS.

Hampshire government in Swanzey, Westmorland, and Chester-field petitioned the General Court for instructions. In Landaff—a township settled under conflicting charters, one owned by Dart-mouth and the other by a group of proprietors including Weare's legislative associate Nathaniel Peabody—efforts were made by friends of the college to have townspeople renounce their allegiance to New Hampshire. A friend of Peabody who witnessed these at-tempts warned the Committee of Safety, "The sentiments of the good people in many of those unhappy towns cannot be determined by the votes in their town meetings as none are allowed to vote but such as solemnly renounce all dependence on . . . the state of New Hampshire and take an oath to support the government and laws of . . . Vermont." Coercion went even further. Some who refused to pay Vermont taxes had their land seized or were thrown in jail. Throughout Grafton and Cheshire counties, those who rejected Ver-mont authority demanded that New Hampshire take quick and effec-tive action.[78]

By now the members of the state legislature were ready to listen. Weare wrote to Philadelphia in June that "unless Congress brings matters to an immediate issue" the state, unable to collect taxes in the west, would not be able "to contribute farther towards the war"; worse still, he feared bloodshed. Three months later the Committee of Safety ordered troops to proceed westward, ostensibly to protect against Indians and the British but prepared, as Bartlett admitted, to prevent greater internal disorder in that part of the state. When it became known that Vermont would not surrender jurisdiction over towns east of the river despite a congressional resolution order-ing it to do so before Congress considered its plea for statehood, the legislators became even more insistent. The act passed, demanding an oath of allegiance from all state inhabitants, was directed at the western rebels as well as Tories. In January 1782 the court resolved to send troops as a "necessary, though disagreeable measure" to bring the rebellion to an end. Soon afterwards a traveler in Exeter wrote to Payne that "the minds of the people are, in this part of the state, much soured against those that have taken up government under the state of Vermont . . . the General Court are determined

78. *NHSP*, XIII, 527, 664, and X, 409, 413 (source of quotation), and 401–485 *passim.*

not to listen to anything but absolute unconditional submission to the government of New Hampshire."[79]

The troops, to the relief of the legislators, were not called into action. Prodded by General Washington, the Vermont Assembly renounced jurisdiction over towns east of the river. The inhabitants of these towns, long tired of the chaos of their affairs, accepted state authority. A strong religious revival which reached Dresden in November and by January had touched "upwards of twenty towns" aided reconciliation: "Long divisions and animosities," reported a correspondent from the valley, "have happily been settled" without "wildness and enthusiasm."[80] The state government soon forgave its lately disaffected brethren. At first appointments in the county courts and militia were reserved for men, like Charles Johnston of Haverhill and Israel Morey of Orford, who had remained loyal throughout the rebellion; but by 1783 Woodward had been reappointed justice of the peace. When Weare, bothered by failing memory and deafness, resigned as chief justice of the superior court and was successful in efforts to make Livermore his successor, it was reported the appointment had "a greater tendency to quiet the counties of Cheshire and Grafton" than any previous act of government. By then all the Grafton County towns except one had begun to participate in assembly elections. Woodward appeared as a member from Hanover in March 1784; the last of the rebellious towns had capitulated.[81]

The leaders of New Hampshire's revolutionary government must have looked back on their experiences with a good deal of self-satisfaction. They had guided the state through a long and fatiguing war, struggled successfully with a complex set of political problems, and ruled in a manner consistent with what they considered the

79. Weare to Livermore and Sullivan, June 20, 1781, *NHSP*, X, 401; *NHSP*, X, 475, 552–558, and XI, 717 (source of court resolution); Batchellor and Metcalf, eds., *Laws of New Hamp.*, IV, 427; Moffatt, Whipple, and Mason Papers, 1; William Page to Elisha Payne, Jan. 8, 1782, New Hamp. Council Correspondence, Force Transcripts.

80. *NHSP*, X, 462, 573–575; Nathaniel Prentice to Weare, Feb. 25, 1782, Weare Papers, X, 120, NHA: *New Hampshire Gazette*, Apr. 13, 1782 (source of quotations); John Phillips to John Wheelock, Feb. 18, 1782, fol. 782168, BLDC.

81. Chase, *Dartmouth*, 502–507; Weare to Livermore, Oct. 30, 1781, Livermore, Memoranda, Livermore Papers; Livermore to Weare, Mar. 12, 1782, and Weare to Livermore, Apr. 2, 1782, Weare Papers, II, MHS; *NHSP*, VIII, 942–944; *New Hampshire Gazette*, Jan. 11, 1783 (source of quotation); fol. 783161, BLDC.

principles of public virtue. To be sure, willingness to assume responsibility for running state affairs had involved personal sacrifice—Weare, Bartlett, Dudley, and several other delegates found themselves much poorer at the end of hostilities than before—but they still had their farms and families. Besides, what happened to them individually made little difference in the long run. Their most important task had been to prove that New Hampshire could govern itself without the aid of arbitrary external authority. And this they no longer doubted.[82]

82. *New Hampshire Gazette,* Feb. 9, 1779, and Aug. 30, 1783; *Essex Journal and Merrimack Packet* (Newburyport), Dec. 1, 1784; Plumer, "Dudley," *NHSP,* XXI, 798; Weare Papers, XI, 20, NHA; will of Meshech Weare, Weare Papers, LC; William Plumer, "The Constitution of New Hampshire," *Historical Magazine,* 14 (1868), 174; Page, "Bartlett," *passim* (esp. 191).

6

Constitutional Reform,

1776–1783

Although the temporary constitution adopted by the fifth provincial congress remained in effect until the summer of 1784, efforts to create a permanent form of government began several years earlier. The leaders of the movement were the same group of Portsmouth residents who constantly condemned the revolutionary legislature and periodically disrupted its proceedings. They sought reform for three mutually reinforcing reasons: to undermine the effective authority of Weare and his associates, to create a government potentially more responsive to their personal, community, and sectional interests, and to make certain New Hampshire's new constitution conformed with what they considered the principles of political justice. They soon discovered, however, that few in the state shared either their dissatisfaction with the existing government or their assumptions about how a republican polity should be organized. Only after the reformers abandoned their most radical proposals was a permanent constitution adopted.

The process of reform began in 1776 with a concerted attack by leading Piscataqua citizens on the existing form of government. One thing that bothered them was the lack of an independent executive. A newspaper correspondent who signed himself "Amicus Republicae" stated his objections in theoretical terms. Under the late government, he noted, people had complained of the Court of Appeals and family-controlled council whose members "shared all the places of honor and profit among themselves and friends." It was true the legislators had abolished "the iniquitous court"; but he wished "the same Assembly would have condemned the dangerous consequences of lodging the legislative and executive powers in the same persons," which was a "political solecism and equally as destructive as the Court of Appeals." Others argued in practical terms. John Langdon—who earlier had recommended that the constitution provide only a bicameral legislature—now thought a governor was needed to bring order into legislative proceedings and permit more decisive governmental action. Several of his merchant friends felt an independent executive might be more sensitive to their commercial needs than the present state authorities.[1]

Many of these same men were disturbed by the plural officeholding which resulted from appointments made in the first and subsequent assembly sessions. Weare, Bartlett, Thornton, Folsom, Dudley, and others held a variety of posts and saw nothing wrong in doing so; in fact, they argued that the government could not operate efficiently in any other way. John Wendell was among the first to condemn the practice. "I know of an Assembly," he complained to Elbridge Gerry, "who have given amongst themselves almost every place of honor or profit in the colony, civil, military, executive, judicial and legislative." Wendell argued that just such a system had led to the undermining of English liberties and worried lest New Hampshire be caught in "the quicksand on which the British state had been cast." The only solution would be an act, by the Continental Congress if necessary, amending all state constitutions so that "every General Assembly . . . consist of gentlemen *unplaced and unpensioned.*" Portsmouth's town meeting offered a less sweeping suggestion when it instructed its delegates to procure a law prohibiting assembly members from holding other offices. Langdon felt so strongly about plural officeholding that when he joined the house he resigned his new commission as justice in the Inferior Court of Common Pleas. Soon thereafter the citizens of both Newmarket and Epping formally congratulated him for acting in accordance with the principles of good government.[2]

Residents in the Piscataqua area also condemned the system of representation adopted in the fourth provincial congress. In a community already critical of the men and institutions of state govern-

1. *Freeman's Journal*, Aug. 3, 1776; Langdon to Bartlett, June 24, 1776, and Aug. 1, 1778, *Historical Magazine*, 6 (1862), 239–242.

2. Wendell to Gerry, June 25, 1776, Elbridge Gerry Papers, vol. 2, MHS; *NHSP*, VIII, 301; *Freeman's Journal*, Aug. 10, 1776, and Jan. 14, 1777; Page, "Bartlett," 463.

ment, the address from Grafton County—which, Weare bewailed, had been "with great assiduity scattered among the inhabitants of this state"—created a mild sensation. "The unequal representation exclaimed against . . . by our friends in the western parts of this unhappy divided state demands a most speedy redress," pleaded "Cato," and his sentiments were echoed by others. But what form the redress should take proved difficult to decide. The westerners' demands that each town be permitted at least one representative and that councilors be elected at large would, if implemented, further dilute seaboard influence in the assembly. The inhabitants of Portsmouth discussed the problem in town meeting and adopted a policy calculated to appeal to all dissenters: they instructed their delegates to seek reduction of the minimum number of voters required for representation to not more than fifty, and, at the same time, to demand that representation be absolutely proportional to population. Had these reforms been adopted, both the size of the house and Portsmouth's influence in it would have doubled.[3]

Eastern critics of state authorities were intrigued by a second argument included in the address that since no legal power existed in New Hampshire a "supreme legislative court for the colony" should be convened to construct a government. The idea was not entirely new—"Amicus Republicae" had suggested something similar when he said plural officeholding should be prohibited "by an Assembly, the members of which had no places themselves by their seats in said Assembly"—but it took on special meaning as time passed. In the first place, the western rebels said they might become loyal citizens if the constitution were rewritten, and some seaboard politicians had begun to think only an alliance with town delegates from the Connecticut River valley could produce needed change in legislative policies. Equally important were events in Massachusetts, where the General Court had voted to resolve itself into a convention for the purpose of writing a constitution. Many citizens objected because they felt no government had the right to create a document which legitimized its own authority. Did not the same logic apply to New Hampshire? Had not the members of the fifth provincial congress usurped authority which in a republic belonged to the people? Should not the people insist, as revolutionists were

3. Misc. MSS, 1778, MHS (source of Weare's statement); *Freeman's Journal*, Nov. 12, 1776 (source of quotation from "Cato"), and Jan. 14, 1777.

insisting in the Bay State, that a new convention be called and its recommendations submitted to the voters for approval? The reformers also pointed out that New Hampshire's present constitution would have to be replaced when the fighting stopped, anyway. Why not, they asked, begin the task now?[4]

The campaign soon produced results. In December 1777 Langdon obtained a house vote asking all towns and parishes to instruct their delegates whether or not the assembly should convene a "full and free representation of all the people of this state . . . for the sole purpose of framing and laying a permanent plan or system for the future government of this state." Although the council refused to concur with the vote—Weare and Bartlett questioned Langdon's motives and wanted to postpone reform until military matters became less demanding—most towns responded to the appeal.[5]

The specific instructions must have encouraged the reformers. A majority of the towns agreed that New Hampshire needed a permanent constitution and that a separate convention made up of delegates from all incorporated towns should frame it. Moreover, many communities expressed dissatisfaction with the present government. Newmarket declared that no government could be considered "free by right . . . when such a multiplicity of offices and employment are conferred on any one person as to interfere with each other, and retard and delay the public service, and when the fees of officers or wages of representatives are voted by themselves, and taken out of the public treasury, and wantonly increased according to their own and sovereign pleasure." The citizens of neighboring Epping put the matter even more bluntly. "We view many members of the Court," they wrote, "to be too nearly interested in several departments of government to establish a constitution upon just and free principle." Fear that present assembly members might control any constitutional convention led the people of Thornton to recommend "that no man belonging to the present Council or House of Representatives have a seat in said convention." And others who cast their

4. *Freeman's Journal*, Aug. 3, 1776; NHSP, VIII, 757, IX, 833, and XIII, 765; Weare Papers, IV, 54–119, NHA. For the debate in Massachusetts see Robert J. Taylor, ed., *Massachusetts, Colony to Commonwealth: Documents on the Formation of Its Constitution, 1775–1780* (Chapel Hill, 1961), 50–73, and Oscar and Mary Handlin, eds., *The Popular Sources of Political Authority: Documents on the Massachusetts Constitution of 1780* (Cambridge, 1966), 169–379.

5. NHSP, VIII, 757–758 (source of quotation), IX, 833, and XIII, 765; Weare Papers, IV, 54–119, NHA.

arguments in less personal terms seemed to have had the same idea in mind; the writing of a new constitution would be a means of removing from power a group of legislators who, like their colonial predecessors, had used their position as public servants to increase their private estate.[6]

The instructions also undermined legislative opposition to a convention. Weare and Bartlett—sensitive to the barbs of their critics —felt obliged to act in accordance with republican principles, and the people as a whole certainly wanted a new constitution. Besides, the two councilors and their associates saw some advantages in reform. Although the western rebels might not be satisfied, the government's organizational problems would be solved: everyone seemed to agree that New Hampshire needed an independent executive. The assembly reconvened in February and issued precepts for a convention to meet at Concord in June. Each town was to send as many delegates as it pleased and to pay them for their services. The new constitution would not go into effect until three quarters "of the people" voted to accept it.[7]

Elections took place that spring. The Portsmouth delegation included two ardent reformers, John Langdon and George King. Exeter sent John Pickering, who had also advocted basic reforms. Weare, Dudley, Whipple, Folsom, Thornton, and Ebenezer Thompson all were chosen. Grafton County boycotted the convention, and twenty other towns decided not to participate, but the total number of representatives still reached about ninety.[8]

The convention disappointed those who wanted the government's organization changed. A member in attendance reported that although a "large number" insisted "upon having the supreme executive authority lodged in one man with advice of a privy council, and some few thought it most proper to be lodged in one man only . . . the greater number thought it most safe in the hands of the Council and Assembly." Weare complained about the decision—"I should have thought," he wrote to Bartlett, "that we have already experienced sufficient to convince anyone of the necessity" of an independent executive—but could do nothing to change it even though

6. Weare Papers, IV, 54–119 (quotations from 86, 89, 102), NHA. *NHSP*, IX, 834–842; Colby, *Manual of the Constitution*, 77–84.
7. *NHSP*, VIII, 757–776, IX, 833, and XIII, 765; Weare to Bartlett, July 3, 20, and Aug. 8, 1778, *Historical Magazine*, 4 (1860), 299, 332.
8. *NHSP*, IX, 834–837.

he served as chairman. Langdon's comment was equally graphic: "It is impossible to give dispatch or keep any dignity in government without some supreme executive power, and to have one branch of the legislature . . . execute those laws which they themselves have made is an absurdity."[9]

The Concord group, however, proved responsive to other eastern demands for reform. Langdon, King, Pickering, and delegates from several more large communities obtained a vote making representation directly proportional to population. The Exeter government had been criticized for paying its own members too much; convention members responded by making towns pay all legislative salaries. Most important, the practice of plural officeholding was curtailed. The document finally submitted for voter approval made it unconstitutional for any member of the General Court to hold an important judicial or military commission. House members were prohibited from serving the state in any salaried capacity. Weare, understandably, objected to these provisions. The constitution was sent out under the signature of John Langdon, president pro tem.[10]

Weare needn't have worried, for the proposals were far too controversial to be ratified.[11] The western rebels ridiculed almost every conclusion reached at Concord and refused to vote on the constitution. Failure to provide for an independent executive provoked an outburst from Jeremy Belknap—he referred to the proposed government as "a lousy chick of the degenerate British breed, vulgarly styled omnipotent"—and so disturbed others in the Piscataqua area that Portsmouth voted 87 to 2 against approval. The provision saddling towns with the expense of the house delegate's salary produced complaints throughout the state. The exclusion clauses alienated many locally influential legislators. Some inhabitants thought

9. [Samuel Philbrick to Bartlett], June 16, 1778, Bartlett Papers, I, BLDC (published in Colby, *Manual of the Constitution*, 78); Weare to Bartlett, July 3, 20, and Aug. 8, 1778, *Historical Magazine*, 4 (1860), 229 and 332; Langdon to Bartlett, June 20, 1778, *Historical Magazine*, 6 (1862), 240.

10. [Philbrick to Bartlett], June 16, 1778, Bartlett Papers, I, BLDC; *NHSP*, IX, 837–842. Since no convention records remain, it is impossible to be precise about what happened. Weare may not even have attended the second session when the limitations on plural officeholding were adopted. He did, however, remark that he was "not much grieved" when voters rejected the constitution: Weare to Peabody, Oct. 25, 1779, Weare Papers, VII, 71, NHA.

11. I have been unable to locate any tabulation of town returns. A spot check of local records proved only that many towns either refused to vote on the constitution or failed to record their decision. Page, "Bartlett," 463a, lists a few returns; at least ten towns rejected the proposal unanimously.

the whole idea of reform suspect. "The mode of attacking our political constitution," wrote a self-styled "Farmer," who also suggested the assembly banish all those guilty of insulting the present government, has been "reduced to a system by our internal enemies." After reading the constitution, Bartlett predicted it would be "some considerable time before we shall have a new government established."[12] He was right. For nearly two years after the 1779 proposals had been rejected, the advocates of constitutional reform remained quiet.

Public apathy toward eastern demands for reform and feuding among leading state politicians, however, could not change the fact that New Hampshire's present plan of government had been enacted only for the duration of hostilities with the British. By 1781 both the legislators and their critics agreed another effort should be made to obtain a permanent constitution. The General Court in April called for a second Concord convention and ordered it to remain in session, amending its proposals until they were ratified. By now the idea of constitutional reforms had lost its popularity. Dozens of towns ignored the precepts completely, while others voted specifically to send no one; all told, only fifty-four delegates were elected. But in Portsmouth, community leaders became excited about the imminent convention. The town chose five representatives, including Langdon, Pickering, another lawyer dissatisfied with state government named Jonathan Sewall, and George King, who recently had had his surname changed to Atkinson in accordance with the terms of his benefactor's will.[13]

The excitement was justified. With the rest of the state indifferent, the Portsmouth delegates might exert a decisive influence over the convention; in any case, they would be operating in a climate favorable to their political ideology. Since the convention of 1778, discussion of constitutional matters in New Hampshire had been dominated by two documents: the Essex Result, written by Theophilus Parsons of Newburyport, and the constitution of Massachusetts, written by John Adams and adopted by state inhabitants in 1780. Both documents emphasized that good government must prohibit

12. Belknap is quoted in Lawrence S. Mayo, "Jeremy Belknap's Apologue of the Hen at Pennycook," *PCSM*, XXVII: *Transactions* (1927–1930), 33. Portsmouth Town Records, NHSL. "Farmer" wrote in *New Hampshire Gazette*, Aug. 5–19, 1779. Bartlett to Whipple, Apr. 3, 1779, Langdon Correspondence, HSP.
13. *NHSP*, VIII, 894–897, and IX, 842–844.

plural officeholding, include an independent executive, and make representation in at least one legislative body directly proportional to population.[14]

The Portsmouth delegates controlled the convention easily, for Bartlett and Weare, whose health had begun to fail, took no part in its proceedings.[15] After Atkinson was elected president and Sewall secretary, even Belknap became optimistic: "The *hen* sat once," he reported; "she was not so large, nor so speckled as heretofore. There is a prospect of something being not only laid, but hatched, that will be clever in itself. Whether it will suit the taste of the people is uncertain."[16] Within three months the convention had submitted for public vote a constitution which, if adopted, would have revolutionized the government of New Hampshire.

The writers of the proposed plan used the Massachusetts Constitution as their model. Copying word for word many of its provisions, they included a bill of rights and elaborate restrictions on plural officeholding. They provided for a governor to be selected annually by the General Court from among the four candidates receiving the highest number of popular votes. The General Court would include house and senate—representation to be proportional to population in the house and to property assessment in the senate—and their members would also be elected annually. No financial qualifications were imposed on house members, but senators had to be worth £400 clear of debt, and the governor £1000. Appointment power was given to the governor and a council of five selected by the legislature from among the citizens of the state. The governor might veto legislation, but three fourths of both houses—in Massachusetts the percentage was only two thirds—might override his veto.[17]

In one important matter Atkinson, Langdon, and the other delegates abandoned their model. House members in the Commonwealth, like those in the existing New Hampshire legislature, represented individual communities or classes of communities. Such a

14. Bartlett to Whipple, Apr. 3, 1779, Langdon Correspondence, HSP; Handlin and Handlin, eds., *Popular Sources*, 324–365, 441–472.

15. *NHSP*, IX, 852. The only two participants in the government's inner circle who attended were Dudley and Folsom. Weare and Bartlett may have felt that as legislators they should not help write the constitution. Neither Hampton nor Kingston sent delegates.

16. Belknap to Ebenezer Hazard, 1781, *Belknap Papers, MHS Collections*, 5th ser., II (1877), 103.

17. *NHSP*, IX, 852–877.

system of town representation had come under increasingly bitter attack by critics of the assembly. Belknap blamed it for introducing men of little education, less virtue, and no sense of public responsibility into power, and he entertained himself and his correspondents with tales of their crude behavior. Others argued that town representation meant an assembly too large for effective operation. The merchant community responded readily to both arguments, for they had long been alienated from a house dominated by local and decidedly nonmercantile interests.[18]

In the Essex Result, Theophilus Parsons had proposed a system he thought would eliminate the problems caused by town representation. He recommended that the Massachusetts House be limited in number, and the members be chosen not by individual towns but by county conventions of town delegates. Although the Massachusetts Constitutional Convention did not seriously consider the plan, the New Hampshire Convention did. Throwing caution to the winds —for Atkinson and his colleagues must have known that the localism proclaimed by western rebels was, if anything, stronger in New Hampshire than in Massachusetts—the constitution-makers wrote the Essex plan of representation into their proposals, with the added proviso that all county delegates must be possessed of an estate worth £200. Rockingham County would have twenty members, Hillsborough ten, Strafford and Cheshire each eight, and Grafton four. And as if to prove their daring they eliminated one other traditional prerequisite of local groups, the right of militiamen to select their own captains and subalterns.[19]

In a lengthy address to the people of New Hampshire, prefixed to the proposed constitution, the reformers explained their reasoning. The present form of government everyone acknowledged to be imperfect, for it lacked an exclusion bill and combined executive and legislative authority in the same body, the General Court. The proposed constitution corrected these defects. It provided for separate legislative, judicial, and executive authority and insured that no man would hold so many offices that he would be unable to fulfill his duties adequately. The fifty-man house would contain "a greater proportion of suitable men" than any larger body. Elimination of

18. Belknap Papers, Apr. 19 and June 5, 1777, MHS; Belknap to Hazard, Dec. 28, 1779, and Mar. 13, 1780, *Belknap Papers, MHS Collections*, 5th ser., II (1877), 26, 43.
19. *NHSP*, IX, 863–869.

town representation would prevent the "interested views . . . party spirit, and zeal for rivalry" of town elections from interfering in state affairs. Publication of assembly journals—a practice not employed by the present court—would keep the people informed of legislative activity. And the governor, who by "the manner of his choice . . . is the most perfect representative of the people," would lend "secrecy, vigor and dispatch" to governmental affairs, while being prevented from usurpation of authority by annual election and privy council control.[20]

The authors of the address—probably Pickering and Sewall—did not limit their considerations to constitutional theory. The two lawyers, warning that the proposed constitution would be opposed by both friends and enemies of the common cause, implied that friends were more dangerous. "The love of power is so alluring," they wrote, "that few have ever been able to resist its bewitching influence." Those in power always try to "enlarge its boundaries" and, even more, "agonize to retain all that is clearly delegated to them." The situation in New Hampshire encouraged such tendencies. Some members of the General Court assisted "in enacting laws, in explaining and applying them, and in carrying them into execution. Can it seem strange," the address continued, "that such persons . . . should be backward in receiving and approving a constitution that so remarkably retrenches them . . . It is not strange, it is perfectly natural; and the fact is fully verified by the length of time which the present form of government has been permitted to continue." The challenge could not have been more pointed: the writers of the proposed constitution intended to destroy the existing state government and replace it with one not only founded on principles of good government but one which Meshech Weare, his associates in the Committee of Safety, and the local delegates of communities in the interior could not easily dominate.[21]

The responses to the address were often just as pointed. Some considered the constitution nothing less than a Tory restoration plot, engineered by George Atkinson, heir and potential successor to colonial tyrant Theodore Atkinson. Others saw in the proposals an

20. *NHSP*, IX, 845–852 (the quotations are from 848, 849, and 850).
21. William Plumer, "The Constitution of New Hampshire," *Proceedings of the Bar Association of the State of New Hampshire*, n.s., II (1904–1908), 233n, identifies Pickering and Sewall as the authors. The quotations are from *NHSP*, IX, 845 and 846. Atkinson signed the address.

attempt by Piscataqua merchants to regain lost power and to prevent state government from adopting measures like the confiscation of estates (one clause in the bill of rights implied such confiscation would henceforth be considered unconstitutional). These critics were doubtless well aware that few outside the Piscataqua area possessed the £1000 free of debt required of the new, independent, and powerful governor.[22]

For the most part, however, debate over the proposed plan of government emphasized constitutional rather than political considerations. Some still resisted the exclusion bill, and many felt the convention had made the governor too strong and the assembly too weak. Others objected to executive control of appointments, particularly the appointment of officers previously elected by local militia groups. But the plan of representation came under the strongest attack. "A True Republican" explained his objection in detail. "An inevitable consequence of adopting the present plan," he wrote, is "that an attention to the interest of particular towns, which now prevents members from forming themselves into parties, will be forgotten, and the members of each county will form an alliance among themselves; the interest of one county will be opposed to that of another, and the most numerous and powerful will command the suffrages of the whole. This mischief," the author continued, "cannot take place where each member has the local attachment confined by the constitution to the particular town he represents . . . should the proposed plan be adopted, a dangerous avenue will be opened for introducing powerful parties." And "an objection even more powerful against this innovation," he concluded, "is that it deprives us of a privilege essential to freemen . . . the power of instructing our representatives." Without such power to bind their delegates to positive instructions, "representation would be but an empty sound."[23]

"A Citizen of New Hampshire" disagreed. He contended that nothing could benefit government more than destruction of local attachments which "confine even good men"; under the county plan, representatives "would learn to measure on a larger scale and to

22. *New Hampshire Gazette,* Dec. 29, 1781, and Jan. 5, 12, 19, 1782.
23. NHSP, IX, 878; the quotations are from *New Hampshire Gazette,* Dec. 1, 15, 1781.

174

move in a nobler sphere." As for instructions to representatives, a true representative of the people should be willing to disobey them and follow "the dictates of his own own conscience and judgment, assisted by the arguments and debates" which his electors could not hear. If each representative felt bound by his instructions, he would be "nothing but a piece of clockwork, and the whole General Assembly one complete puppet show!" But such arguments received little support among people long accustomed to town representation and in the habit of instructing their assembly members. The citizens of Concord voted 48 to 0 not to accept the constitution and cited the system of representation as their first objection; town meetings throughout the state did the same. The constitution was overwhelmingly rejected.[24]

By August of 1782 a second plan of government had been readied for popular scrutiny. Belknap reported, "Our hen has laid again . . . We have a constitution as often as we have an almanac, and the more we have the worse. They have now spoiled the plan of representation . . . and lowered the pecuniary qualifications of the officers of government and of the voters." Others were less disappointed, for the convention had thrown out the Essex plan and restored town representation; each community or class of community with 150 ratable polls would have one delegate, and one more for each additional 300 polls. In response to critics who claimed that only the wealthy could hold office under the former proposals, Atkinson and his colleagues halved estate requirements for the governor and senators and eliminated the "clear of debt" clause. In other changes they further abandoned their attempt to erect a patrician government with a strong executive. Power to appoint captains and subalterns was taken from the governor and council and given to general field officers; rather than being "established by the standing laws" the governor's salary would be granted annually. Furthermore, convention leaders assumed a far more humble pose in their address supporting the new proposals. All references to the misuse of power by present legislators were eliminated.[25]

24. Quotations are from *New Hampshire Gazette*, Dec. 8, 22, 1781. *Concord Town Records* (Concord, 1894), 279; NHSP, IX, 877. No voting tabulations are available for this or the other constitutions proposed by the second convention.
25. Belknap to Hazard, Nov. 10, 1782, *Belknap Papers, MHS Collections*, 5th ser., II (1872), 161; NHSP, IX, 878–895.

In spite of the changes, the reformers remained worried. In the address they pleaded passionately for an independent executive and emphasized every check against the governor's authority built into the new plan of government. They felt obliged to defend the appointment of militia officers by their superiors: "electing officers by the voice of tumult, dissension and party spirit," as did the existing militia, undermined military discipline. But the pleas were unsuccessful. To the convention's "great grief and surprise," Atkinson later reported, "not half the towns within the state made any returns, and of those that did, not a fifth part of the inhabitants voted." Of those who did vote, most offered amendments.[26]

The leaders of the convention, however, could not be sure how unpopular their proposals actually were. They thought that their inability to "find enough voters either to establish or set aside the constitution," as Belknap put it, stemmed from another source: town inhabitants refused to vote because the house had required an oath of allegiance from all voters in town meeting, and many refused to take the oath. The oath had caused much confusion. In Portsmouth, Newington, and New Ipswich, local townsmen balked at the requirement, arguing that it deprived them of their rightful privileges and did nothing to separate enemies of the state from patriots. Many returns to the convention blamed the small vote on the oath. The infuriated convention members voted to resubmit the constitution, directed the towns to proceed as though the oath had never been passed, and promised to accept any votes given in town meeting. Such disregard of state authority delighted Belknap. "This . . . will make a clashing when the Court meets again with old *Vacation of Ty*"—Belknap referred to Dudley's description of the capture of Fort Ticonderoga—"in the Speaker's chair, who is a great stickler for the test. Don't you think we are in a curious situation," he asked, "with two supreme dictatorial bodies subsisting, and independent of each other?"[27]

Eastern ridicule of state government became increasingly frequent

26. *NHSP*, IX, 878–882 (the quotation is from 881). Atkinson's report is in *New Hampshire Gazette*, Feb. 8, 1783.

27. All quotations are from Belknap to Hazard, Jan. 8, 1783, *Belknap Papers*, *MHS Collections*, 5th ser. II (1877), 175. *NHSP*, XII, 725, 741, and XIII, 48; Batchellor and Metcalf, eds., *Laws of New Hamp.*, IV, 473, 516; *New Hampshire Gazette*, Jan. 4, Feb. 8, and Apr. 5, 1783.

during the campaign for adoption which followed resubmission. "Republican," who published a series of seven articles in support of the constitution, repeated the earlier accusations that the members of the General Court, "who have gained an unbounded influence in the towns where they reside, and others adjacent have influenced them to reject the proposed constitution and to vote for continuing that under which they are sure to rule with unlimited sovereignty." Angered by the second confiscation act, the oath of allegiance, and the frustration of their attempts at constitutional reform, Portsmouth instructed its delegates to take measures to circumscribe the power of the court. "Quibus" demanded that the powers of the Committee of Safety "be exactly ascertained or totally annihilated, for at present both the people and the laws seem to be the sport of their will." Joseph Whipple (William's brother) ascribed New Hampshire's inability to pay taxes to the unwillingness of state authorities to "give power and energy to their laws." John Wendell, writing as "A Soldier's Friend," declared that he earnestly wished to see the present state authorities impeached "and the new constitution take place, where men and measures will be changed." But men and measures were not to change just yet. In June the members of the convention met and, after reviewing the latest returns, reluctantly concluded they had to make further amendments.[28]

At first they voted that, instead of two thirds, only a majority of votes for approval would be necessary for adoption. But doubting that even a majority could be convinced to accept the constitution, they agreed to more extreme changes. A few convention members thought that if the executive were given the title "president" rather than "governor"—a term still associated with restoration politics— the recently rejected plan of government might pass. Most, however, felt that still more alterations must be made. After brief debate the convention did change the executive's title and, in addition, eliminated his veto powers. His privy council was to be elected by and

---

28. "Republican's" articles were published from Feb. 8 to Mar. 22, 1783, in the *New Hampshire Gazette*. The first quotation appears in the Mar. 1 issue; "Quibus's" in the Sept. 20, 1783, issue; and Wendell's on Aug. 23, 1783. See also the *Gazette*, Mar. 9–30 and May 11–25, 1782, and Jan. 25 and Apr. 5, 1783. William Whipple to J. T. Gilman, July 14, 1782, Langdon Papers, 175, HSP; Joseph Whipple to Robert Morris, Jan. 25, 1783, Lowell Papers, 108, MHS.

from the General Court. Neither president nor council members would have a permanent salary.[29]

In an address to the people, the convention announced that expediency rather than conviction had caused them to weaken executive authority. Further delay in adopting a new plan of government could not be tolerated: war had ended, and the assembly which had arbitrarily extended the authority of the 1776 constitution could not legitimately remain in power. Although convention members did not believe the plan they offered to be in accordance with principles of good government, they reluctantly recommended adoption. This time the constitution received the votes needed for ratification.[30]

Adoption of a permanent constitution settled the last of the political disputes which had plagued the leaders of New Hampshire since the collapse of imperial authority. It created a structure of government which, most revolutionists agreed, would be an improvement on the old. The provision for an independent executive satisfied Weare and Bartlett as well as their critics. The exclusion bill promised to eliminate the plural officeholding which men throughout the state had condemned. Removal of appointment powers from the assembly to a privy council pleased those who felt legislative authority should be limited. The bill of rights protected liberties denied the revolutionists under British rule. Moreover, many of the "feuds, animosities and divisions" which, one *Gazette* correspondent five months earlier had warned, might "lay a foundation for future calamities," and give ambitious men a chance to seize power, disappeared after ratification. Langdon, Atkinson, and Pickering bided their time, waiting for the new constitution to go into effect. Weare and his associates in the legislature accepted their lame-duck status and avoided any behavior which might be controversial. Adoption did little to sweeten Belknap's disposition—he thought the people incapable of self-rule and doubted whether the new constitution would bring into power the better sort of men on whom the future of republicanism rested—but few shared his pessimism. A congregation of his fellow ministers expressed more widely held sentiments when it congratulated Weare on having discharged his duties with

29. *New Hampshire Gazette*, Aug. 30, Sept. 13, and Oct. 4 and 25, 1783; *NHSP*, IX, 896–919.
30. *New Hampshire Gazette*, June 28, 1783; *NHSP*, VIII, 969, and IX, 918.

"disinterested integrity" and applauded the "new form of government, rising from the united wisdom of the state and established by the free voice of the people in which their nobles are themselves and their Governor from the midst of them."[31] With the war over, independence won, the state's western boundaries fixed, and a permanent constitution adopted, the people of New Hampshire could look to the future with optimism.

31. *New Hampshire Gazette*, May 10, 1783; Belknap to Hazard, Mar. 3, 1784, *Belknap Papers, MHS Collections*, 5th ser., II (1877), 309–315. The ministers' address is in *Essex Journal*, Dec. 1, 1784. See also Joseph Buckminster, Jr., *Discourse ... after the Ratification of the Peace Treaty* (Portsmouth, 1784), and Samuel McClintock, *A Sermon Preached before the Honorable Council ...* (Portsmouth, 1784), for expression of general optimism.

Part III
Crisis and Resolution

7

Republicanism on Trial,

1783–1787

Two years after the constitution had gone into effect, many inhabitants of New Hampshire felt their experiment in republicanism was in deep trouble. The state government had been unable to offer effective remedies for their pressing economic problems. The newspapers carried stories ridiculing the behavior of state leaders and accusing them of corruption and wastefulness. Towns refused to pay taxes or to send delegates to the General Court. A few residents had begun to talk of rebellion if their demands for reform were not met. The government itself, torn by bitter factionalism, could not decide how to respond to its critics. Increasing evidence of depression, disillusionment, and disorder elsewhere in America heightened the general mood of anxiety.

The present difficulties seemed particularly distressing because of the circumstances in which they took place. In previous years the revolutionists had been able to blame the inadequacies of their government on the war and all its attendant confusion. Now, however, they expected more, and when, as the townspeople of Atkinson explained in an address to the assembly, they looked about in "search for the golden prize—the dear, earned, promised happy day . . . to their chagrin and disappointment" they could not find it. Could republicanism itself be at fault? Was it possible that the people were incapable of self-government except when threatened by external conquest? In winning independence, wrote one worried inhabitant, we apparently "collected all our virtue to one point, and it was just equal to attaining it, for it expired the moment the prize was gained."[1] Not everyone, of course, shared these concerns, and few men thought the political system as a whole appeared ready to collapse. Nevertheless, a serious crisis in faith had developed.

Collapse of the prosperity which war had brought to all parts of New Hampshire except the Piscataqua area precipitated the crisis. After the victory at Yorktown in October 1781, the market for agricultural goods and new land decreased. Fiscal retrenchment by the state government accelerated the development of economic troubles, for the land boom had been financed with paper money. When the legislature repealed the legal-tender laws, creditors became aggressive; debtors who had avoided payment for years and found "the interest of many years had accumulated far beyond their expectations" hastened to retrench. But with prices falling and money scarce they had little success. The assembly received petitions asking relief from pressing court suits as early as December 1782. Eleven months later, twenty-three towns in the interior presented a long list of complaints about their economic difficulties: "the war with all its calamities," they observed bitterly, "did not seem near so distressing as the present times."[2]

Initially, large landholders suffered most seriously from the deterioriation in values. Burdened with heavy property taxes, they were unable to sell at a profit, and some large speculators who could not collect from their own debtors helplessly watched their fortunes disappear. Jonathan Moulton, a militia general thought to be one of the richest men in the state, provided the most extreme case. In January 1783 he began calling in his debts because of the "exceeding large taxes" he paid and two months later advertised lands at reduced prices for cash. Pressed by creditors, he had become frantic by 1786. "Having for more than twenty years been encouraging settlement," the general explained in huge full-column advertisements in two state newspapers, "and expending very large sums of money while flattering himself, from a very long course of success, with the idea that while the community was served his own interest was vastly accumulating," he now found himself embarrassed by

1. *NHSP*, XI, 122; *Essex Journal*, May 31, 1786.
2. *New Hampshire Gazette*, Sept. 7, 1786; Autobiography of William Plumer, 21, Plumer Papers, LC; *NHSP*, XI, 91–92, 317, XII, 762–766, and XVIII, 721–724. The quotations are from Plumer and *NHSP*, XII, 765.

"the sudden stagnation of the disposal of new lands." Unable to meet his own obligations, Moulton pleaded for payment from his debtors and promised to accept anything they could offer. "Had his expectations from his landed interests" alone been "but a small degree adequate to what he reasonably" expected, he would not have been forced to such action; "but it is a known truth," he grieved, "that landed interest in the country is now but a poor resource for present and pressing exigencies."[3]

The collapse of land prices and curtailment of trade in the interior soon affected seaboard merchants. They and their English competitors had flooded the province with goods when the fighting stopped and, encouraged by heavy consumer demand, continued to import heavily. As long as credit and specie—much of it hidden during the war—remained plentiful, high prices held. But the specie soon disappeared, for the favorable balance of trade to which provincial merchants had been accustomed before the war was destroyed by English regulations limiting American exports to the West Indies. Without specie, merchants could not finance further imports. To make matters worse, they dared not sell to inland traders, many of whom owned large tracts of undisposable land, lacked money, and could buy only on credit. Thomas Sheafe expressed the frustrations of the entire Portsmouth merchant community when he explained in 1785 that "trade in a great measure is cut off and many persons [are] drawing for goods without any means of paying for them but in the goods they import, and selling them at such a low rate as to be in debt when the goods are gone."[4]

As soon as signs of distress appeared, state inhabitants sought relief through their government. Towns in Cheshire and Hillsborough counties and the western portion of Rockingham County petitioned for a reduction in direct taxation and suggested an impost on imported goods plus levies on money at interest and stock in trade to replace lost revenue. Debtors in these areas—and less frequently

3. *New Hampshire Gazette*, Jan. 4, Mar. 22, 1783, and Sept. 7, 1786; *New Hampshire Mercury* (Portsmouth), Aug. 23, 1786.
4. *New Hampshire Gazette*, Mar. 20, 1784; merchant statistics, Toscan Papers, NHHS; Thomas Sheafe to Lane, Son, and Fraser, Sept. 14, 1785, Thomas Sheafe Letter Book, NYPL. For a general description of economic conditions in the mid-eighties see Merrill Jensen, *The New Nation: A History of the United States during the Confederation, 1781–1789* (New York, 1950), 179–193.

from other parts of the state—demanded protection against aggressive creditors and a reduction in exorbitant legal fees. Many simultaneously recommended that grain, livestock, and lumber be made legal tender for private debts and state taxes. Those rich in land but unable to meet pressing obligations proposed a land bank where the state would mortgage private property and issue paper currency. They argued that if it acted boldly, the state government could prevent such paper from depreciating.[5]

Measures recommended by Portsmouth inhabitants differed from those of countrymen, for the decline in commerce left many merchants helpless. "Since the establishment of independence," wrote one, "as total a revolution has taken place in the system of our commerce as in the administration of our government; and an entire new code of laws is now as necessary for the regulation of the one as a new constitution was for the adminstration of the other." The writer requested laws to limit the liability of bankrupt merchants. Others, probably in less desperate straits, advised navigation acts to improve the balance of trade and to prevent English merchants from engrossing the little remaining Piscataqua trade. Since they understood that New Hampshire alone could not retaliate effectively against British trade measures, they supported the Continental Congress in its requests for authority to impose a national impost. Those among the commercial community holding notes from the state government sought accelerated retirement of the public debt and more efficient tax collection.[6]

The distress of state citizens and the multiplicity of possible solutions placed the legislators in a serious dilemma. Eager to reduce the public debt, which had reached eighteen dollars for every state resident, they hesitated to lower taxes. Laws which favored debtors or made anything except specie legal tender for private or public obligations would surely alienate those who throughout the war had been unable to collect previous loans. An issue of paper money might satisfy some, but the money was certain to deteriorate in value, since state securities presently circulated at 80 per cent below par.[7] Naviga-

5. NHSP, XI, 91–92, 317–321, XII, 762–768, and XVIII, 721–724, 755; *New Hampshire Gazette*, July 20, 1782, and Mar. 20, 27, 1784.

6. *New Hampshire Gazette*, Aug. 23, 1783, and Mar. 20, 27, June 5, Oct. 21, 1784. The quotation is from "Aristides" in the Oct. 21, 1784, issue.

7. Plumer, Autobiography, 23, Plumer Papers.

tion laws might improve the balance of trade, but they would also raise the price of goods already too expensive for people to purchase. Each remedy had its supporters and its opponents. Eventually the government explored almost every possibility.

The legislators first voted not to press collection of back taxes and gradually reduced new taxation from £110,000 in 1782 to £22,000 in 1785. Early in 1784 they prohibited public auction of debtor estates, empowered local justices of the peace to handle all cases of less than £10 value, and voted an import tax. The first assembly to meet under the new constitution agreed on one further measure, designed to appease state creditors while increasing the amount of money in circulation: interest on the state debt would in the future be paid in certificates acceptable for payment of taxes. In 1785 after merchant distress had become acute and John Langdon had replaced Weare as president, the court instituted still stronger measures. It passed regulations against British shipping and enacted a law to improve the quality of exported lumber (which, theoretically, could then be sold for cash in the French West Indies). To ease the problem of debtors, the court, by a 64 to 17 vote, authorized them to offer personal estate in lieu of specie for payment of existing debts; creditors were prohibited from jailing those who tendered such offers. Finally, early in 1786 the legislators canceled many outstanding taxes.[8]

Some measures instituted by the court were designed not to quiet popular complaints but to improve the general economic circumstances of the state. Most legislators agreed with the Portsmouth merchants that only a favorable balance of trade could right the state economy. Navigation acts provided some protection against excessive imports which drained specie from the province; a second necessary step was to stimulate internal manufacturing. Accordingly, the legislators encouraged the people of New Hampshire to produce iron, steel, wool, tobacco, linseed oil, and other goods. The inhabitants of Portsmouth responded by forming a Society for the Encouragement of Arts and Promotion of Industry. The legislators

8. New Hampshire Tax Books, 1775–1787, NHA; Batchellor and Metcalf, eds., *Laws of New Hamp.*, IV, 543, 544, 562, and V, 8, 69, 78, 98, 101. *NHSP*, XX, 420–534, contains the legislative records for the period discussed in this paragraph. The court vote is on pages 434–435.

applauded such efforts and hoped their enactments would soon show results.[9]

But assembly action neither improved economic conditions nor stilled complaints. Taxes, though reduced, remained burdensome. Debtors and inland traders claimed that outstanding interest certificates were hoarded by the rich to pay their own taxes, thus leaving the province without currency; only a land bank, they argued, would solve the need for a circulating medium. Creditors condemned and labeled unconstitutional the £10 act and debtor laws. Portsmouth merchants found that the impost increased prices and placed them at a competitive disadvantage with traders who smuggled goods from Massachusetts and Connecticut. The inhabitants of Strafford County—where Belknap said there was "nothing to be seen but timber and boards"—blamed the total collapse of their business on the new navigation acts.[10]

As soon as it became evident that legislative enactments had in no manner alleviated the "unhappy check on trade and business" (as the unfortunate Jonathan Moulton called it), court members began feuding among themselves about future policy. The representatives from Strafford County, led by John Sullivan, sought and eventually obtained suspension of shipping and lumber regulations. In February 1786, and again in June, the members from Portsmouth tried unsuccessfully to repeal the laws protecting debtors from imprisonment. Assemblymen from the Connecticut Valley, where the severe depression caused communities to complain that "the whole" of their "goods and chattels" were insufficient to pay outstanding obligations, gained enough support from other areas to push through a house bill making state currency good for back taxes; but the senate, which included merchants Atkinson and Joshua Wentworth, nonconcurred. The legislators considered new methods of taxation and tax collection, debated the merits of a land bank, and argued about future commercial regulations without coming to any decision. By the summer of 1786 court members had reached such an impasse they could agree on nothing, except to encourage manufactures and

9. *NHSP*, XX, 359, 512, 518; Batchellor and Metcalf, eds., *Laws of New Hamp.*, V, 146, 163, 172; letter to John Rogers, July 20, 1786, Rogers Papers, Hudson Collection, box 3, NYPL.

10. *NHSP*, XIII, 299, 341, XX, 197, and XXI, 75; *New Hampshire Gazette*, Feb. 21, 1784, Dec. 2, 1785, Jan. 13, 20, and Feb. 3, 1786; *New Hampshire Mercury*, Jan. 3, 1786; Belknap to Sally Belknap, Aug. 16, 1784, Belknap Papers, NHHS.

promote the import of specie.[11] Such measures, however, did nothing to relieve the anxiety of those who suffered from economic difficulties. They had expected the government established under the reformed constitution to promote even greater and more general prosperity than had the wartime legislature. Now the opposite seemed to be true.

Confidence in the government was further undermined by the public accusations that some elected officials had abused their political privileges. The members of the privy council, a group of five chosen by and from the legislature to join with the president in making appointments, came under the most serious attack. According to one correspondent whose articles appeared in the state's two most widely circulated newspapers, Nathaniel Peabody gained control of nominations mainly because President Weare trusted him and could not attend legislative sessions regularly. Whether or not Peabody actually dominated the council, there can be no doubt he and his fellow members took care of themselves handsomely.[12] Joseph Badger of Gilmanton was made judge of probate. Francis Blood—like Badger a patriotic inland farmer who had been a house representative for nearly a decade—became an inferior court judge and militia colonel. Peabody asked to be made general of the cavalry and a justice of the peace after deciding not to seek a judicial appointment which would remove him from the legislature. The other two councilors were content with justice-of-the-peace commissions.[13]

The councilors also took care of their friends and relatives. John Dudley, who had cooperated closely with Peabody in the wartime legislature, replaced Leverett Hubbard on the superior court.[14] Most

11. *New Hampshire Gazette*, Sept. 7, 1786. The second quotation is from Chase, *Dartmouth*, 520. NHSP, X, 502–706, contains legislative records for this period.

12. *Essex Journal*, Mar. 2, 16, and Apr. 6, 1785; *New Hampshire Gazette*, Mar. 18 and May 27, 1785. For additional evidence of Peabody's influence see Ebenezer Thompson to Peabody, June 20, 1785, Ebenezer Thompson Papers, NHHS; Langdon, Peabody, and Kittery Papers, 130, 136–138, NHHS; Diary of Stephen Peabody, II, Mar. 17 to June 1, 1785, American Antiquarian Society, Worcester, Massachusetts.

13. *Essex Journal*, Mar. 2, 16, and Apr. 6, 1785; *New Hampshire Gazette*, Mar. 18 and May 27, 1785; William Plumer to John Hale, Oct. 14 and 22, 1786, PCSM, XI: *Transactions* (1906–1907), 398–403; NHSP, XX, 229–297, 549–569.

14. Hubbard had long been a critic of Weare, Bartlett, Peabody, and other Committee of Safety members: Hubbard to Committee, April 2, 1780, Weare Papers, VIII, 1, NHA. His dismissal angered inhabitants of Portsmouth: *New Hampshire Gazette*, June 3 and Sept. 23, 1785; Hubbard to Langdon, Feb. 3, 1786, NHSP, XVIII, 763; Adams, *Annals*, 302.

of Peabody's other political cronies—described by William Plumer, a young lawyer who later became governor of New Hampshire, as men "noted for perjury, forgery . . . counterfeiting . . . horse stealing, breaking gaols, and such high-handed offenses"—received justice-of-the-peace commissions. Badger's son became a militia colonel, his son-in-law an inferior court justice, and so many of his other relatives Strafford County officeholders that a critic of the council queried: "Is it not an attempt to establish a nobility in the state . . . or can we suppose that the wisdom of the county is centered in the pitiful village of Gilmanton?" Such use of political power reminded him of the colonial days when a man who "had married the great-grandchild of the great aunt of a Governor" needed no further qualifications for officeholding. By the summer of 1785 several public pleas for the impeachment of the council had been made.[15]

Accusations were also leveled at the legislature. "Observator" described it as a place where "honor and profit, pensions and sinecures, are avariciously fought after by designing men and disposed of by others, equally designing, with a liberal hand." Plumer, the only representative who had voted against the £10 act, which increased the jurisdiction of justices of the peace, told his friends that the law had been passed "at a time when there was scarce a quorum in the House . . . and the number of justices who were members was more than ten to one who was not in commission." One writer accused the assemblymen of appropriating for their personal use what little specie came into the treasury. Others expressed the conviction that state government expended its revenues improperly, and that unless waste and corruption were eliminated the people of New Hampshire would soon be like Englishmen, the helpless victims of burdensome taxes needed to pay the salaries of political sycophants. In addition, the unwillingness of the house and senate to act on public demands for some of the paper money generated a widespread belief that wealthy men, more interested in protecting their own private fortunes than in promoting general prosperity, had gained control of the government.[16]

15. Plumer to Hale, Oct. 14, 1786, *PCSM*, XI: *Transactions* (1906–1907), 398; *New Hampshire Gazette*, Mar. 18 (source of second quotation) and May 27 (source of third quotation) 1785; *Essex Journal*, Mar. 2, 16, Apr. 6, May 18, 25, and June 1, 8, 1785. For the details of Plumer's life see Lynn W. Turner, *William Plumer of New Hampshire, 1759–1850* (Chapel Hill, 1962).

16. *New Hampshire Gazette* May 20 (source of Observator's criticism), Oct. 14, 1785; Plumer to William Coleman, May 31, 1786, *PCSM*, XI: *Transactions* (1906–

Once specific scandal lent credence to these suspicions. During the war Peabody had begun accumulating deeds granted by Benning Wentworth to land later regranted by his nephew, hoping to have them validated by the legislature.[17] Later he and several other state officials went after bigger game by purchasing from the heirs of Samuel Allen an old claim to the Masonian patent. The Masonian proprietorship, in part because some rights had been purchased by active patriots, remained uncontested during the war. When the "Allenites," instead of taking their claim to court, advertised and sold land in the proprietorship, property holders grew worried. Some demanded legislative repudiation of the Allen claim. Others decided that neither the Allen nor the Mason claim was valid and asked the state to assume title to previously unsold land and then sell it to erase the state debt. Eventually Peabody and two other assembly members were overheard discussing their plans to gain support for both the Benning Wentworth grants and the Allen claim through distribution of civil and military appointments, and their conversation—which had been well-flavored with outspoken attacks on religion—was reported in the local newspapers. Some citizens became so irate that they surrounded Peabody's house and demanded he give up the Allen claim. Although such activity temporarily cost Peabody much of his influence—he gained no elective office in the spring elections of 1786 and that summer was criticized in a house resolution which asked the council to remove him from his state office—popular distrust of the legislature remained. So did Peabody, for the senate refused to approve the house resolution.[18]

1907), 384; *Exeter Chronicle*, June 10, 17, and Oct. 28, 1784; *Essex Journal*, July 5, 1786.

17. Weare, Bartlett, and Dudley cooperated with Peabody in his land speculations until at least 1781. The man who worked most closely with Peabody was Silas Hedges, a counterfeiter and perjurer who so duped the Committee of Safety that it employed him during the war to prevent counterfeiting. See correspondence between Hedges, Weare, and Peabody, and also Weare to Governor Trumbull, Hampton Falls, June 4, 1781, in Weare Papers, I and II, MHS; Weare Papers, *passim*, especially July 1778 to July 1779, LC; Weare Papers, IV, 28a, 55, NHA; NHSP, XII, 655, and XVIII, 694; Kenneth Scott, "New Hampshire Counterfeiters," *New York Historical Society Quarterly*, 34 (1950), 43; PCSM, XI: *Transactions* (1906–1907), 239–242.

18. NHSP, XX, 658, 661, and XXIX, 313–340; *New Hampshire Gazette*, Apr. 20 and May 18, 1786; *Essex Journal*, Mar. 22, 1786; Plumer to Hale, Oct. 14, 1786, PCSM, XI: *Transactions* (1906–1907), 398; Diary of Stephen Peabody, III, June 1–15, 1786; Belknap, *History*, III, 15–16. At various times Whipple, George Atkinson, Woodbury Langdon, and John Hancock were Masonian proprietors: NHSP, XXIX, 346, 564–593.

The behavior of New Hampshire's presidential aspirants added to the growing dissatisfaction. The retirement of Meshech Weare in 1785 resulted in a scramble among the politically ambitious to attain the "chief seat" of government. Atkinson (who had gained influence after replacing Dudley as Speaker of the house), Sullivan, and the two Langdons sought the office. None of these candidates could possibly have gained the general popularity of the man they would succeed. They all came from the Portsmouth area, and sectional antagonisms remained high in the state. Secondly, each man possessed distinct political liabilities. Woodbury Langdon and Atkinson, as their opponents pointed out, had been unwilling to support the revoluton in its initial stages. Sullivan, the state's attorney general, came under attack for having accepted gifts from the refugee George Boyd while refusing to confiscate his estate, and for acting as legal adviser for the Allen claimants. Besides, Sullivan had many enemies in the legislature. A vain and easily offended man—Washington once told him that "no other officer of rank in the whole army has so often conceived himself neglected, slighted and ill-treated as you have done, and none I am sure has had less cause than yourself to entertain such ideas"—Sullivan had for the past several years been feuding with the state government about its unwillingness to pay him for past military services. John Langdon had to combat his reputation as one whose patriotism had been tarnished by avariciousness and gross favoritism toward his brother.[19]

The campaign itself did nothing to dispel growing anxiety about political developments in the state. Contemporary ethical assumptions dictated that a man seeking elective office remain passive so that voters could act without passion or prejudice. In fact, many felt that it was improper for a candidate to publicly admit his ambitions; rather, he could be recommended by others and in response express only a reluctant willingness to serve.[20] Of course, the revolutionists

19. *New Hampshire Mercury,* Mar. 2–June 28, 1785; *New Hampshire Gazette* Aug. 3, 1783, and Jan. 28–Mar. 25, 1785; Washington to Sullivan, Mar. 15, 1777, in Hammond, ed., *Sullivan Papers,* I, 328; NHSP, XVIII, 748; Charles P. Whittemore, *A General of the Revolution, John Sullivan of New Hampshire* (New York, 1961), 206 and *passim;* "John Sullivan" in Shipton, *Biographical Sketches,* XIV, 318–338.

20. Sullivan wrote his main political backer in Portsmouth that he did not desire "the chair" but would not "refuse the office if elected" because he wanted to please his friends and serve his country. Two weeks later he was giving the same man advice on campaign tactics: Sullivan to John Wendell, Feb. 7, 18, 1785, in Hammond, ed.,

had violated these principles—courting voters in local elections was a common practice—but never before had New Hampshire men witnessed open statewide competition for public office. Weare had had no opposition in 1784, and before that the legislature had selected its own leaders. Now the candidates and their backers found it necessary to be aggressive. Sullivan used the *Gazette* to announce his availability, to defend himself against the accusations of his critics, and to expose the practices employed by his opponents to gain votes. Writers in the newly formed *Mercury* promoted Woodbury Langdon, emphasizing his well-known antagonism to Governor Wentworth as proof of his patriotism. All four candidates sought support among state legislators, who in turn campaigned at the local level. Woodbury Langdon, and perhaps his competitors, sent agents into inland communities to solicit votes.[21]

More than a few men found the whole spectacle disheartening. The "party spirit" manifested by the candidates, particularly Sullivan and Woodbury Langdon, could only foment political divisions in the state. The willingness of campaigners to attract potential voters by offering them free liquor not only violated the constitution but suggested that bribery and corruption would become as prevalent in New Hampshire as in Great Britain; one writer who expressed such fears reminded his readers that "the man who would give one hogshead of port to be chosen a president of the state would give fifty to become a despot, and the man who spends money to obtain power will use that power to repay himself with interest." Some inhabitants probably suspected that Woodbury Langdon had entered the race only to split the "Tory" vote, thus improving his brother's chance of victory. Atkinson's supporters, who included many of the state's most-educated and wealthy citizens, deplored what they considered the demagogic efforts of his opponents to identify him with the colonial aristocracy. Others considered his candidacy an insult to the state, nothing less than an overt attempt at restoration politics.[22] They could hardly have been encouraged when Atkinson received a plurality of the votes and was prevented from taking office only

Sullivan Papers, III, 397–398. See also *Essex Journal*, Mar. 9, 1785, and Jan. 24, 1787; *New Hampshire Mercury*, June 21, 1785.

21. *New Hampshire Gazette*, Feb. 25–Mar. 25, 1795; *New Hampshire Mercury*, Mar. 2, Apr. 5, 1785; Hammond, ed., *Sullivan Papers*, III, 415–419.

22. *Essex Journal*, Mar. 9, 1785 (source of quotation); *New Hampshire Mercury*, June 21, 1785; *New Hampshire Gazette*, Jan. 28–Mar. 25, 1785.

because the whig-dominated legislature selected John Langdon as president.[23]

Langdon's performance as president proved controversial. The main palliatives for economic distress he sponsored were navigation laws and restrictions on British shipping, both of which protected the interests of the small community of revolutionary merchants. Advocates of paper money and debtor legislation criticized him for his refusal to support such measures and for using his influence over nominations to reward council and assembly members who agreed with him. The most serious outburst, however, came when in February 1786 Langdon forced through the council his brother's appointment as a justice of the superior court and nearly succeeded in making him chief justice. The incident received a good deal of publicity throughout the state and raised again the specter of nepotism. Sullivan, who served both as Speaker of the house and as a council member and whose absence from the council had made the appointment possible, became so furious he resigned as head of the militia and vowed to oust Langdon in the coming elections. "The big fellows cannot agree," reported Belknap. "I suppose our Major General expects to be the biggest of all next year, and there will be a pull for it between him and J. L."[24]

Sullivan's political position was far stronger in the spring of 1786 than it had been a year earlier. Atkinson decided not to seek the presidency again and lent his support to the former general. Sullivan's work in the legislature had given him political experience and gained him the respect of many locally influential delegates. Furthermore, Sullivan understood what his political liabilities were and took steps to correct them. He repudiated Peabody, apologized for the aggressiveness of the Allenites, and promised that no matter which of the competing claimants gained legal title to the patent, existing deeds would not be violated. He publicized his role as an antagonist of merchant-inspired economic legislation, opposed the effort by the president to have repealed an act protecting debtors against imprisonment (originally he had voted against the act), and, in general, tried

23. *NHSP*, XX, 306–308. The vote totals were Atkinson 2755, John Langdon 2497, Sullivan 777, Josiah Bartlett (who had announced his retirement from politics) 720, and 330 scattered. The paucity of records makes it impossible to analyze the vote.

24. *NHSP*, XX, 353–354; Langdon to Sullivan, Nov. 13, 1780, in Hammond, ed., *Sullivan Papers*, III, 199; *New Hampshire Mercury*, Mar. 8, 1786; the quotation is from Belknap to Hazard, Mar. 9, 25, 1786, *Belknap Papers*, MHS *Collections*, 5th ser., II (1877), 433–434.

John Langdon (1741–1819), leader in the movement for independence, Speaker of the House of Representatives during the war, president of New Hampshire 1784–1785 and 1788–1789, and a member of the United States Senate throughout the 1790s. Portrait by Edward Savage ca. 1795.

to cultivate a "man of the people" reputation. His backers intimated that their candidate might well support the increasingly popular idea of a land bank. When all the returns were in, the "Sullivan-Atkinson-tory interest," as Langdon labeled it, had won an overwhelming victory.[25] Sullivan received heavy support everywhere except in the Merrimack Valley and raised the 777 votes he had received in 1785 to 4309, a majority of those cast.[26]

25. *New Hampshire Gazette*, May 11, 1786; NHSP, XX, 434, 518; Max Farrand, ed., *Records of the Federal Convention*, (New Haven, 1911–1937), III, 232; *Essex Journal*, Jan. 24, 1787; letter from John Langdon, Apr. 5, 1787, John Langdon Papers, NHHS.
26. NHSP, XX, 614; Whittemore, *Sullivan*, 196; *New Hampshire Gazette*, Mar. 25, Apr. 1, 1786. Sullivan's identification with the Allenites undoubtedly cost him many votes in the Merrimack Valley. His reputation for backing lumber interests and seeking a strong militia helped him along the frontier.

Although Sullivan's victory set off a wave of enthusiasm among his numerous supporters, it soon subsided. The president failed to mention a land bank in his first recommendations to the legislature, and the house, where Langdon had replaced his adversary as Speaker, took no action on the petitions for some form of paper money. The failure of the government to work out a solution to the Allen-Mason controversy made many feel that Sullivan still favored the group which had already thrown the state's land-deed situation into turmoil. Those who since the ratification of the peace treaty in 1783 had opposed compliance with the provisions recommending repeal of all laws militating against loyalists feared that he and Langdon both might support such "Tory" legislation. Even some of those who agreed with Sullivan on policy matters found his behavior as president distasteful. "I never knew a mortal so greedy of flattery," complained one supporter in the fall of 1786, "his knowledge as a lawyer and his talents as a man are rated too high." The following spring when he and Langdon again sought election, Sullivan's vote declined by more than 15 per cent.[27]

Finally, the administration of state justice came under attack. "Junius" claimed that most justices of the peace were so "ignorant" of the law that to submit property to their judgment would be a "wanton sacrifice of liberty." Belknap and Sullivan agreed and entertained each other with the story of a local magistrate who, when asked to determine which of two men should pay for a disputed horse, so bungled the job that he ended up buying the animal himself before turning it over to the rightful owner. More frequent were attacks on the inferior courts of common pleas. The depression had forced creditors to retrench at a time when debtors had no ready cash. The resulting rash of lawsuits created a heavy demand for legal services, which in turn permitted lawyers not only to raise their fees but to demand payment before taking on a case. Pressure on the courts and the burden of legal fees were both increased by litigants appealing decisions made by local justices of the peace. Soon men throughout New Hampshire, especially in the newly settled towns, were demanding a fundamental restructuring of the state's judicial system.[28]

27. Hammond, ed., *Sullivan Papers*, III, 454; *New Hampshire Gazette*, July 20, 1786; Plumer to Hale, Oct. 22, 1786, PCSM, XI: *Transactions* (1906–1907), 401 (source of quotation); NHSP, XXI, 41.

28. *New Hampshire Mercury*, Apr. 19, Sept. 6 (source of quotation), Oct. 5,

The government soon came under pressure to change its ways. Community petitions to the legislature and informal instructions to the assemblymen provided the most common forms of protest, but as the depression intensified and the government remained indecisive in the face of popular demands for action, new tactics were adopted. Delegates from western towns met in county conventions which then submitted their own petitions. Instructions to house representatives were made binding rather than informal.[29] In the summer of 1786 groups of irate citizens began meeting on their own to think up still more effective ways of influencing their leaders.

The first such meeting, held at Concord in June 1786, turned into a fiasco. When the first delegates arrived, a group of hard-money lawyers posed as malcontents and convinced the early arrivals to draw up a list of such exorbitant demands—including an emission of three million dollars, annihilation of inferior courts, and expulsion from office of all Allen and Masonian claimants (with the exception of President Sullivan)—that when the real convention leaders arrived they retired in shame without presenting their more moderate proposals. The absurdity of such proceedings may have played a decisive role in convincing the assembly to resolve that it was "not practicable at this time to make a bank of paper money."[30]

Subsequent meetings proved more effective. Early in July about 150 men gathered at Londonderry and, after resolving "to adopt such measures as would force the General Court to emit paper money," adjourned to meet later at Chester. News that Sullivan and two others had petitioned the house to examine the validity of the Allen deed lent momentum to the movement. At Rochester a Strafford County convention elected Jonathan Moulton president, and the local militia escorted him to the second meeting. So serious were the implications of these developments—civil disorder had already

1786; Sullivan to Belknap, Dec. 5, 1785, in Hammond, ed., *Sullivan Papers*, III, 438; Belknap to Hazard, Jan. 10, 1786, *Belknap Papers*, MHS Collections, 5th ser., II (1877), 422; Plumer to J. Plumer, June 8, 1784, Plumer Letter Book, I, 42, LC; *New Hampshire Gazette*, Dec. 16, 1785, and June 1, 1786.

29. Whittemore, *Sullivan*, 199, has found petitions from forty-one different towns and groups of towns. For discussions of binding instructions see Parker, *Londonderry*, 114, and Belknap to Hazard, Dec. 1, 1783, *Belknap Papers*, MHS Collections, 5th ser., II (1877), 282.

30. Belknap, *History*, II, 468–469; Nathaniel Bouton, *History of Concord* (Concord, 1856), 298; Turner, *Plumer*, 20–21; Plumer to Samuel Plumer, Jr., June 9, 1786, PCSM, XI: *Transactions* (1906–1907), 384; NHSP, XX, 630 (source of quotation).

broken out in neighboring Massachusetts—that the General Court which convened on September 6 tried to placate the discontented. It took up the matter of a land bank and by the thirteenth had voted to submit for town approval a plan which provided for £50,000 of paper money, most of it to be loaned against the value of land; the currency was not to be legal tender for private debts or state taxes. The plan, however, satisfied no one, for not only did £50,000 seem insufficient, but convention leaders, like Moulton, had no use for a currency which would not satisfy their creditors. Moreover, town meetings would take months to discuss the proposal. After the terms of the assembly plan became known, rumors circulated that the Chester convention intended "to adopt coercive measures."[31]

A secondary matter precipitated violence. After the assembly voted, as some had long feared, to repeal all laws militating against peace treaty provisions and to guarantee that British subjects would "meet with no lawful impediment to the recovery of . . . debts," men in lower Rockingham County gathered in protest. Rumors that the General Court had voted an additional tax to repurchase confiscated estates led them to take up arms and set off for Exeter. Upon entering the capital, they presented the court with demands for paper money and, when the legislators refused to consider their petition, surrounded the meeting house. Some of the rioters, reported Plumer, "were clamouring against the Court for passing a law authorizing the return of the refugees, declaring that those who voted for it ought to be punished with death. Some demanded paper money; others an equal distribution of property, some the annihilation of debts, freedom from taxes, the abolition of lawyers, the destruction of the inferior courts, the reduction of salaries, and all of them exclaimed against law and government." But the mob was without leadership or a plan of action; they retired in confusion after the townspeople rallied in support of the legislature. The next day a hastily mustered militia regiment routed them completely.[32]

31. Plumer to Plumer, July 22, 1786 (source of first quotation), and Plumer to Hale, Aug. 13, Sept. 18, 1786 (source of second quotation), *PCSM*, XI: *Transactions* (1906–1907), 385–390. See also *New Hampshire Mercury*, Sept. 20, 1786; Plumer, Autobiography, 24–26, Plumer Papers; Diary of Stephen Peabody, III, July 16–Sept. 20, 1786; *NHSP*, XX, 687–696.

32. Batchellor and Metcalf, eds., *Laws of New Hamp.*, V, 195 (source of first quotation); *NHSP*, XX, 697–713; Plumer to Hale, Sept. 18, 20 (source of second quotation), 1786, *PCSM*, XI: *Transactions* (1906–1907), 389–392; Belknap, *History*, II, 470–475.

Despite the praise which most citizens accorded their political leaders for dispersing the rioters, the crisis of confidence in New Hampshire's republican institutions continued. Sullivan issued a proclamation advising citizens not to countenance future county conventions because they had "a tendency to overturn and destroy constitutional authority and government."[33] Those who had participated in the conventions and otherwise supported reform felt that officials still remained unsympathetic to their needs, a feeling which increased after the legislature refused to consider further the matter of a paper currency and instead raised taxes, demanded payment for back levies, and repealed the debtor act. When an inferior court judge declared the £10 act unconstitutional and his fellow magistrates refused to enforce it despite the legislature's reaffirmation of the law, criticism of the courts intensified. The spring elections of 1787 made clear how embittered were vast numbers of state voters. Nearly a fourth of the towns resolved not to send delegates to the General Court, and another 15 per cent simply failed to elect anyone. Travelers reported that inhabitants in the interior didn't care who became president; neither Sullivan nor Langdon would satisfy them. The residents of Wolfboro returned nineteen votes for former Governor John Wentworth.[34]

Economic depression, the behavior of public officials, widespread alienation from the state government, and civil disorder forced the citizens of New Hampshire to reassess their assumptions about the adequacy of the existing political system and triggered a series of ideological debates more intense and widespread than any since the collapse of imperial authority. Indeed, the intensity of debate is the best indication of the degree to which the revolutionists considered their experiment in republicanism endangered. Newspapers, private correspondence, sermons, press publications, and the discussions

33. Plumer to Coleman, May 31, 1786, PCSM, XI: *Transactions* (1906–1907), 384; Nicholas Gilman to James McClure, Mar. 28, 1787, McClure Papers, NHHS; *New Hampshire Gazette*, Sept. 28, 1786; "Amicus Republicae" [probably Benjamin Thurston], *An Address to the Public, Containing Some Remarks on the Present Political State of the American Republics* (Exeter, 1787). The quotation is from Hammond, ed., *Sullivan Papers*, III, 484.

34. NHSP, XX, 761, and XXI, 35, 78–83, 117; Jeremiah Libbey to Belknap, Apr. 20, 1787, *Belknap Papers*, MHS Collections, 5th ser., IV, 333, and June 18, 1787, Belknap Papers, 161.A.138, MHS; *New Hampshire Spy*, Mar. 13, Apr. 13, May 19, June 12, 30, 1787; Gilman to McClure, Mar. 28, 1787, McClure Papers.

which took place among individual inhabitants all reflected political disillusionment and in some cases a sense of impending doom. Proposed solutions to the state's political crisis only seemed to accentuate disagreement. As late as the spring of 1788, the people of New Hampshire remained as divided in their attitudes toward what would constitute an ideal or even acceptable structure of public authority as they were about the state government's policies.

Much of the discussion focused on why the establishment of republican institutions had not produced the anticipated utopia. To some the answer seemed quite obvious: their government had been taken over by the same type of wealthy aristocrats who had dominated colonial politics. How else could the assessment of taxes to pay off already affluent creditors, or, more important, the refusal of the legislature to issue paper money, be explained? "Monitor" argued that the opponents of a land bank wanted to make "the poor and needy their vassals" and to "reduce the farmer who fought the revolution while they remained cool"; in their opinion, he observed bitterly, "the tradesmen are not made of the same cloth with themselves." Another writer described debtors' motives for wanting a paper medium as reasonable, honest, and patriotic, and those of the creditors "not only unjust and cruel, but anti-republican." "Philopatriae" explained the logic which supported such conclusions: lack of a currency prevented the ordinary man from "enlarging his views" and thus forced him either to divide his estate among his sons or to make them "labor and toil on the farms of the rich and spend the prime of their lives in a state of despondency. These situations," he emphasized, "a plenty of money would soon remedy and enable men to live more upon a level."[35]

Those who interpreted state policies in class terms and thought the government controlled by men of aristocratic tendencies experienced no difficulty in understanding how this had taken place. Like most Americans, they believed that power by its very nature corrupted those who held it and that any form of government, especially republicanism, was subject to the self-seeking factionalism of the avaricious. Events in the eighties had confirmed such beliefs. Had not Atkinson, Langdon, and their associates in the constitutional convention tried to establish a system in which only the rich

35. The three quotations are from *New Hampshire Gazette*, July 20, 1786, *New Hampshire Mercury*, Sept. 6, 1786, *Exeter Chronicle*, Oct. 28, 1784.

could hold power? Did not the activities after 1784 of these same men, the Allenites, the lawyers who had made a mockery of the June convention in Concord, legislators who voted against reform, and judges who refused to enforce laws designed to help the people add additional proof? Indeed, the behavior of their own elected representatives suggested how irresistible was the tendency of power to corrupt. Once in the legislature they forgot the public interest, succumbed to the arguments of state leaders, voted for taxes and against paper money, and returned home having been appointed to some state office.[36]

It was difficult, however, to recommend any effective solution to the problem. Traditional assumptions dictated that the rich, well-born, and educated should rule, and these were the very men who for the most part held positions of profit and honor. Boycotting the legislature increased the relative power of those who needed to be restrained. Refusal to pay taxes smacked of irresponsibility; few wanted the state to renege on its debts. Extralegal activities like the county conventions degenerated into mob action which threatened public welfare even more than did rule by men of aristocratic tendencies. Frustrated, the discontented resorted to what seemed the only remaining alternatives. They yearned for greater local autonomy —the inhabitants of Plaistow, for example, recommended that town clerks be authorized to receive and record land deeds, local constables take over duties now handled by state-appointed sheriffs, and excise revenues be collected by selectmen[37]—refused to elect delegates despite the consequences, and in general became resigned to their fate.

Langdon, Sullivan, Belknap, Plumer, and others who supported governmental policies agreed upon after the Exeter riot explained the political crisis in quite different terms. The success of republicanism, they believed, depended ultimately on the willingness of men to sacrifice personal interests for public good, to accept the decisions made by those in power, and to elect wise and disinterested leaders. On all three counts the people of New Hampshire had failed.

Demands for paper money, lower taxes, and debtor legislation indicated that the public had gone soft. The solution to economic

36. *New Hampshire Spy,* Apr. 13 and May 19, 1787; *New Hampshire Gazette,* Oct. 14, 1785, June 8, July 20, 1786; *New Hampshire Mercury,* Sept. 6, 1786; *Exeter Chronicle,* Oct. 28, 1784.
37. *NHSP,* XIII, 220.

problems lay not in increasing the money supply but in "diligence, economy, patience, honesty and perseverence" on the part of every citizen. The government had done what it could. The traffic in such luxuries as "gauzes, ribbons, silk, feathers and flowers" had been checked by the navigation laws; taxes had been used to reduce the public debt; the legislature had assumed its responsibility to protect private property and the sanctity of written contracts by repealing the debtor law, and it had tried to redress the unfavorable balance of trade by encouraging internal manufactures. The rest was up to the people. "We are complaining of hard times and at the same time revelling in extravagance," lamented one writer; "there was a time when to be noble was to be virtuous, when patriots were willing to sacrifice all for the public weal; but now avarice encircles all." When a people degenerate into licentiousness and debauchery, he warned, "virtue and public spirit must of course give way, and when these go liberty cannot long tarry."[38]

Republicanism was also threatened by the refusal of the people to accept the decisions of constitutionally elected officials. Ever since the spring of 1776, worry lest the "levelling spirit" generated by the revolution undermine civil order had been a constant theme in political commentaries written by New Hampshire men. The activities of the county conventions and the Exeter rioters proved that those expressing such thoughts had not exaggerated. Ministers, statesmen, lawyers, and town officials spoke out now, demanding that the people not violate their responsibilities. One writer summarized their arguments in a *Gazette* article entitled "On the Respect due to Office." "Revolution and public commotions," he explained, "imperceptibly lead us to forget this duty because government being relaxed and broken down," magistrates can only unite the community through "flattery, affability and even familiarity." This in turn makes every man "suppose himself a ruler, privy councillor or assistant, and brings all men upon a level," civil order then collapses, and either tyranny or anarchy results. "It is the office which dignifies the man," he concluded, and therefore rulers should be obeyed. "What an age we do live in," exclaimed another writer. "Everyone is a politician and believes himself could guide the helm

38. The quotations are from "Amicus Republicae," *An Address*, 20, 22, and *New Hampshire Spy*, Nov. 10, 1786. See also Plumer to Moses Neal, Jan. 16, 1787, Plumer Letter Book, I, 116, LC; *New Hampshire Gazette*, July 21, 1787; *New Hampshire Mercury*, July 12, 1786.

of state . . . Antiquity could furnish seven wise men, but in our days there are hardly seven to be found who do not think themselves wise."[39]

Somewhat inconsistently, the same men who supported government economic policy and demanded respect for those in office often cited the poor quality of New Hampshire's officials as another index of the people's failure to assume their proper role in republican society. "A. M." spoke of the "ignorance and imbecility of those in power." Plumer noted cryptically that "if talents and extensive information are a requisite to form the statesman, you will in vain look for them in the General Court." Sullivan complained it was difficult to get the legislature to pass laws essential to the public welfare and probably shared the sentiments expressed by one resident who applauded the refusal of towns in the interior to elect representatives because it would improve the quality of government. Men throughout the state agreed with the general proposition that one of the greatest dangers to republicanism lay in the ability of designing men like Nathaniel Peabody and Jonathan Moulton to deceive the people, gain elective office, and use it for their own purposes.[40]

Those disillusioned with public behavior suggested a number of ways in which the political problems they recognized might be solved. Belknap used his election sermon in the spring of 1785 to put in a strong plea for the education of youth, which would lead to the acceptance of wise political institutions and in time produce the informed electorate and intelligent public officials on which the future of republicanism rested. Others thought a show of strength by the government would put fear into the hearts of the disorderly and reduce lawlessness; they applauded President Sullivan when he made a grand tour of the state to review the militia, and they urged the government to mete out stiff punishments to the Exeter rioters. Many of these same men began to urge strengthening of the judiciary. Belknap asked grand jurors to stop being "deaf and blind

39. The quotations are from *New Hampshire Gazette*, Sept. 4, 1788, and *New Hampshire Recorder* (Keene), Sept. 4, 1787. See also "Amicus Republicae," *An Address*, 18; *New Hampshire Mercury*, Mar. 21, 1787.

40. The quotations are from *Essex Journal*, May 31, 1786, and from Plumer to Samuel Plumer, Jr., June 6, 1786, PCSM, XI: *Transactions* (1906–1907), 385–386. See also Sullivan to Belknap, Feb. 26, 1788, in Hammond, ed., *Sullivan Papers*, III, 566; *New Hampshire Spy*, May 19, 1787; *New Hampshire Gazette*, Sept. 4, 1788; *New Hampshire Mercury*, Mar. 21, 1787.

and dumb" about "flagrant omissions of the duties enjoined by law." "Junius" warned against the dangers of a situation in which legislators appointed one another justices of the peace and then gave themselves the power to pass on all civil cases involving £10 or less; he implied that county and state courts should be given more power. Plumer believed that "if our elective government is long supported it will owe its existence to the judiciary . . . the only body of men who will have an effective check upon a numerous assembly." When an inferior court judge declared the £10 act unconstitutional, he commented, "Our courts of law are firm, and in these degenerate days dare to be honest."[41]

There was one other hope. As early as 1784, Portsmouth merchants and others who thought the solution to economic stagnation lay in cooperation among the states had advocated broadening the regulatory, taxing, and treaty-making powers of the Continental Congress. The idea of a strengthened central government had taken on additional importance by the summer of 1786. Joshua Wentworth feared that unless some dramatic commercial reforms were adopted —none of the proposed amendments to the Articles of Confederation had gained the unanimous approval needed for adoption—eastern states would be ruined and "the whole confederacy broken up"; Belknap prayed for "some common danger pressing hard upon us to make us feel our need for union." The Exeter riot and Shays' rebellion raised troublesome doubts about the future of the confederacy as well as the stability of state governments. Under such circumstances it was natural to think of congressional reform as a vehicle for bolstering state authority. "The insurgents . . . appear to threaten the destruction of what little government we have," wrote Portsmouth's postmaster, Jeremiah Libbey, "and what will be the event of such proceedings God only knows . . . If the Convention in May next can strengthen, or rather unite us in a federal government . . . it will be a happy event."[42]

41. Jeremy Belknap, *An Election Sermon Preached before the General Court of New Hampshire* (Portsmouth, 1785), 12–23 (quotation from p. 22); *New Hampshire Gazette*, Dec. 2, 1786; *New Hampshire Mercury*, Sept. 6, 1786; Plumer to Coleman, May 31, 1786, *PCSM*, XI: *Transactions* (1906–1907), 384.
42. John Wendell to Edmund Quincy, Oct. 4, 1785, Misc. MSS Bound, XVIII, MHS; Joshua Wentworth to Sullivan, Aug. 29, 1786, *NHSP*, XVIII, 772; Belknap to Hazard, Mar. 9, 1786, *Belknap Papers*, *MHS Collections*, 5th ser., II (1877), 431; Libbey to Belknap, Apr. 20, 1787, *Belknap Papers*, *MHS Collections*, 5th ser., IV (1891), 333. See also Langdon Papers, 177, HSP; Mayo, *Langdon*, 198–201.

By the spring of 1787, then, the people of New Hampshire had become sharply divided in their assessment of what had gone wrong with their experiment in republicanism. On the one hand there were those who blamed present troubles on the unwillingness of the rich and wellborn who ruled the state to sacrifice personal for public interest, who chose to disassociate themselves from a government which by its very nature seemed corrupt and inflexible, and who tended to yearn for the good old days when disinterested men like Meshech Weare had administered a weak but just law. Opposed to them were the merchants, ministers, lawyers, political leaders, and others who condemned the people themselves and considered the strengthening of government essential to the preservation of republican institutions. To be sure, the two groups had some things in common: both deplored civil disorder and both had lost faith in the ability of the state government to protect the general public welfare. But the areas of agreement were negative and in no way promoted consensus on reform. And few men expressed confidence that New Hampshire—indeed all of America—could survive unless major political reforms were adopted.

8

Republicanism Triumphant,
1787–1794

"It is here . . . that we have the most abundant testimony from experience that man is capable of governing himself; a position which the sages of old acknowledged to be beautiful in theory, but denied its reducibility in practice." Most men in the audience which had gathered in the summer of 1794 to hear a Rochester justice of the peace deliver the traditional Fourth of July oration shared his feelings of self-satisfaction. For the past four years the citizens of New Hampshire had enjoyed a political tranquillity unknown since the days of Benning Wentworth. Local governments continued to serve the needs of town residents. State officials, only eight years earlier the object of widespread suspicion and criticism, now commanded both respect and allegiance. The newly formed federal government had adopted policies instrumental in restoring economic prosperity and protecting America from foreign intervention. Indeed, the whole system of politics seemed to be functioning in such a stable and effective manner that even Jeremy Belknap was satisfied. In the last volume of his *History of New Hampshire*, published in 1792, he noted that the state "after a long dissention" had become "better united." Those who either directly or indirectly wielded power were becoming daily more knowledgeable and judicious. "Prejudices are wearing away," he concluded, "and the political character of the people is manifestly improving."[1]

1. Joseph Clark, *An Oration Delivered at Rochester on the Fourth of July, 1794* (Dover, 1794), 7; Belknap, *History*, III, 256–257. For other expressions of self-satisfaction see *New Hampshire Recorder*, Oct. 21, 1790; *New Hampshire Spy*, June

Several developments helped resolve the crisis in faith which reached its peak in the summer of 1786 and remained serious for more than a year afterward. Ratification of the proposed federal constitution played an important role in the process, as did the economic recovery which began while the struggle for ratification was still in progress. Cooperation among acknowledged political leaders, rationalization of legislative procedures, and reduced taxes all helped restore confidence in the state government. For those dissatisfied with the existing institutional structure the convention which met in 1791 to amend the state constitution offered opportunity for further reform. People who initially had condemned the "party spirit" which marked annual elections came to accept the necessity of such behavior. To be sure, each specific change affected men differently, and many citizens remained indifferent to both state and national politics. But in a general sense events in the years between 1787 and 1794 convinced the revolutionists that their experiment in republicanism had finally succeeded.

The call for a constitutional convention to revise the Articles of Confederation provided the first ray of hope. Most state residents had long felt that one way to combat the depression would be to strengthen congressional economic powers, and consequently they had been disappointed when the various amendments proposed for that purpose had been defeated. The General Court, reflecting public sentiment, had supported every effort to amend the articles and in 1786 had appointed delegates to the convention at Annapolis. Now the legislature reaffirmed its position. In January 1787 the house and senate passed a joint resolution authorizing any two of the state's congressional representatives to join the convention and to discuss "all such alterations and further provisions" necessary to make the central government "adequate for the exigencies of the union." Bickering between the house and senate and the failure of the impoverished government to provide adequate expense funds delayed the delegates' departure, but in July John Langdon and Nicholas Gilman left for Philadelphia. Speculation about what the convention would recommend increased throughout the spring and

---

4, 1791; *NHSP,* XXII, 53, 326; Israel Evans, *A Sermon Delivered at Concord before the Honorable General Court . . . at the Annual Election* (Concord, 1791), 2–11.

summer.[2] The proposed constitution reached New Hampshire late in September; debate over its merits and weaknesses soon dominated political discussion in the state.

From the beginning the constitution had many ardent supporters. Most of them emphasized the economic benefits of ratification. "It is in the interest of the merchants to encourage the new constitution," one correspondent proclaimed in the *Gazette*, "because commerce may then be a national object and nations will form treaties with us. It is in the interest of the landholders because thousands in Europe with moderate fortunes will migrate to this country if an efficient government gives them a prospect of tranquillity . . . It is in the interest of the mechanics to join the mercantile interest, because it is not to their interest to quarrel with their bread and butter. It is in the interest of the farmer, because the prosperity of commerce gives vent to his produce—raises the value of his lands—and commercial duties will alleviate the burden of his taxes." The federal government, another writer argued, would so stimulate business that the unemployed would find work, the scarcity of specie would disappear, debtors would be able to pay their creditors, and prosperity would soon return to New Hampshire. In his first address to the General Court in June 1788, John Langdon, who had finally regained the presidency, noted the derangement of state finances and virtual "annihilation of our commerce"; but, he added optimistically, "I look forward with pleasure to the time . . . when . . . we shall be relieved in a great measure from those and many other embarrassments by the adoption of the proposed federal constitution . . ."[3]

The federalists also predicted that ratification would resolve the present political crisis. Prosperity would allay discontent and reduce the threat of further civil disorder. Creation of a strong central government would make the individual states "united and powerful, each supporting the dignity of the other" instead of "each seeking and contending for its own local advantages." Furthermore, the effective authority of undependable elected officials would be diminished. "There is an absolute necessity of establishing a more efficient

2. Batchellor and Metcalf, eds., *Laws of New Hamp.*, IV, 379, 537, and V, 25, 81, 203; *NHSP*, XX, 839–847 (quotation from 840), and XXI, 869–878; *New Hampshire Gazette*, July 7, 1787. Neither Langdon nor Gilman exercised much influence in the Philadelphia convention.
3. *New Hampshire Gazette*, Oct. 20 and Dec. 26, 1787; *NHSP*, XXI, 299. See also *New Hampshire Spy*, Oct. 27, 1787.

system of government than the present," Plumer told a friend. "Our liberties, our rights and property are now the sport of ignorant, unprincipled state legislators." After describing one recently re-elected Portsmouth representative as "conspicuous for ignorance, impertinence and loquacity," a Portsmouth merchant took solace in the thought that "after the much wished for federal constitution is in motion it will not matter much who are sent to our Court, as their wings will be pretty well clipped." A relative of the influential antifederalist legislator Joseph Badger made the same point when he argued that the constitution gave Congress power only over things "of great national concern, which requires a large comprehensive view . . . Heaven knows," he continued, "our House of Representatives were never capable of judging whether they were acting right or wrong" on these matters. "The regard I have for my children, my kinsmen, my friends, my neighbors, posterity and my country makes me bless God that these objects are likely forever to be taken out of such hands, two thirds of whom were never from their fireside before, and never comprehended in their view more than their own farms and their own little private interest."[4]

The commitment of the federalists was heightened by still another conviction. The anxiety of the revolutionists about recent civil disorders and the weakness of Congress stemmed in part from their belief that, as one inland resident put it, "the inhabitants of the old world have been looking at America to see whether liberty and a republican form of government are worth contending for." If America failed as a nation, the whole idea would be discredited. Ratification, then, became the vehicle not only for restoring the unity and sense of purpose which had existed in the early years of the war but also for providing mankind with an alternative to political corruption and tyranny. "Rise to fame among all nations as a wise and understanding people"—so urged the Reverend Samuel Langdon in a sermon delivered shortly before New Hampshire's ratification convention was to meet, and others in the state echoed his sentiments.[5]

4. *New Hampshire Gazette*, Apr. 16, 1788; Plumer to Tilton, Dec. 16, 1787, Plumer Letter Book, I, 154, LC; William Gardner to Nicholas Gilman, June 14, 1788, Misc. MSS, NYHS; Nathaniel Sargeant to Joseph Badger, NEHGR, 1 (1847), 237. See also *New Hampshire Gazette*, Sept. 15 and Dec. 26, 1787.
5. *New Hampshire Recorder*, Oct. 30, 1787; Samuel Langdon, *The Republic of the Israelites, an Example to the American States* (Exeter, 1788), 29–35; *New Hampshire Spy*, Oct. 13, 1787.

Such arguments had a mutually reinforcing impact. The more the federalists talked and wrote, the more they came to believe that ratification and ratification alone could prevent disaster. At times they tended to exaggerate the seriousness of present difficulties, but they did so because they had convinced themselves that the fate of New Hampshire, America, and ultimately the whole world was at stake. Earlier in the decade political discussions had been marked by a pervasive pessimism: no one thought the state constitution perfect, yet it had been impossible to obtain a better one; ignorant and dishonest men would have the means of rising to power in any elective government; republican institutions by their very nature were too feeble to protect liberty and property. Now, however, at least one segment of the population had something positive to fight for, a practical alternative that promised to resolve all the tensions, anxieties, and conflicts which had been responsible for their discouragement. "The present object," wrote a correspondent from Keene, "is of more consequence than our emancipation from tyranny." Another writer noted that "many people look upon the adoption of the new constitution as the millennium of virtue and wealth."[6]

But those who supported the constitution were in the minority. Most inhabitants thought of New Hampshire as an independent and sovereign polity, joined loosely with other states for practical military and diplomatic purposes. They had been suspicious even when the Articles of Confederation, which acknowledged state sovereignty, had been proposed. At that time the citizens of Hawke felt that to bind all the states by a vote of only nine was "too prerogative" and refused to consent to "so small a majority." Numerous other communities expressed fears that any central government might be dominated by individuals and states whose interests conflicted with those of New Hampshire. The town of Wilton protested that the article giving Congress the right to determine war and peace bestowed "a power greater than the King of Great Britain in Council ever had" and warned against any governing body whose members held such authority.[7] To be sure, the behavior of the Congress had dispelled

6. *New Hampshire Recorder*, Jan. 1, 1788 (source of first quotation); *Freeman's Oracle*, Dec. 22, 1787, and Jan. 18, 1788 (source of second quotation).
7. Weare Papers, IV, 82 (the Hawke resolutions), and 54–119 *passim*, NHA. The Wilton resolution is in *NHSP*, XIII, 680. For a classic expression of belief in decentralization, see *Freeman's Journal*, June 29, 1776.

some of this distrust, but the general fear of central government remained, and the federal constitution promised to establish a government far more powerful than any previously contemplated. Even many of those who agreed that some kind of national government was needed and thought that New Hampshire, with its exposed frontier and economic dependence on Massachusetts and Connecticut, would benefit from union found it difficult to accept what they read. "We are not drove to such great straits to be obliged to swallow down every portion offered us by wholesale or else die immediately by our disease," wrote a state legislator; "We can form a constitution at our leisure." Tobias Lear, a kinsman of John Langdon who had become Washington's secretary, visited New Hampshire and reported the people felt that "if the Constitution obtained, the rights and liberties of all American citizens would be destroyed, and that the people of this state, as a part of the community, would suffer in the general wreck."[8]

In addition, local circumstance made the people of New Hampshire relatively immune to one of the federalists' strongest arguments and receptive instead to the ideas of those who opposed ratification. The assumption that a federal government, by increasing commerce, would promote general prosperity had little impact on the thousands of independent farmers who distrusted merchants and thought themselves capable of economic self-sufficiency. They wanted reduced taxes, a paper currency, and relief from debtor suits: the federal government promised none of these.[9] Furthermore, their experience with the state government had made them particularly suspicious of all political authority. If annual elections in New Hampshire had not prevented state legislators from abusing the privileges of power, what could be expected of national officials

---

8. *Freeman's Oracle*, Jan. 11, 1788; Lear to Washington, June 2, 1788, in Jared Sparks, ed., *Correspondence of the American Revolution* (Boston, 1853), IV, 221. See also Plumer, "Plumer's Biographical Sketches," IV, 539, NHHS. There is a brief biography of Lear by Timothy L. Tullock in *Granite Monthly*, 6 (1883), 4–14, 60–62.

9. *New Hampshire Gazette*, Nov. 9, 1787. Although exact tabulations cannot be made, I estimate that about 60 per cent of the towns known to have favored a land bank selected antifederalist convention delegates. Orin G. Libby, *Geographical Distribution of the Vote of the Thirteen States on the Federal Constitution, 1787–1788* (Bulletin of the University of Wisconsin, Economics, Political Science, and History Series, I [1894–1896], 53–54), has reached the same conclusion.

whose terms were even longer? The proposed judiciary threatened to make justice even more oppressive than at present. A citizen might have to travel four or five hundred miles at his own expense to attend a case appealed to a federal court, only to face a judge totally unfamiliar with the issues at stake. Finally, the lack of religious qualifications for national officeholding—New Hampshire's constitution made only Protestants eligible for elective state office —seemed fraught with dangerous implications to the state's predominantly Congregational population.[10]

The federalists understood that unless they played their cards carefully New Hampshire's ratification convention would vote against the constitution. President Sullivan refused to call the state legislature into immediate session for the purpose of deciding when and where the convention would meet, reasoning that unless the people were exposed to arguments in favor of adoption and saw that the constitution received strong support elsewhere, particularly in Massachusetts, the chances for a favorable outcome would be small. When the assembly did meet—in early December—he publicly announced that even though New Hampshire men might have written a better one, the constitution provided "one of the best systems of government that ever was devised" and urged his fellow legislators to adopt a set of convention regulations which he felt would maximize the chances for ratification. The legislature complied. It voted to have each town send as many delegates to the convention as it sent representatives to the assembly; antifederalists, led by Nathaniel Peabody, had supported a plan to have the number doubled, in an effort to dilute the effectiveness of the group of vocal and influential federalists expected to dominate discussion of the constitution. The house and senate also agreed that state constitutional provisions against plural officeholding would not apply to the ratification convention delegates, thus making it possible for known federalists like Superior Court Judges Samuel Livermore and Josiah Bartlett and State Treasurer John Taylor Gilman to attend. Sullivan's delaying

10. *Freeman's Oracle,* Jan. 11, Feb. 1, 8, June 6, 13, 1788; *New Hampshire Spy,* Feb. 15, 23, 1788; Libbey to Belknap, Feb. 22, 1788, and Sullivan to Belknap, Feb. 26, 1788, *Belknap Papers, MHS Collections,* 6th ser., IV (1891), 390, 394. For the general argument describing antifederalist distrust of political authority, see Cecelia M. Kenyon, "Men of Little Faith: The Anti-Federalists on the Nature of Representative Government," *WMQ,* 3d ser., 12 (1955), 3–43.

tactics had already made it impossible for the convention to meet until after Massachusetts had made its decision.[11]

The federalists stepped up their campaign as soon as precepts for the election of delegates went out. Ministers, most of whom supported ratification, delivered sermons emphasizing the importance of the present issue and joined in community discussions dealing with the constitution; a few even decided to defy the tradition against clerical involvement in politics and made known their eagerness to serve in the convention. The editors of the state's five newspapers filled their pages with letters and articles favoring the constitution. Sullivan and Langdon suspended their feud and joined forces in urging their political associates both to seek election and to fight for ratification. At the same time, spokesmen in parts of the state where antifederalist sentiment was strong tried to prevent towns from fettering their delegates with instructions to vote against adoption. "As the question will require much discussion and as the opinion of most of the gentlemen who will compose the convention will depend in some measure upon the light and information which this free discussion will throw upon the subject," explained "Probus," "it seems necessary that the representative should be entirely unshackled by any instructions from his constituents."[12]

The campaign met with some success but not enough. So many inhabitants feared the consequences of adoption and the persuasive powers of federalist leaders that at least fifteen and probably closer to thirty delegates, most of them from the Merrimack Valley, showed up at the Exeter convention with orders to vote against ratification.[13] Several who appeared without final instructions knew that sentiment in the communities they represented was overwhelmingly antagonis-

11. Libbey to Belknap, Oct. 24, 1787, *Belknap Papers, MHS Collections,* 6th ser., IV (1891), 341; *New Hampshire Spy,* Dec. 11, 1787 (source of quotation); NHSP, XXI, 157–169.

12. *Freeman's Oracle,* Dec. 22, 1787 (source of quotation); *New Hampshire Recorder,* Sept. 18, 1787, and Feb. 5, 1788; NHSP, X, 2–7. Only one state newspaper, the *Freeman's Oracle,* published any antifederalist arguments.

13. State Convention, Federal Constitution, 1788, Election of Delegates (also referred to as Goodwin Town Papers), NHA; Libby, *Geographical Distribution,* 70–75; Nathaniel J. Eiseman, "The Ratification of the Federal Constitution by the State of New Hampshire," unpub. thesis Columbia University, 1937, mimeograph, NHSL, 27–36. Belknap heard that forty towns had issued instructions to vote negatively: Belknap to Hazard, Feb. 17, 1788, *Belknap Papers, MHS Collections,* 5th ser., III (1877), 20.

tic to the constitution and hesitated to defy their constituents. Many others opposed ratification from personal conviction. In all, if Sullivan's estimates are accurate, only 30 per cent of the convention delegates were prepared to vote yes before debate began.[14]

The federalists, however, were equal to the task. With Sullivan in the chair they pushed through a set of rules which included a provision permitting adjournment before any final vote on the constitition had been taken. Bartlett, Langdon, Sullivan, Livermore, Gilman, and others who, because of their past political services, commanded both respect and influence conferred privately with opposition delegates and spoke out frequently in floor debate. The two most articulate clergymen who had gained election—Samuel Langdon and Benjamin Thurston—urged their fellow Congregationalists not to condemn the constitution because it included no religious qualifications for officeholding; religion, they argued, should be detached from civil power. After Joshua Atherton, an Amherst lawyer who became the most vocal antifederalist spokesman, had delivered a lengthy attack on the judiciary, the former state attorney general, John Pickering, responded by pointing out that all federal judges would be "appointed by men, all of whom are chosen mediately or immediately by the people, accountable to their constituents for their conduct, and removable at certain periods if they have betrayed the rights of their countrymen." All the federalists emphasized the limitations placed on federal authority and tried to show how America in general and New Hampshire in particular would benefit from ratification.[15]

Such arguments, and the fact that by now six other states including Massachusetts had ratified the constitution, gained a number of converts. When all the key constitutional provisions had been dis-

14. Sullivan to Belknap, Feb. 26, 1788, in Hammond, ed., *Sullivan Papers*, III, 566. See also Eiseman, "Ratification," 36; Langdon to Washington, Feb. 28, 1788, in Sparks, ed., *Correspondence*, IV, 211; Langdon to Rufus King, Feb. 23, 1788, in Alfred L. Elwyn, ed., *Letters by Washington, Adams, Jefferson, and Others Written . . . to John Langdon* (Philadelphia, 1880), 117.

15. *NHSP*, X, 12–15. No record of convention debates has survived. The excerpts included in this paragraph were reported in the *New Hampshire Spy*, Feb. 22, 23, 1788, the *American Herald* (Boston), Mar. 3, 1788, and the *New Hampshire Recorder*, Mar. 25, 1788. Jonathan Elliot, ed., *Debates on the Several State Conventions on the Adoption of the Federal Constitution*, 2d ed., II (Philadelphia, 1836), 203–204, reports an antislavery speech by Atherton which is probably apochryphal: see Joseph B. Walker, *A History of the New Hampshire Convention . . .* (Boston, 1888), 4–5.

cussed, the federalist leaders calculated that 45 of the 100-plus members would vote for approval and that eleven more who were bound by contrary instructions wanted to do the same. John Langdon quickly moved for an adjournment. It passed 56 to 51 and the delegates dispersed after agreeing to reconvene at Concord in June.[16]

Between conventions the federalists intensified their campaign. They flooded the press with proconstitution arguments, many of them carefully edited excerpts from out-of-state newspapers. In private conversations and public debate they reiterated the reasons which had led the Philadelphia delegates to propose a federal government. At the same time they tried to discredit the opposition. Atherton provided a particularly inviting subject. At the beginning of the revolution he, from personal friendship with the British colonel, Edward Lutwyche, and from dislike of patriot mobs, had refused to sign the loyalty oath. Now the federalists accused him of "wishing to prevent the adoption of a system only because it will put it out of the power of Britain to subjugate us." Aspiring poets had a field day identifying the "bouncing old tory" and his associates with efforts to subvert the revolution. And although, as a few writers admitted, many former Tories supported ratification—of the eight elected to the convention four voted yes—the federalists kept up their attacks as long as the issue remained in doubt.[17]

State officeholders who opposed ratification were also treated roughly. Long before the February convention a writer in the *Gazette* had warned that "interested politicians . . . and certain factions composed of salary and prerequisite men" in the legislature would oppose the constitution. Subsequent events only reinforced such fears, for several of the leading antifederalists did hold justice-of-the-peace and militia appointments. Furthermore, many house members who had fought for paper money and restrictions on creditor lawsuits criticized the proposed constitution because it prohibited the state governments from establishing currency and by implication outlawed debtor legislation. The citizens of New Hampshire were reminded,

16. Libbey to Belknap, Feb. 26, 1788, *Belknap Papers, MHS Collections*, 6th ser., IV (1891), 396; Langdon to King, Feb. 23, 1788, in Elwyn, ed., *Letters*, 117; *NHSP*, X, 15.

17. *New Hampshire Spy*, Mar. 11 (source of first quotation), Apr. 12, 1788; *New Hampshire Gazette*, Apr. 16, 1788 (source of second quotation); *Freeman's Oracle*, Feb. 29, 1788. *New Hampshire Recorder*, Oct. 30, 1787, and Jan. 1, 1788. The tabulation has been made from biographies in Eiseman, "Ratification," 45–48 and 89–97.

for example, that Nathaniel Peabody—who helped organize the opposition—was heavily in debt. Another federalist claimed to have overheard Peabody and an associate asking: "What will become of our commissions? Will not the appointment of officers rest with Congress?"[18]

It is impossible to measure the effectiveness of these accusations, but it is clear that by June a significant shift had taken place in public sentiment. Lear informed Washington the people now felt that "as they have more to hope and less to fear" from the constitution "than almost any other state, it would be doing an injustice to themselves not to accept it." A few communities had released their representatives from instructions, and in other towns proratification delegates had been elected to replace antifederalists. Furthermore, at least three towns not represented at Exeter had decided to send federalists to the Concord convention. When news arrived that South Carolina had become the eighth state to ratify and New Hampshire now had the opportunity to provide the ninth and final vote needed for adoption, the "constitution men" became positively jubilant.[19]

The convention went smoothly. In the first session, delegates approved the credentials of two federalist delegates whose election had been contested. Later the convention agreed to recommend a bill of rights which several antifederalist members had indicated would conciliate them. Atherton's motion to "ratify the constitution, together with said amendments, but that said Constitution do not operate in the state of New Hampshire without said amendments," was postponed, as was his motion for adjournment. Livermore asked for a vote on the main question and Langdon seconded it. Fifty-seven delegates voted "yes" and forty-seven "no."[20]

Ratification had an instantaneous and dramatic impact on the public. A wave of political optimism engulfed the seaboard area and a few inland communities where the vast majority of townsmen had been federalists.[21] Portsmouth held a massive celebration with a

18. The quotations are from *New Hampshire Gazette*, Dec. 26, 1787, and June 19, 1788. See also *New Hampshire Recorder*, Oct. 30, Nov. 27, 1787.
19. Lear to Washington, June 22, 1788, in Sparks, ed., *Correspondence*, IV, 221; Eiseman, "Ratification," 73–77.
20. Lear to Washington, June 22, 1788, in Sparks, ed., *Correspondence*, IV, 224; *NHSP*, X, 16–22.
21. Delegates from towns within ten miles of Great Bay voted 13 to 1 for ratification. Most residents in this area were engaged directly or indirectly in external com-

parade, fireworks, free liquor, and thirteen toasts, one for each of the new United States. Langdon reported his friends in "high spirits" and "every order of people . . . highly pleased." Sullivan credited the constitution with eliminating any future military threat to the state government. In Stratham a farmer observed that although "money remained scarce and business dull" adoption had made the people expect "relief from their difficulties" soon.[22] Men who earlier in the decade had begun to wonder whether the revolutionary experiment in republicanism could survive now professed renewed hope in the future of their own state and of the nation as a whole: "The foundations of peace, opulence and even power are deep laid," wrote a correspondent to the *Gazette*, "the sun of American glory is just rising above a delightful horizon." Paine Wingate, a Hampton Falls minister who had abandoned the pulpit and become involved in state politics, agreed with Pickering that it was "a most fortunate circumstance, as well as surprising, that so great a revolution in the government of the United States . . . should be effected by mere force of reasoning and persuasion, without confusion or bloodshed. I think this," he added, "may be adduced to evidence that this country is not prone to anarchy, however far a zeal for liberty may sometimes carry them." Indeed, enthusiasm was so widespread a few men became alarmed. Wingate told Belknap in the spring of 1789 he feared the historian's "expectation . . . respecting the new government" and "that of the public in general" had been "raised too high . . ."[23]

In other parts of New Hampshire the reaction was different in kind but no less encouraging to those who emphasized the need for political stability. Inhabitants along the Connecticut River and the northern frontier had been divided in their attitude toward the constitution and only with difficulty had been convinced by community

merce. The few citizens who would benefit from the appreciation of public securities expected after ratification were also concentrated here but, with the exception of Langdon and Gilman, had little convention influence: Forrest MacDonald, *We the People: The Economic Origins of the Constitution* (Chicago, 1958), 243–251.

22. *New Hampshire Spy*, July 5–22, 1788; Langdon to Nicholas Gilman, June 28, 1788 in the manuscript version of James F. Cooper, "History of the Navy of the United States," I, Part 2, 84, NYHS; Sullivan to Nicholas Gilman, Sept. 5, 1788, in Hammond, ed., *Sullivan Papers*, III, 593; *Journal of Samuel Lane*, ed. Hansen, 92.

23. *New Hampshire Gazette*, Sept. 16, 1788; Wingate to Pickering, Apr. 27, 1789, in Wingate, *Life of Wingate*, II, 298; Wingate to Belknap, May 12, 1789, *Belknap Papers*, MHS *Collections*, 6th ser., IV (1891), 431.

leaders, Samuel Livermore especially, that they had much to gain and little to lose through ratification;[24] now they accepted the decision and waited to see what would happen. Pretty much the same attitude predominated in the Merrimack Valley and other sections of the interior where community sentiment had remained adamantly antifederalist. The influential Joseph Badger urged all those who had joined him in opposing adoption to obey the new government. Other antifederalist legislators and their fellow townsmen gradually overcame their disappointment; they too realized the state was in trouble, and although they thought the new government an excessive antidote they were willing to suspend judgment. Eight months after the constitution had gained approval, Atherton reported to a friend in New York that in the assembly "where for a long time there was a decided majority against the new system," opposition had ceased. "The language," he lamented, "is 'it is adopted, let us try it.' "[25]

Political and economic developments in the next five years justified the optimism of the federalists and erased the remaining doubts of those disappointed by ratification. To begin with, none of the gloomy antifederalist predictions came to pass. George Washington and John Adams, both Protestants and heroes of the revolution, gained election as the nation's chief executive officers. Creation of a federal judiciary had almost no impact upon the administration of justice in New Hampshire; if anything, it improved conditions by permitting state residents who otherwise might have been forced to appear before out-of-state courts to defend themselves before supposedly less biased national judges. Speculation in public securities by members of Congress evoked some criticism, and a few probably agreed with the disgruntled state representative in Philadelphia who complained that his associates were as much interested in "creating offices and getting themselves and friends appointed to them" as anything else, but in general the behavior of national

24. Grafton County produced eleven affirmative votes against one negative. Residents had been subjected to heavy profederalist arguments by their friends in Connecticut. Legend credits Livermore with converting several Grafton County delegates who had been instructed to oppose ratification, but there is no evidence any of the delegates ever received such instructions. See *Connecticut Courant* (Hartford), Mar. 3, 10, 1788; Charles R. Corning, *Samuel Livermore* (Concord, 1888); Eiseman, "Ratification," 27–36.
25. Eiseman, "Ratification," 96; Atherton to John Lamb, Feb. 23, 1789, Lamb Papers, box 5, no. 38, NYHS.

legislators seemed consistent with the principles of republicanism.[26]

Several specific actions by the federal government helped bolster public confidence. Citizens throughout the state were flattered by Washington's visit to New Hampshire and celebrated the occasion with enthusiasm. The selection of John Langdon as the Senate's temporary presiding officer met with favorable comment, as did the decision to reappoint under federal authority customs and post-office officials who previously had held office under state commissions. Submission to the states of a bill of rights and its subsequent ratification helped dissipate anxiety that the federal government would usurp powers better handled by state authorities; the General Court accepted all but one of the recommended amendments.[27]

Another important factor in generating enthusiasm was the business revival which began late in the 1780s. European wars stimulated demand for the fish, lumber, and agricultural products which New Hampshire had available for export. The revival in commerce, in turn, created a market for new ships: eight were built in the Piscataqua during 1790, twenty the following year, and even more after that. At the same time the money supply increased so quickly that by the summer of 1791 "knowing men" agreed it was "full plenty enough for the benefit of the trade," and a year later farmers' produce was reported to fetch "the highest prices and quickest money ever known." Merchants and others with capital offered loans on reasonable terms. Credit, high prices for agricultural goods, continued immigration, and the need for investment outlets produced a new land boom.[28] Exactly how much federal policies were responsible for the recovery no one knew; but most men probably thought the national government had a great deal to do with New Hampshire's economic prosperity.[29]

26. *New Hampshire Gazeteer* (Exeter), Feb. 26, 1791; the Jeremiah Smith to John Smith, Mar. 29, 1792, quoted in John H. Morison, *Life of Hon. Jeremiah Smith* (Boston, 1845), 50.

27. *New Hampshire Gazette*, Nov. 5, 11, 1789; Adams, *Annals*, 295–298; NHSP, XXI, 545, 732.

28. McKinley, "Portsmouth," 233–238 and 293–295; Belknap, *History*, III, 209; *Journal of Samuel Lane*, ed. Hansen, 96 and 57 (sources of quotations); *New Hampshire Gazette*, Mar. 28, 1792. State population, probably about 100,000 in 1786, had risen to over 140,000 five years later: NHSP, X, 639–689, and XIII, 767–772.

29. See, for example, William K. Atkinson, *An Oration Delivered at Dover, New Hampshire, on the Fourth of July, 1791* (Dover, 1791), 10–13; William Jones, *An Oration Pronounced at Concord the Fourth of July, 1794* (Concord, 1794), 15; NHSP, XXII, 141–143.

The way in which some inhabitants viewed the French revolution and attendant political upheavals across the Atlantic also helped to cement allegiance to the new system. In the mid-eighties many in New Hampshire had been embarrassed by the sharp contrast between political stability in Europe and disorder in republican America. Now the tables had been reversed. America enjoyed unprecedented prosperity and unity, while, as one resident smugly announced, "bloodshed and devastation attend the revolutions of government in the old world." And what had been responsible for the change? The establishment of "an energetic national government" which not only had eliminated domestic discontent but kept the United States from becoming embroiled, as the colonies had, in conflicts generated by corrupt and ambitious European rulers. As thirteen separate polities the states might have succumbed to foreign intrigue; together they had the strength to remain free and independent. When in 1793 Washington came under attack in other parts of America for his refusal to aid France in her struggle with England, the people of New Hampshire applauded his decision. President Josiah Bartlett informed the General Court that Washington's "strict neutrality" had avoided "giving any just cause" for the European powers "to disturb the peace and tranquillity of these states," and he warned against the "dangerous effects of foreign politics and influence." The legislators in their reply expressed complete agreement with his sentiments.[30]

Finally, the general success of the experiment in federalism made it easier for residents to accept the few congressional policies with which they disagreed. One problem arose when state leaders supported militia reforms recommended by national authorities, and legislators balked because the reforms reduced local influence in the appointment of officers; in the end those who advocated change won in a close contest, and their opponents accepted defeat without becoming distraught.[31] More serious was antagonism generated by Alexander Hamilton's fiscal program. Few except hard-money men who for other reasons were totally committed to federalism opposed the national bank, and no protest at all arose over tariffs and excise

30. *New Hampshire Gazette,* Nov. 11, 1789 (source of first quotation), and Jan. 18, 1792; *New Hampshire Recorder,* Oct. 21, 1790; *A Journal of the Proceedings of the Honorable Senate of the State of New Hampshire . . . December . . . 1793* (Portsmouth, 1794), 8 (source of second quotation), 29.
31. Page, "Bartlett," 552–556; *NHSP,* XXII, 624–638 and 687.

taxes; but refunding domestic debt at par and federal assumption of state debts incurred during the revolution were far from popular. The refunding gave speculators who had purchased discounted securities from soldiers and other original holders a quick windfall. The assumption of state debts, some argued, aggrandized federal powers at the expense of the states; in addition, details of the assumption plan seemed unfair to New Hampshire, which through taxation had already paid off most of its debts. One of the state's federal representatives lost his office in the next election in part because he had voted for both policies, and another—Samuel Livermore—was made a senator largely because he had voted against them; the legislature passed a resolution criticizing the principle of assumption as well as the unequal treatment received by New Hampshire. In time, however, the controversy subsided. By 1794 most political leaders and many of their constituents had accepted the logic of Hamilton's entire program.[32]

Developments at the state level further bolstered the revolutionists' confidence in the political system. For one thing, the Sullivan-Langdon feud which had disrupted the legislature and been a matter of concern to all who thought unity essential to the success of republicanism gradually subsided. Langdon resigned as president to serve in the national senate. His successor and close friend, senior Senator John Pickering, possessed neither the prestige nor the legislative connections to remain in office: in the spring of 1789 Sullivan won a plurality of the votes and was chosen president by the senate for a third term. The 1790 elections were the last in which the old alignment dominated. Langdon and his backers supported Pickering again. Failing in health, embarrassed by a well-publicized dispute with former councilor Ebenezer Thompson, and much criticized for insisting that his appointment as federal district judge did not violate constitutional restrictions on plural officeholding, Sullivan decided not to run; instead he promoted the candidacy of his merchant friend Joshua Wentworth. Pickering received the most votes and Wentworth was close behind, but neither became president: the legislators, fed up with the bickering which had gone on since the

32. *Concord Herald*, Aug. 24, Nov. 23, 1790; *New Hampshire Gazette*, Dec. 4, 1790, and Oct. 18, 1792; Mayo, *Langdon*, 237–240; Morison, *Smith*, 52–64; Nobel Cunningham, *Jeffersonian Republicans: The Formation of Party Organization, 1789–1801* (Chapel Hill, 1957), 31; NHSP, XXII, 239–241.

war, chose the man who without soliciting votes had received the third highest total.[33]

Josiah Bartlett could not have been better suited to the task of restoring public faith in the institutions of government. He had joined the revolutionary movement early, served in the Continental Congress, acted as Meshech Weare's closest and most trusted political associate, and, as a superior court judge after the war, had gained a statewide reputation for fairness and sensitivity; even Plumer, who had few good words to say about any politician in New Hampshire except himself, described the new president as "a man of integrity, firmness, economy and a general knowledge of the interests of the state—a man in whom I have extreme confidence." Bartlett's performance as chief executive only enhanced his popularity. In the next two elections he received over 95 per cent of the popular vote and in 1793 almost 75 per cent despite a challenge from John Langdon. Before that election one newspaper correspondent expressed what must have been widely held sentiments when he wrote: "New Hampshire has been quiet and happy under President Bartlett; why should she be convulsed unnecessarily with . . . any remains of the old contention between Presidents Sullivan and Langdon?"[34]

The postratification period also witnessed a marked improvement in the effectiveness of the legislature as a whole. To some extent the new conditions in which state officials operated made their task in providing for the public welfare an easy one. Economic prosperity reduced both the level of discontent and the number of petitions demanding reform. The national government assumed responsibility for many of the problems which had divided the assembly.[35] Sullivan's fiscal reforms, the rise in security prices which followed ratification, and Hamilton's assumption program all helped to decrease

33. NHSP, XXI, *passim*; Whittemore, *Sullivan*, 221–225; *New Hampshire Spy*, Mar. 6–20, 1789; *New Hampshire Gazetteer*, Jan. 15, 1790; *Concord Herald*, Jan. 13–Feb. 17, 1790.

34. Plumer to Abiel Foster, June 28, 1790, Plumer Letter Book, I, 161; NHSP, XXII, 281, 519; *A Journal of the Proceedings of the Honorable Senate of the State of New Hampshire . . . June, 1793 . . .* (Portsmouth, 1793), 8; *Concord Herald*, Feb. 14, 1793. See also *New Hampshire Gazetteer*, Jan. 30, Feb. 13, 1793.

35. Bartlett considered this last point to be of major importance. In 1791 he explained to the General Court that "the great national affairs that concern the United States in general which formerly occupied a considerable part of the time and attention of the state legislatures having by the adoption of the general government devolved on the national legislature has afforded us a favorable opportunity to attend with more deliberation to those matters that principally concern the interest of this state in particular . . .": NHSP, XXII, 142.

Josiah Bartlett (1729–1795), member of the council and the Committee of Safety during the war, president and governor of New Hampshire 1790–1794. Painting by Alonzo Slafter from a pencil sketch made by John Trumbull in 1790.

and finally eliminate the public debt; by 1791 the treasury contained such a surplus it was possible to announce that no taxes would be needed the following year. The restoration of faith in established political processes tended to attract better men to the assembly. In 1787, 43 per cent of the house delegates had had no previous legislative experience, while only 13 per cent had served for more than three years; five years later the first figure had been halved and the second more than doubled. Furthermore, there were more delegates to share the work. By 1792 the percentage of towns not sending delegates had declined by half, to slightly over 20 per cent.[36]

Whatever the reasons, the assembly sessions became more and more productive. The members passed an act guaranteeing that no citizen would lose property because of the Mason-Allen controversy, then decided the state owned much of the disputed land, and finally arranged a compromise settlement which eliminated confusion about the rest; in 1789 they established legal procedures for dealing with other conflicting land claims stemming from the colonial period. A joint committee of the house and senate in cooperation with the treasurer brought order into the state's previously chaotic revolutionary accounts. The government authorized and surveyed roads to facilitate the transportation of goods, chartered a state bank, and passed other measures designed to stimulate the state's burgeoning economy. Private petitions which occupied the legislators a good part of the time were handled quickly and fairly by specially appointed committees; only rarely did the assembly reject the recommendations of such committees. After Bartlett became president, the legislature conducted a survey of property within the state, reapportioned taxes, and refined collection procedures. Legislation based on public demands for a tax on public securities was passed. Several hard-working representatives assumed responsibility for rewriting and codifying state laws; when they finished, the assembly published the results along with the treaty of peace, the state constitution, and the Constitution of the United States. This done, the legislators relaxed and began to congratulate one another on their success. In 1792 Bartlett announced in his inaugural address that "the general revision of the laws of the state and the several regulations that have taken place has rendered the situation of our public affairs more eligible than they have been in years past." He informed the General Court a year later that it had carried out its duties so effectively he could think of no further specific actions to recommend.[37]

36. Sullivan to Belknap, Feb. 26, 1788, in Hammond, ed., *Sullivan Papers*, III, 566; Plumer, Autobiography, 47–51, Plumer Papers; *NHSP*, XXII, 177, 231–237; *New Hampshire Gazette*, Mar. 19, 1796. The statistics are based on assembly records in *NHSP*, XXI and XXII.

37. *NHSP*, XXI, XXII, and Batchellor and Metcalf, *Laws of New Hamp.*, V, *passim*; *Journal of the Senate, December 1793*, 11. The quotation is from *NHSP*, XXII, 638.

Moreover, the assembly managed to resolve its internal disputes peacefully and without alienating significant segments of the population. Before Bartlett became president, there had been a number of controversies. The choice of a second national senator pitted federalists and antifederalists in the state government against one another. The house voted for Nathaniel Peabody while the senate supported Bartlett; in the end the house changed its mind and when Bartlett refused to accept the office joined the senate in appointing the uncontroversial Paine Wingate. A struggle involving the choice of New Hampshire's presidential electors kept the two legislative bodies at loggerheads for weeks. The house insisted the decision be made in joint session, which its members would dominate; the senate demanded concurrent action. Public anxiety increased when it became apparent the conflict might not be settled before the deadline established for selecting electors. The house, however, gave in at the last minute. Equally dramatic were the debates triggered by efforts to obtain an assembly resolution criticizing Sullivan for not resigning as president when he accepted his federal appointment. Much to the relief of Sullivan's supporters and others who thought the action an unnecessary affront to one who had served his nation and state so well, the resolution was defeated.[38]

The most serious battle during Bartlett's administration began soon after he took office. The house, with his approval, impeached Judge Woodbury Langdon for failing to attend sessions of the superior court held in Grafton County. Langdon didn't deny the charge; instead he criticized the legislature for not giving him a permanent and honorable salary, accused it of unconstitutional behavior in passing laws to nullify court decisions, refused to appear for trial before the senate, and, after obtaining a federal appointment through the influence of his brother, resigned. Langdon's response infuriated his many enemies and split the assembly into opposing camps. About three fifths of the house members united in declaring his actions contemptuous and his resignation illegal; they then asked Bartlett and the council formally to remove him from office. Cooler heads, however, prevailed. At Bartlett's urging the senate nonconcurred the house resolutions, and the council accepted the resignation. The outcome gave everyone involved some satisfaction. Friends

38. For a description of assembly controversies between 1789 and 1791, see Turner, *Plumer*, 37–43.

of the controversial judge thought him vindicated by the senate and council decisions; his foes could point to their success in ridding the state of an undependable public servant; Langdon himself probably considered the affair partly responsible for passage a year later of an act to give superior court judges a permanent salary and for the legislature's increased reluctance to overthrow judicial decisions.[39]

After "this mighty fuss"—the phrase is Plumer's—affairs in the assembly went more smoothly. Bartlett helped prevent further disputes between the house and senate. He and the council developed procedures which gave every legislator and many outside the government the opportunity to recommend civil and military appointments. The house members improved the efficiency of their operations by appointing a special committee to act as a clearing house for the private petitions which now absorbed much of their time and energy. Plumer, elected Speaker, prevented the special interest groups from obstructing popular legislation. Late in December 1791 he informed a friend that "the unanimity, harmony and dispatch in the legislature was never greater than at the present session."[40] Conditions remained substantially the same in subsequent meetings.

All this—Bartlett's presidency, the responsiveness and efficiency of the assembly, the disappearance of bitter feuding among public officials—helped give both voters and politicians a renewed confidence in the state government.

The end result of efforts to reform New Hampshire's institutional structure added to the general sense of political self-satisfaction. A provision in the constitution obligated the General Court in 1791 to issue election precepts for an assembly "to make such alterations" in the form of government "as from experience may be found necessary." At the convention a group of young delegates, led by William

39. Plumer to Smith, July 6, 1790, and Plumer to Woodbury Langdon, Jan. 24, Mar. 26, 1791, Plumer Letter Book, I, 162–176; Plumer, Autobiography, 41–45, Plumer Papers; *NHSP*, XXI, 813, and XXII, 76–93, 171–177, 241–242, 749–756; Walter F. Dodd, "The Constitutional History of New Hampshire, 1775–1792," *Proceedings of the Bar Association of the State of New Hampshire*, n.s., 2 (1904–1908), 399–400.

40. Plumer to Langdon, Mar. 26, 1791, and Plumer to Smith, Oct. 27 and Dec. 10, 1791, Plumer Letter Book, I, 174–183; *NHSP*, XXII, 145 and *passim*. Three recognizable political cliques existed in the house, one led by Exeter's John Taylor Gilman, another representing Portsmouth interests, and a third which Peabody had organized. None was powerful or stable enough to control the assembly: Turner, *Plumer*, 37–43.

Plumer, urged that every branch of the state government be fundamentally reorganized, that relationships among the departments be redefined, and that constitutional provisions limiting the autonomy of local communities be adopted; others sought less sweeping changes.[41] Although the convention rejected many suggestions and the public—a two-thirds majority was needed for ratification—voted against some submitted for their approval, enough amendments survived to convince the reformers their efforts had been worthwhile. A sufficient number were defeated to remind the revolutionists that in a republican society political power remained ultimately in the hands of the voters. And almost everyone agreed that the constitution had been altered in a manner consistent with the principles of good government.

A few of the proposals were almost universally popular. The memory of Sullivan's plural officeholding and a recently passed house resolution permitting its members to hold federal commissions made it possible to obtain convention support and voter approval of an amendment prohibiting such practices in the future. There was no significant opposition to Plumer's suggestion that assemblymen be prohibited from accepting fees for sponsored legislation, or to an amendment which opened assembly sessions to the public. Over 70 per cent of those voting agreed that the state, not the towns, should pay legislative salaries, and that judges should retire when they reached the age of seventy. The latter decision was especially pleasing to attorneys in the convention, because it later removed from the bench at least two men—John Dudley and Joseph Badger—notorious for their willingness to ignore the letter of the law while administering justice.[42]

The reformers' most important victories altered relations between the legislative and executive departments. In the early 1780s those who tried to create an independent and strong executive had been defeated: the president presided over and voted in the senate, could not veto legislation, and in most matters was required to act only with the consent of his councilors, who were drawn from the General Court and served simultaneously in both bodies. Moreover, the house and senate selected the president when no candidate received

41. *NHSP*, XX, 30 (source of quotation); Turner, *Plumer*, 44–53. The records of the convention are in *NHSP*, X, 24–196.
42. *NHSP*, X, 113–142, and XXI, 779, 797.

a majority of the popular vote. The arrangement had come under attack for several reasons. Some said it forced the executive to favor legislators and their relatives in making civil and military appointments. Others decried the inflexibility of a system which made it difficult to respond to emergencies like the Exeter riot. Many felt that had Presidents Sullivan and Langdon been able to veto legislation the confusion of the mid-eighties would have been reduced. The main criticisms, however, were more theoretical. By the 1790s most thoughtful Americans had been convinced the abuse of political power could best be prevented by keeping executive, legislative, and judicial authority as distinct and separate as possible: "The blending of these powers together or uniting them in one man, or in one body of men," argued a *Gazette* correspondent, " 'makes the *essential* difference between a free and *despotic* government.' " Knowledge of other state constitutions and the debates over ratification of the federal Constitution made many in New Hampshire aware of the degree to which their system violated this principle.[43]

Plumer and his associates experienced only minimal difficulties in obtaining convention approval of a series of amendments to improve the situation. In the first session the delegates voted by an overwhelming margin both to remove the president from the senate and to symbolize his independent stature by changing his title to governor. Plumer and the other nine men on the committee appointed to meet between sessions to frame specific amendments cautiously recommended a veto which could be overridden by four sevenths of the house and a majority in the senate; to his surprise and glee the convention as a whole raised both figures to two thirds. The delegates also agreed the council should be elected directly by the people and should contain neither senators nor house representatives. Another alteration gave the governor and council a negative on each other in making both nominations and appointments. The only reform which met defeat was one which actually violated the separation-of-powers principle: the committee proposal to create a lieutenant governor who would preside over the senate.[44]

Gaining public approval of the amendments proved more troublesome, but not because of serious opposition to the idea of a strong

43. *NHSP*, XX, 21–25; *New Hampshire Gazette*, Dec. 11, 1790; *New Hampshire Spy*, June 9, 1792; *Concord Herald*, Aug. 3 and Sept. 14, 1791; *New Hampshire Gazetteer*, Sept. 23, 1791.
44. *NHSP*, X, 47–48, 55–56, 64, 68, 93, 94.

and independent executive. Many in populous Rockingham County criticized the provision giving each county one representative on the council, despite the convention's attempt to undermine such sentiment by including another amendment which gave the legislature the authority to divide the state into districts for future council elections. Throughout the state there were objections to the property qualification for councilors and to the clauses which failed to exclude from office men who were not Protestants. The amendments changing the president's title to governor and prohibiting councilors from holding seats in the legislature gained approval when first submitted; the others did not. After analyzing the returns, a committee chaired by Plumer decided to eliminate the controversial property requirement and added a phrase limiting the governor and council to men of the Protestant religion. This time, even though several town leaders in Rockingham County continued to resist, the amendments passed.[45]

Attempts to reform the senate met with only partial success. The convention in its first session voted down a proposal to increase the property qualification from £200 to £500 and later rejected a committee recommendation to extend the term in office to two years. Major disputes arose over how to make the senate more independent of the house. Under the old constitution, counties provided the basis for senatorial representation, a majority vote was needed for election, and when no candidate received a majority the house, for all practical purposes, filled the vacant seat; as a result most of the senators were selected by the house rather than the voters. Two solutions to the problem were offered. The convention first voted that a plurality would be sufficient for election. Plumer and others on the committee appointed to draw up amendments took a different tack, probably because they feared the plurality arrangement would favor candidates from large towns: five Portsmouth men, for example, might win in Rockingham County if voters in other communities favored their own local leaders. To avoid such a possibility and to keep the house from influencing the selection of senators, the committee recommended that the state be divided into districts, each representing an equal amount of taxable property and each to elect one senator; if no candidate received a majority, there would be a run-off between the two men with the highest number of votes. The con-

45. *NHSP*, X, 121, 142–167; *Concord Herald*, Feb. 29 and Mar. 3, 1792.

vention accepted the first idea but insisted that the assembly determine the winner when voters failed to give anyone a majority. This
arrangement gained the necessary two-thirds approval after the convention had added a religious requirement for officeholding and
eliminated an unpopular provision changing the time of the General
Court's first meeting from June to October.[46]

Plumer failed completely in his efforts to reorganize the house.
His motion to limit the membership to 60 received support from only
21 of the 100 or so men present. Another motion to increase the
minimum number of polls required before a town could elect a
house delegate lost by a similar margin, as did a proposal—sponsored
by men from the larger towns—to make representation proportional
to population. Plumer cajoled the committee of ten into recommending an upper limit of 110 house members, but that too was voted
down. The negative response of the convention is not surprising. The
inhabitants of New Hampshire had rebelled against British authority
and some of them had refused to accept state authority in part
because their communities lacked representation in the legislature;
their leaders were by no means eager to relinquish that right now.
In addition, many delegates undoubtedly disagreed with the assumption that "the few" must rule. One man who heard the debate over
Plumer's original proposal questioned whether "that kind of rats/
Which some folks term aristocrats/Will never bite—like bugs and
fleas/And slily eat—the public cheese." It may be so, he concluded,
"but yet, perhaps/Tis better to keep . . . a cat . . . and traps."[47]

Reform of the courts met a similar fate, although not so quickly.
Plumer and other young lawyers had long complained of inefficiency
and injustice in New Hampshire's judicial system. The lack of an
equity court, they felt, forced citizens to turn to the legislature for
justice, which not only violated separation of powers but corrupted
assemblymen who accepted fees for sponsoring such action. The
inferior courts of common pleas only encumbered legal processes.
Plumer claimed after examining court records that only 5 per cent
of the cases on lower court dockets ever reached trial, and, of that
5 per cent, three fourths were later appealed to the superior court.
Another attorney pointed out that awareness of these statistics,
plus distrust of many inferior court justices, made litigants hesitant

46. *NHSP*, X, 44, 52, 66, 94–95, 142–167.
47. *NHSP*, 48–50, 67, 96; the quotation is from *Concord Herald*, Oct. 19, 1791.

to reveal their best arguments; thus trials became farcical. The county courts of general sessions came under attack too, mainly because they determined serious criminal cases without trial by jury.[48]

The campaign to reorganize the courts started well. The first session of the convention voted to establish an equity court, to eliminate the inferior courts, to give justices of the peace final jurisdiction in all civil cases involving less than £4 and the superior court jurisdiction over all others, and to prohibit legislators from receiving private payment for their services. Although the delegates refused by a small margin to abolish the courts of general sessions, Plumer convinced the committee of ten to recommend the creation of a new county court to handle criminal cases. The committee also voted to give the superior court equity jurisdiction and added two new reforms: judges should retire at age sixty-five, and justice-of-the-peace commissions would have to be renewed every five years.[49]

The proposals stimulated widespread public criticism. Thomas Cogswell, a convention member who also sat on the Strafford County Inferior Court, published a lengthy and effective pamphlet attacking the logic of the reformers. How, he asked, could justice be improved by increasing the jurisdiction of the least-qualified authorities in the system—the justices of the peace? Would not that, in fact, further reduce citizen access to trial by jury? Were not the lower tribunals useful since they forced so many to compromise their differences outside the courtroom? To the argument that inferior court judges sometimes ignored the law, Cogswell had a simple and direct response: men of common sense often made better judges than those "brought up in the study of books." Others accused the convention of trying to usurp authority and pointedly remarked that the federal Constitution, which the reformers used as a model for many of their recommendations, gave Congress the responsibility for establishing lower courts. Still others used personal attacks. "A Freeman" noted that two outspoken advocates of change, William Page and Elisha Payne, had been active in the western rebellion and accused them of seeking to gain through subterfuge power they had earlier been

48. "A Member of the Convention," *Observations Occasioned by Writings against Alterations Proposed in the Convention, to be Made in the Judiciary System* (Portsmouth, 1792), 5, 23; *Concord Herald*, Feb. 24, Apr. 6, 19, 1790; *New Hampshire Spy*, Mar. 30, 1791; Smith to Plumer, Dec. 20, 1791, Plumer Collection, NHSL; Turner, *Plumer*, 48–49.
49. *NHSP*, X, 56–57, 69.

denied; he added that the one man who dared defend the convention decisions in print was a former Tory. Cogswell wrote of Plumer, who for a brief period in the eighties had toured New Hampshire as an itinerant Baptist preacher: "I am afraid he will be found as erroneous in politics as he has been enthusiastic in religion."[50]

The opponents won a complete victory. In the second session the delegates put aside the controversial committee report, then substituted a series of amendments which charged the General Court with the "duty to make a reform in the judiciary system" and suggested what shape the change might take. Even this proved too much for the voters: they rejected the whole idea of reorganization by a small margin and decisively defeated the amendments implying criticism of the lower courts.[51]

More antagonistic still was the response to recommended alterations in church-state relations. The 1784 constitution contained not only a Protestant qualification for officeholding—which the convention tried unsuccessfully to eliminate—but an ambiguous bill-of-rights article forcing many residents to support Congregationalism against their will. Plumer's motion to expunge the article lost so decisively he apparently decided not to present a prepared amendment declaring that no man should "ever be obliged to pay taxes . . . for the maintenance of a minister . . . contrary to what he believes is right or had deliberately or voluntarily engaged himself to perform." When the convention submitted a more moderate proposal —citizens might support the denomination of their choice—people made it abundantly clear they wanted no change. Town leaders warned against infringements on traditional local autonomy. Although some ministers supported the amendment, far more considered it a threat both to their livelihood and to public morality. A "Friend to the Common-Wealth" thought the arguments of "freedom of conscience" overstated and that nothing should be allowed to undermine communal harmony. The proposal lost by a four-to-one margin.[52]

50. [Thomas Cogswell], *Some Remarks on the Proceedings of the Late Convention with a Few Observations on Our Present Government* (New Hampshire, 1791), 12, 27, and *passim*; "A Freeman," *Strictures upon the Observations of a Member of Convention in Answer to the Author of Some Remarks* (New Hampshire, 1792), 6–9; *New Hampshire Gazetteer*, Feb. 4, 1792.

51. NHSP, X, 97, 98 (source of quotation), 123–125, 141–142.

52. NHSP, X, 41, 113–114, 141; Turner, *Plumer*, 47 (source of first quotation); *Concord Herald*, Oct. 5, 1791 (source of second quotation). For arguments on the

Economic prosperity, the ability of elected officials to solve many of New Hampshire's special problems, and successful constitutional reform at both the national and state level dissipated the general mood of anxiety which had dominated the mid-1780s. Some revolutionists, however, continued to worry about one condition which had contributed to the earlier crisis in faith: the prevalence of "electioneering" by the politically ambitious and their supporters. "Amicus Libretati Populi," for example, complained about the way in which rum and the fast talk of politicians undermined the good sense of voters. Another writer described at length the "incredible" means men would use in order to "purchase the suffrage of a freeman," condemning especially the practice of "ascribing to their favorites qualifications which they do not possess" and "overrating those that they do"; in free governments, he explained, "the presumption is that candidates for public office in which people have a voice in their appointment are so generally known to them that it would supersede the necessity of investigating their characters by individuals who for the most part have various passions to consult in disquisitions of that sort." In the winter of 1790 "Watchman" cited electioneering as one of the reasons why for the past five years the state government had been marked by "caballing, intriguing, party spirit, calumniating and then coalescence, all the tricks of low cunning, artifice, dissimulation, and every species of chicanery." Several spokesmen repeated the familiar warning that any man who had to buy political power would be sure to abuse it once in office.[53]

Such complaints seemed justified, for despite Bartlett's stranglehold on the presidency, open competition for public office had increased in the years after 1788. "Parties" formed in the General Court each time it was necessary to select a federal senator. The annual election of federal House representatives afforded a new opportunity for inhabitants to promote the interests of their favorites. Because the legislature had decided to have these delegates chosen at large, some of the state's most influential politicians drew up lists of preferred candidates and had them distributed among local

---

amendment see *New Hampshire Spy*, Mar. 2, Apr. 25, 1792; *New Hampshire Gazetteer*, June 6, 1792. Kinney, *Church and State*, 122–129, analyzes the religious implications of the constitutional controversy.

53. The quotations are from *New Hampshire Gazette*, Mar. 12, 1791, and *Concord Herald*, Feb. 17, 1790. See also *Concord Herald*, Aug. 18, 1792.

leaders. Similar slates for the state senate were circulated in counties with more than one post to be filled. Correspondents bombarded newspaper editors with eulogies of prospective officeholders. On election day the liquor flowed freely, and men used various other tactics to influence the voters. It became an accepted practice in some communities to hand out premarked ballots to citizens as they went into town meetings.[54]

But those who condemned political manipulation were in an increasingly small minority. Indeed, many New Hampshire men had begun to think of electioneering as a necessary and even desirable part of the political system. The state's leading politicians—Bartlett excepted—had long accepted the necessity of courting voters aggressively: Sullivan, for example, helped establish the *New Hampshire Spy* to promote his political ambitions, and John Taylor Gilman became a master at the game of sponsoring candidates in the early 1790s. Others who had once considered themselves above politics soon joined in. Plumer began to practice the same tactics he had condemned a decade earlier; two of his close friends—William Page and Jeremiah Smith—did the same. Local leaders felt fewer compunctions about entertaining their fellow townsmen on election day, and prospective voters undoubtedly enjoyed all the attention. Even some critics reflected the shift in attitude. They apologized for seeming overly concerned, talked of politics as an "inconvenience" rather than a threat, and punctuated their complaints by recommending someone for office.[55]

Several factors help account for the increased acceptance of electioneering. In the first place, the political climate had changed: it was much easier to criticize both voters and politicians when government seemed incapable of solving felt problems than when the system was functioning smoothly. Secondly, a group of younger men, less conditioned by the ideological commitment of the war years than their predecessors, had come to power. Plumer once wrote that people were "much more interested in good administration than in the theory or form of government"; Jeremiah Smith thought the development of factions inevitable in a republican society; Gilman

54. Plumer-Page correspondence, 1792, Plumer Letter Book, I, 208–213, Plumer Papers; John T. Gilman to Peabody, Aug. 24, 1792, Misc. MSS, box 17A, fol. 9, NHHS; Dudley Papers, 89, NHHS; *New Hampshire Spy*, Mar. 19, 1791.

55. Whittemore, *Sullivan*, 206; Plumer correspondence, Plumer Letter Book, I *passim*, Plumer Papers; *New Hampshire Gazette*, Mar. 12, 1791.

was capable of the pragmatic statement, "what remains to be done is to turn out and vote." Thirdly, campaigning often assumed a form which seemed consistent with traditional republican beliefs. Only in communities where the secret ballot—which supposedly protected against political manipulation—had been adopted could premarked votes be distributed. Newspapers provided the primary means of soliciting votes, and who could argue against freedom of the press?[56]

Moreover, the increased availability of information about the behavior of public officials helped undermine the notion that inhabitants knew nothing about the political attitudes of those whom they were asked to elect. Ever since the colonial assembly had refused to join in protests against the Stamp Act, governmental secrecy had been under attack. State leaders had responded by authorizing the regular publication of assembly journals, by manifesting a greater willingness to discuss new political activities, and eventually by supporting a constitutional amendment opening assembly sessions to the public. But newspapers proved the most effective vehicle for keeping the public informed.

Before 1787 relatively few residents had regular access to news: the *Gazette* circulated largely around Portsmouth; the only other paper published in the state—the *Mercury*—competed in the same area; and Newburyport's *Essex Journal,* which many in the Merrimack Valley read, concentrated on Massachusetts politics. After that, however, matters began to change. Controversy over state policies and interest in the federal Constitution led to the establishment of three additional state publications by the end of 1787. The success of these ventures, general prosperity, and rapid population growth in the interior added to the number. By 1794 the citizens of both Portsmouth and Concord—where the state government met most frequently—could boast of two newspapers; Dover, Exeter, Keene, Walpole, and Hanover each had one.[57]

The editors of these papers considered political reporting a public responsibility as well as good business. They printed lengthy excerpts

56. Plumer to Jesse Johnson, Dec. 23, 1794, Plumer Letters, no. 27, Plumer Papers; Smith to Peabody, Feb. 27, 1792, Jeremiah Smith Papers, NHHS; Gilman to Peabody, Aug. 24, 1792, Misc. MSS, box 17A, fol. 9, NHHS. For discussion of the secret ballot see *New Hampshire Spy,* Aug. 28, 1790, and *New Hampshire Gazette,* Mar. 26, 1791. The use of such ballots probably was not widespread.

57. Brigham, *American Newspapers,* I, 439–491.

from congressional records, often emphasizing the activities of New Hampshire's own political representatives. At election time they accepted articles discussing not only the personal virtues of prospective officeholders but also their stance on controversial issues. They published the presidential speech given at the beginning of each state legislative session, reported some house and senate debates, listed new laws, and often repeated rumors of political scandal. No resident who cared about constitutional reform could legitimately have complained about lack of information. Almost every issue of every paper printed in the first six months of 1788 contained something about the proposed national government. Later the Concord papers gave the state constitutional convention full coverage; publishers elsewhere reprinted many of the Concord articles.[58]

Finally, the revolutionists began to think of campaigning as a vehicle for solving one long-term threat to the continued success of their experiment in republicanism: public indifference to anything but local politics. New Hampshire contained in 1790 about 25,000 qualified voters, less than 40 per cent of whom voted in statewide elections; only 3,100 votes were cast on the final amendments sent out by the state constitutional convention.[59] There can be no doubt some inhabitants considered the problem serious. One man, for example, complained that people were "grossly negligent" in exercising their privileges. Such behavior had dangerous implications, for it could lead to the loss of liberty or the election of men like "Judas Arnold or even the Prince of Devils." The solution, he argued, lay in the willingness of good men to "make an interest for themselves"; only then would responsible citizens be encouraged to vote. Another writer, observing the multitude of candidates for federal representative, considered the competition healthy, in part because it suggested a renewed interest in the national government but also because it generated enthusiasm for public affairs in general. A vigilant and involved citizenry, he implied, was the best protection against political abuse.[60]

58. These generalizations are based on a reading of copies of almost all newspapers printed in New Hampshire before 1795.

59. *NHSP*, X, 167. There were about 36,000 males above 16 years of age. All men 21 and over who paid town taxes could vote: *NHSP*, XX, 17–21.

60. *New Hampshire Journal* (Walpole), Dec. 30, 1794 (source of quotations); *New Hampshire Gazetteer*, Aug. 20, 1790. See also *New Hampshire Recorder*, Aug. 26, 1790; *New Hampshire Journal*, Dec. 20, 1793, and Feb. 14, 1794.

Thus by 1794 the anxiety of a decade earlier had all but disappeared. The people of New Hampshire were happy with the formal structure of government, the system of politics which determined who should rule, and the style and policies of men presently in power. Public officials—whether elected or appointed—found their authority respected. The state as a whole was united by the mutual commitment of virtually every citizen to the ideals and ethics of republicanism.

Those who had lived through the entire revolutionary era viewed conditions with particular satisfaction. They could recall the chaos which had followed passage of the Stamp Act, the hopes and fears kindled by the declaration of independence, the discouragement and excitement of the war years, and the disillusionment of the eighties. "Our government appears at last to be happily settled," wrote Jeremy Belknap to former governor John Wentworth in the spring of 1791, "and every friend to virtue and good order must wish it permanency. I hope that twenty-five years of controversy and revolution will be sufficient for the space of time which I have to exist on this globe. Were I to live to the age of Methuselah," he concluded, "I should not wish to see another such period."[61] His sentiments were shared by many.

61. Belknap to Wentworth, Mar. 21, 1791, *Belknap Papers, MHS Collections,* 6th ser., IV, 484.

Bibliography
Index

Bibliography

MANUSCRIPT COLLECTIONS

Bartlett Josiah, Correspondence and Photostats, 1775–1792. 1 vol. and 1 box. NHHS.
Bartlett, Josiah, Papers, 1774–1794. 3 vols. and 2 folders. BLDC.
Belcher, Jonathan, Correspondence, 1730–1753. 3 vols. NHHS.
Belknap, Jeremy, Papers, MHS.
Belknap, Jeremy, Papers, 1760–1790. 1 box. NHHS.
Bowdoin-Temple Papers. 3 vols. MHS.
Boyd, George, Letter Book, 1773–1775. NHHS.
Buccleuch and Queensberry Muniments: The Charles Townshend Papers. Intro. [and ed.] by T. C. Smoot. East Ardsley, Yorkshire: Micro Methods, 1964. 3 reels of microfilm of original documents in Dalkeith House.
Dartmouth College Archives. BLDC.
Dreer Collection, 1492–1917. HSP.
Dudley Papers. 1 box. NHHS.
Gerry, Elbridge, Papers, 1772–1782. 2 vols. and 1 box. MHS.
Gratz Collections, 1383–1921. HSP.
Lamb, John, Papers, 1765–1795. 6 boxes. NYHS.
Langdon Correspondence, 1777–1782. HSP.
Langdon Correspondence, 1775–1781. NYPL.
Langdon Papers, 1777, 1781. HSP.
Langdon, John, Papers, 1770–1819. 3 boxes, 1 envelope. NHHS.
Langdon, Woodbury, Papers. 1 box. NHHS.
Langdon, Peabody, and Kittery Papers. NHHS.
Larkin, Thomas, Papers, 1750–1798. PA.
Livermore, Samuel, Papers, 1780–1786. 1 vol. and 1 envelope. NHHS.
Livius, Peter, Letter Book, 1764–1766. NHHS.
McClure, James, Papers. NHHS.
Masonian Papers, 5 vols. NHA.

241

Bibliography

Miscellaneous Manuscripts. NHHS.

Miscellaneous Manuscripts. NYHS.

Miscellaneous and Miscellaneous Bound, 1200–1952. 20 boxes and 21 vols. MHS.

Moffatt, Whipple, and Mason Papers. NHHS.

New Hampshire Colonial Court Records. NHA.

New Hampshire Council Correspondence, 1776–1779. LC.

New Hampshire Loyalist Claims. 5 vols. NHSL. Transcripts from the Public Record Office, London.

New Hampshire Miscellaneous. 2 boxes, NYPL.

New Hampshire Miscellaneous Manuscripts, ca. 1680–1800. 4 vols. LC.

New Hampshire Tax Books. 5 vols. NHA.

New Hampshire Town Records. NHSL. Microfilms of transcripts from Town Records.

Peabody, Nathaniel, Papers, 1767–1785. NHHS.

Peabody, Stephen. Diaries and Accounts, 1777–1794. American Antiquarian Society, Worcester, Mass.

Peirce Papers, 1730–1780. PA.

Plumer Collection, 1782–1854. 121 vols. and 81 bundles. NHSL.

Plumer, William, Papers, 1759–1844. 7 vols., 1 box, and 11 folders. LC.

Portsmouth Tax Records. City Hall, Portsmouth, N.H.

Province Papers, Correspondence. 3 vols. NHA.

Province and Revolutionary Papers, 1754–1780. NHA.

Queens Chapel Parish Records. Vol. IV. NHHS.

Rockingham Letters, Ramsden Papers, Sheepscar Library, Leeds, England.

Rockingham Papers. Wentworth-Woodhouse Muniments, Sheffield City Library, Sheffield, England.

Rogers, John, Papers, 1781–1790. NYPL.

Sheafe, Thomas, Letter Book, 1784–1794. NYPL.

Smith, Jeremiah, Papers, 1791–1841. NHHS.

Society for the Propagation of the Gospel Papers, 1732–1864. Vol. IV. NHHS.

Sparks Transcripts and Manuscripts. 266 vols. and 9 boxes. Houghton Library, Harvard University, Cambridge, Mass.

State Convention, Federal Constitution, 1788, Election of Delegates (also referred to as Goodwin Town Papers). NHA.

State Papers. 9 boxes. NHA.

State Papers, 1620–1789. 1 box. NHA.

State Papers, Documents, Series of 1901. 55 vols. NHA.

State Papers, Revolution. 11 vols. NHA.

Thompson, Ebenezer, Papers. NHHS.

Tolford-Patten Papers, 1714–1795. 10 boxes. NHSL.

Toscan Papers. 2 boxes. NHHS.

Waldron Family Papers, 1713–1753. 2 vols. NHHS.

Walker Papers, NHHS.

Weare, Meshech, Papers, 1769–1807. 3 vols. and 1 box. LC.

Weare, Meshech, Papers, 1776–1785. 2 vols. MHS.
Weare, Meshech, Papers, 1647–1837. 14 vols. NHA.
Wendell Family Papers. Wendell Collection, Baker Library, Harvard Business School, Boston, Mass.
Wentworth, John, Letter Book, 1767–1778. NHA. Transcript of 3 vols. in Nova Scotia Public Records, Halifax.
Wentworth Papers, 1765–1798. 3 boxes. NHHS.
Whipple, William, Papers, 1774–1789. 2 vols. LC.

(In addition, I have used transcripts and microfilms of miscellaneous material from the Public Record Office, London. These were in BLDC, NHHS, LC, and my personal possession.)

NEWSPAPERS

American Herald (Boston), 1787–1788.
Columbian Informer (Keene), 1793–1794.
Concord Herald, 1790–1794.
Courier of New Hampshire (Concord), 1794.
Dresden Mercury, 1779.
Essex Journal and Merrimack Packet (Newburyport, Mass.), 1773–1777.
Essex Journal and New Hampshire Packet (Newburyport, Mass.), 1784–1794.
Exeter Chronicle, 1784.
Freeman's Journal (Portsmouth), 1776–1778.
Freeman's Oracle (Exeter), 1786–1789.
Herald of Liberty (Exeter), 1793–1794.
Mirrour (Concord), 1792–1793.
New Hampshire Gazette (Portsmouth), 1756–1795. (The paper was also published in Exeter between 1778 and 1781.)
New Hampshire Gazetteer (Exeter), 1789–1793.
New Hampshire Journal (Walpole), 1793–1794.
New Hampshire Mercury (Portsmouth), 1784–1788.
New Hampshire Recorder (Keene), 1787–1791.
New Hampshire Spy (Portsmouth), 1786–1793.
Political and Sentimental Repository (Dover), 1790–1792.
Portsmouth Mercury, 1765–1768.

PRINTED PRIMARY SOURCES

Adams, John. *Diary and Autobiography of John Adams,* ed. Lyman H. Butterfield. 4 vols. Cambridge, Mass.: Harvard University Press, 1961.
Adams, John Quincy. "Diary of John Quincy Adams," *Proceedings of the Massachusetts Historical Society,* 16 (1902), 295–463.
Adams, Joseph. *The Necessity and Importance of Rulers, Civil and Ecclesiastical . . .* Portsmouth, 1769.

Bibliography

"Amicus Republicae" [probably Benjamin Thurston]. *An Address to the Public, Containing Some Remarks on the Present Political State of the American Republics.* Exeter, 1787.

Atkinson, William K. *An Oration Delivered at Dover, New Hampshire, on the Fourth of July, 1791* . . . Dover, 1791.

Batchellor, Albert S., and Henry H. Metcalf, eds. *Laws of New Hampshire.* 8 vols. Manchester and elsewhere, 1904–1920.

Belknap, Jeremy. *An Election Sermon Preached before the General Court of New Hampshire* . . . Portsmouth, 1785.

Belknap Papers (*Collections of the Massachusetts Historical Society*, 5th ser., II and III, 6th ser., IV). 3 vols. Boston, 1877–1891.

Bouton, Nathaniel, *et al.*, eds. *Documents and Records Relating to New Hampshire.* 40 vols. Concord and Manchester, 1867–1941. (The titles of this series vary. They are grouped in general as follows. Vols. I–VII, XVIII, and XIX: Provincial Papers, 1623–1776; VIII, X, and XVIII–XXII: State Papers, 1776–1793; XIV–XVII, and XXX: Revolutionary Papers; IX, XI–XIII, and XXIV–XXIX: Town Papers; XXXI–XL: Probate Records. Volume XXIII is a list of New Hampshire documents in the Public Record Office, London. The series includes legislative records, public and private correspondence, petitions to the assembly, town charters, records of the Masonian proprietors, probate court records, and a mass of miscellaneous material. Although poorly edited, inadequately indexed, and frequently lacking in apparent organization, these volumes are the best single source of information on political life in eighteenth-century New Hampshire.)

Bowdoin-Temple Papers (*Collections of the Massachusetts Historical Society*, 6th ser., IX, 7th ser., VI). 2 vols. Boston, 1897–1906.

Buckminster, Joseph, Jr. *A Discourse Delivered in the First Church of Christ at Portsmouth, on Thursday, December 11, 1783* . . . *after the Ratification of a Treaty of Peace* . . . Portsmouth, 1784.

———— *A Sermon Preached before His Excellency the President, the Honorable Council, and the Honorable House of Representatives of the State of New Hampshire, June 7, 1787.* Portsmouth, 1787.

Burnaby, Andrew. *Travels through the Middle Settlements in North America in the Years 1759 and 1760.* 3d ed. London, 1798.

Burnett, Edmund C., ed. *Letters of the Members of the Continental Congress.* 8 vols. Washington, D.C.: The Carnegie Institution of Washington, 1921–1936.

Chastellux, Marquis de. *Travels in North America in the Years 1780, 1781, and 1782*, trans. with intro. and notes by Howard C. Rice, Jr. 2 vols. Chapel Hill: University of North Carolina Press, 1963.

Clark, Joseph. *An Oration Delivered at Rochester on the Fourth of July, 1794.* Dover, 1794.

(Cogswell, Thomas). *Some Remarks on the Proceedings of the Late Convention with a Few Observations on Our Present Government.* New Hampshire, 1791.

Bibliography

Collections of the New Hampshire Historical Society. 15 vols. Concord, 1824–1939.

Concord Town Records. Concord, 1894.

Elliot, Jonathan, ed. *The Debates in the Several State Conventions on the Adoption of the Federal Constitution*, 2d ed. 5 vols. Philadelphia and Washington, 1836–1845.

Elwyn, Alfred L., ed. *Letters by Washington, Adams, Jefferson, and Others Written during and after the Revolution to John Langdon, New Hampshire.* Philadelphia, 1880.

Evans, Israel. *A Sermon Delivered at Concord before the Honorable General Court . . . at the Annual Election . . .* Concord, 1791.

Farmer, John, and Jacob B. Moore, eds. *Collections, Topographical, Historical and Biographical Relating Principally to New Hampshire.* 3 vols. Concord, 1822–1824.

Farrand, Max, ed. *Records of the Federal Convention of 1787.* 4 vols. New Haven: Yale University Press, 1911–1937.

Force, Peter, comp. *American Archives.* 9 vols. Washington, 1837–1853.

"A Freeman." *Strictures upon the Observations of a Member of Convention in Answer to the Author of Some Remarks.* New Hampshire, 1792.

Gay, Bunker. *The Accomplished Judge; or a Compleat Dress for Magistrates.* Portsmouth, 1773.

Grant, William L., and James Munro, eds. *Acts of the Privy Council, Colonial Series.* 6 vols. Hereford and London, 1908–1912.

Hall, Aaron. *An Oration Delivered at the Request of the Inhabitants of Keene, June 30, 1788; to Celebrate the Ratification of the Federal Constitution by the State of New Hampshire.* Keene, 1789.

Hammond, Otis G., ed. *Letters and Papers of Major-General John Sullivan (Collections of the New Hampshire Historical Society, XIII–XV).* 3 vols. Concord: New Hampshire Historical Society, 1930–1939.

Handlin, Oscar, and Mary Flug Handlin, eds. *The Popular Sources of Political Authority: Documents on the Massachusetts Constitution of 1780.* Cambridge: Harvard University Press, 1966.

Haven, Samuel. *An Election Sermon, Preached before the General Court of New Hampshire at Concord, June 8, 1786.* Portsmouth, 1786.

Historical Magazine. 23 vols. Boston and elsewhere, 1857–1875. (Vols. 4–6 and 15 include important revolutionary correspondence.)

Howard, Robert M., ed. *Records and Letters of the Family of the Longs of Longville, Jamaica, and Hampton Lodge, Surrey.* 2 vols. London: Simpkin, Marshall, Hamilton, Kent & Co., 1925.

Hutchinson, Peter O., comp. *The Diary and Letters of His Excellency Thomas Hutchinson, Esq.* Boston, 1884.

Jones, William. *An Oration Pronounced at Concord the Fourth of July, 1794 . . .* Concord, 1794.

A Journal of the Proceedings of the Hon. House of Representatives of the State of New Hampshire . . . Portsmouth, 1793 and 1794.

Bibliography

A Journal of the Proceedings of the Honorable Senate of the State of New Hampshire . . . Portsmouth, 1793 and 1794.

Lane, Samuel. *A Journal for the Years 1793–1803 by Samuel Lane of Stratham, New Hampshire,* ed. Charles L. Hanson. Concord: New Hampshire Historical Society, 1937.

Langdon, Samuel. *The Republic of the Israelites, an Example to the American States* . . . Exeter, 1788.

MacClintock, Samuel. *Herodias: Or Cruelty and Revenge, the Effects of Unlawful Pleasure. A Sermon on the Death of John the Baptist* . . . Portsmouth, 1772.

———— *A Sermon Preached before the Honorable Council, and the Honorable the Senate, and House of Representatives* . . . Portsmouth, 1784.

McClure, David. *Diary of David McClure,* ed. Franklin B. Dexter. New York, 1899.

"A Member of the Convention." *Observations Occasioned by Writings against Alterations Proposed in the Convention, to be Made in the Judiciary System.* Portsmouth, 1792.

Morrison, William. *A Sermon Delivered at Dover* . . . *at the Annual Election* . . . Exeter, 1792.

Munro, James, ed. See Grant, William L.

New England Historical and Genealogical Register. 117 vols. Boston: New England Historic Genealogical Society, 1847–1963. (Vols. 1, 22, and 23 contain New Hampshire correspondence.)

New Hampshire Provincial and State Papers. See Bouton, Nathaniel, *et al.,* eds. *Documents and Records Relating to New Hampshire.*

Patten, Matthew. *Diary of Matthew Patten of Bedford, New Hampshire, 1754–1788.* Concord: Published by the Town of Bedford, 1903.

Paullin, Charles O. *Outletters of the Continental Marine Committee and Board of Admiralty.* 2 vols. New York: Printed for the Naval History Society by the DeVinne Press, 1914.

Plumer, William. "Letters of William Plumer," *Publications of the Colonial Society of Massachusetts,* XI: *Transactions* (1906–1907), 383–403.

Proceedings of the Massachusetts Historical Society. 72 vols. Boston, 1879–1963.

Sanger, Abner. "Ye Journal of Abner Sanger," *The Repertory* (Keene), December 1924 through June 1927.

Sewall, Jonathan M. *An Oration Delivered at Portsmouth, New Hampshire on the Fourth of July, 1788, Being the Anniversary of American Independence.* Portsmouth, 1788.

Sparks, Jared, ed. *Correspondence of the American Revolution.* 4 vols. Boston, 1853.

Stearns, Josiah. *Two Sermons, Preached at Epping* . . . *on a Public Fast Appointed by Authority on Account of the Unnatural and Distressing War with Great Britain, in Defense of Liberty.* Newburyport, 1777.

Taylor, Robert J., ed. *Massachusetts, Colony to Commonwealth: Documents* on the Formation of Its Constitution, 1775–1780. Chapel Hill: University of North Carolina Press, 1961.

Walker, Timothy. *Diaries of Reverend Timothy Walker*, ed. Joseph B. Walker. Concord, 1889.

Walton, Eliakim P., ed. *Records of the Council of Safety and Governor and Council of the State of Vermont.* 8 vols. Montpelier, 1873–1880.

SECONDARY SOURCES

Abbott, Wilbur C. *Conflicts with Oblivion.* New Haven: Yale University Press, 1924.

Adams, Charles T. *Matthew Thornton of New Hampshire.* Philadelphia: Dando Printing and Publishing, 1903.

Adams, Nathaniel. *Annals of Portsmouth . . .* Portsmouth, 1825.

Adams, Randolph G. *Political Ideas of the American Revolution.* Durham: Trinity College Press, 1922.

Akagi, Roy H. *Town Proprietors of the New England Colonies: A Study of Their Development, Organization, Activities and Controversies.* Philadelphia: Press of the University of Pennsylvania, 1924.

Albion, Robert G. *Forests and Sea Power: The Timber Problem of the Royal Navy, 1652–1862.* Cambridge, Mass.: Harvard University Press, 1926.

Alden, Timothy, Jr. *An Account of the Several Religious Societies in Portsmouth.* Boston, 1808.

Aldrich, Edgar. "The Affair of the Cedars and the Service of Colonel Timothy Bedel in the War of the Revolution," *Proceedings of the New Hampshire Historical Society,* 3(1895–1899), 192–231.

Anderson, George P. "Land Grants Made in New Hampshire by Governor Benning Wentworth to Boston Men," *Publications of the Colonial Society of Massachusetts,* XXV: *Transactions* (1922–1924), 33–38.

Andrews, Charles M. *The Colonial Background of the American Revolution.* New Haven: Yale University Press, 1924.

Bailyn, Bernard. *The Ideological Origins of the American Revolution.* Cambridge, Mass.: Harvard University Press, 1967.

Baker, Henry M. "General Nathaniel Folsom," *Proceedings of the New Hampshire Historical Society,* 4 (1899–1905), 253–267.

Baldwin, Alice M. *The New England Clergy and the American Revolution.* Durham: Duke University Press, 1928.

Barrow, Thomas C. *Trade and Empire: The British Customs Service in Colonial America, 1660–1775.* Cambridge, Mass.: Harvard University Press, 1967.

Barstow, George. *History of New Hampshire.* Concord, 1842.

Baxter, William T. *The House of Hancock.* Harvard Studies in Business History, vol. X. Cambridge, Mass.: Harvard University Press, 1945.

Beaven, Alfred B. *The Aldermen of the City of London.* 2 vols. London: E. Fisher & Co., 1908–1913.

Bibliography

Belknap, Jeremy. *History of New Hampshire*. 3 vols. Philadelphia and Boston, 1784–1792.

——— *History of New Hampshire*, with notes by John Farmer, Dover, 1831.

Bell, Charles H. *The Bench and Bar of New Hampshire* . . . Cambridge, Mass., 1894.

——— *History of the Town of Exeter, New Hampshire*. Exeter, 1888.

Bellows, Henry W. *Historical Sketch of Colonel Benjamin Bellows*. New York, 1855.

Bouton, Nathaniel. *History of Concord*. Concord, 1856.

Boyd, Julien P. "Silas Deane: Death by a Kindly Teacher of Treason," *William and Mary Quarterly*, 3d ser., 16(1959), 165–188, 319–343, 515–551.

Boylston, Edward D. *The Hillsborough County Congresses, 1774 and 1775*. Amherst, 1884.

Brewster, Charles W. *Rambles about Portsmouth: Sketches of persons, localities and incidents of two centuries: principally from tradition and unpublished documents*. 2 vols. Portsmouth, 1859–1869.

Bridenbaugh, Carl. *Mitre and Sceptre: Transatlantic Faiths, Ideas, Personalities, and Politics, 1689–1775*. New York: Oxford University Press, 1962.

Brigham, Clarence S. *History and Bibliography of American Newspapers, 1690–1820*. 2 vols. Worcester: American Antiquarian Society, 1947.

Brown, Ralph A. "New Hampshire Editors Win the War," *New England Quarterly*, 12(1939), 35–51.

Brown, Wallace. *The King's Friends: The Composition and Motives of the American Loyalist Claimants*. Providence: Brown University Press, 1965.

Brown, William H. *Colonel John Goffe*. Manchester: L. A. Cummings Co., 1950.

Burns, John F. *Controversies between Royal Governors and Their Assemblies*. Privately printed. Boston, 1923.

Burrage, Henry S. "Colonel Nathaniel Sparhawk of Kittery," *Collections and Proceedings of the Maine Historical Society*, 2d ser., 9(1898), 225–264.

Butters, Avery J. "New Hampshire History and the Public Career of Meshech Weare, 1713 to 1786," unpub. diss. Fordham University, 1961.

Chambers, William N. *Political Parties in a New Nation: The American Experience, 1776–1809*. New York: Oxford University Press, 1963.

Chase, Frederick. *The History of Dartmouth College and the Town of Hanover*, ed. John K. Lord. Cambridge Mass., 1891.

Coffin, Charles C., comp. *The History of Boscawen and Webster from 1773–1838*. Concord, 1878.

Colby, Fred M. "Moffatt-Whipple Mansion," *Granite Monthly*, 13(1890), 219–227.

Colby, James F. *Manual of the Constitution of the State of New Hampshire*. Concord, 1912.

Cooper, James F. "History of the Navy of the United States." 8 vols. NYHS.

Corning, Charles R. *John Fenton*. Concord, 1886.

——— *Samuel Livermore*. Concord, 1888.

Bibliography

Cunningham, Nobel. *Jeffersonian Republicans: The Formation of Party Organization, 1789–1801.* Chapel Hill: University of North Carolina Press, 1957.

Cushing, Harry A. "The People the Best Governors," *American Historical Review,* 1(1896), 284–287.

Cutter, William R. A *History of the Cutter Family of New England.* Boston, 1871.

Daniell, Jere R. "Reason and Ridicule: Tea Act Resolutions in New Hampshire," *Historical New Hampshire,* 20(Winter 1965), 23–28.

Dodd, Walter F. "The Constitutional History of New Hampshire, 1775–1792," *Proceedings of the Bar Association of the State of New Hampshire,* n. s., 2 (1904–1908), 379–400.

———— *The Revision and Amendment of State Constitutions.* Baltimore: The Johns Hopkins Press, 1910.

Donoughue, Bernard. *British Politics and the American Revolution: The Path to War, 1773–1775.* New York: St. Martin's Press, 1965.

Douglass, Elisha P. *Rebels and Democrats.* Chapel Hill: University of North Carolina Press, 1955.

Downs, Charles A. *History of Lebanon, New Hampshire, 1761–1787.* Concord: Rumford Printing Co., 1908.

Eiseman, Nathaniel J. "The Ratification of the Federal Constitution by the State of New Hampshire," unpub. thesis Columbia University, 1937. Mimeograph, NHSL.

Ells, Earnest E. "An Unpublished Journal of George Whitefield," *Church History,* 7(1938), 297–346.

Fairchild, Byron. *Messrs. William Pepperrell: Merchants at Piscataqua.* Ithaca: Cornell University Press, 1954.

Ferguson, E. James. *The Power of the Purse.* Chapel Hill: University of North Carolina Press, 1961.

Foote, Henry W., et al., eds. *Annals of King's Chapel from the Puritan Age of New England to the Present Day.* 3 vols. Boston: Little, Brown & Co., 1882–1940.

Forbes, Harriette M. *New England Diaries, 1620–1800.* Privately printed. Topsfield, 1923.

Fry, William H. *New Hampshire as a Royal Province.* Columbia University Studies in History, Economics, and Public Law, vol. XXIX. New York, 1908.

Garrett, Wendell D. *Apthorp House, 1760–1960.* Cambridge, Mass.: Harvard University Press, 1960.

Gemmill, John K. "The Problems of Power: New Hampshire Government during the Revolution," *Historical New Hampshire,* 22(Summer 1967), 27–38.

Gipson, Lawrence H. *Jared Ingersoll.* New Haven: Yale University Press, 1920.

Goldthwait, James W. "The First Province Road; the Road from Durham to Co-os," *New Hampshire Highways,* April 1931, 1–5.

———— "The Governor's Road, From Rochester to Wolfboro," *New Hampshire Highways*, May 1931, 2–5.

———— "The Road to Conway and the Upper Cohos," *New Hampshire Highways*, August 1931, 1–5.

Graham, Ian C. C. *Colonists from Scotland*. Ithaca: Cornell University Press, 1956.

Grant, Charles S. *Democracy in the Connecticut Frontier Town of Kent*. New York: Columbia University Press, 1961.

Greene, Evarts B. *The Revolutionary Generation, 1763–1790*. New York: Macmillan, 1945.

Greene, Jack P. "Martin Bladen's Blueprint for a Colonial Union," *William and Mary Quarterly*, 3d ser., 17(1960), 516–530.

———— "The Role of the Lower Houses of Assembly in Eighteenth-Century Politics," *Journal of Southern History*, 27(1960), 451–474.

Hale, Selma. *Annals of the Town of Keene*. Keene, 1851.

Hammond, Otis G. "The Mason Title and Its Relations to New Hampshire and Massachusetts," *Proceedings of the American Antiquarian Society*, 26(1916), 245–263.

———— *Tories of New Hampshire in the War of the Revolution*. Concord: New Hampshire Historical Society, 1917.

Henderson, Herbert J. "Political Factions in the Continental Congress," unpub. diss. Columbia University, 1962.

Hunt, Agnes. *Provincial Committees of Safety of the American Revolution*. Cleveland: Press of Winn and Judson, 1904.

Hunt, Elmer, and Robert A. Smith. "The English Background of Some of the Wentworth Town Grants," *Historical New Hampshire*, 6(1950), 2–52.

Jensen, Merrill. *The New Nation: A History of the United States during the Confederation, 1781–1789*. New York: Knopf, 1950.

Jervey, Theodore D. "Barlow Trecothick," *South Carolina Historical and Genealogical Magazine*, 32(1931), 157–169.

Jones, Matt B. *Vermont in the Making, 1750–1777*. Cambridge, Mass.: Harvard University Press, 1939.

Jordan, Chester B. "Colonel Joseph Whipple," *Proceedings of the New Hampshire Historical Society*, 2(1888–1895), 289–320.

Kenyon, Cecelia M. "Men of Little Faith: The Anti-Federalists on the Nature of Representative Government," *William and Mary Quarterly*, 3d ser., 12(1955), 3–43.

———— "Republicanism and Radicalism in the American Revolution: An Old-Fashioned Interpretation," *William and Mary Quarterly*, 3d ser., 19(1962), 165–168.

Kinney, Charles B., Jr. *Church and State: The Struggle for Separation in New Hampshire, 1630–1900*. New York: Teachers' College, Columbia University, 1956.

Knollenberg, Bernhard. *Origin of the American Revolution: 1759–1766*. New York: Macmillan, 1960.

Bibliography

Labaree, Benjamin W. *Patriots and Partisans: The Merchants of Newbury-port, 1764–1815*. Cambridge, Mass.: Harvard University Press, 1962.

Leyburn, James G. *The Scotch-Irish: A Social History*. Chapel Hill: University of North Carolina Press, 1962.

Libby, Orin G. *Geographical Distribution of the Vote of the Thirteen States on the Federal Constitution, 1787–1788*. Bulletin of the University of Wisconsin, Economics, Political Science, and History Series, I, no. 1. Madison, 1894.

Lilly, Edward P. *The Colonial Agents of New York and New Jersey*. Washington, D.C.: The Catholic University of America, 1936.

Looney, John F. "The King's Representative: Benning Wentworth, Colonial Governor, 1741–1767," unpub. diss. Lehigh University, 1961.

Lyford, James O. *History of the Town of Claremont*. Manchester, 1895.

McAnear, Beverly, ed. "An American in London, 1735–1736: The Diary of Robert Hunter Morris," *Pennsylvania Magazine of History and Biography*, 64(1940), 164–217, 365–406.

McClintock, John N. *History of New Hampshire*. Boston, 1888.

MacDonald, Forrest. *We the People: The Economic Origins of the Constitution*. Chicago: University of Chicago Press, 1958.

McKinley, Samuel J. "Economic History of Portsmouth," unpub. diss. Harvard University, 1931.

MacMillan, Margaret B. *War Governors in the American Revolution*. New York: Columbia University Press, 1943.

Main, Jackson T. *The Anti-Federalists: Critics of the Constitution, 1781–1788*. Chapel Hill: University of North Carolina Press, 1961.

———— "Government by the People: The American Revolution and the Democratization of the Legislatures," WMQ, 3d ser., 23(1966), 391–407.

———— *The Upper House in Revolutionary America, 1763–1788*. Madison: University of Wisconsin Press, 1967.

Malone, Joseph J. *Pine Trees and Politics: The Naval Stores and Forest Policy in Colonial New England, 1691–1775*. Seattle: University of Washington Press, 1964.

Martin, Margaret E. *Merchants and Trade of the Connecticut River Valley, 1750–1820*. Smith College Studies in History, vol. XXIV. Northampton, 1939.

May, Ralph. *Early Portsmouth History*. Boston: C. E. Goodspeed and Co., 1926.

Mayo, Lawrence S. "Jeremy Belknap's Apologue of the Hen at Pennycook," *Publications of the Colonial Society of Massachusetts*, XXVII: *Transactions* (1927–1930), 31–35.

———— *John Langdon of New Hampshire*. Concord: The Rumford Press, 1937.

———— *John Wentworth, Governor of New Hampshire, 1767–1775*. Cambridge, Mass.: Harvard University Press, 1921.

Morgan, Edmund. "The Puritan Ethic and the American Revolution," *William and Mary Quarterly*, 3d ser., 24(1967), 3–43.

Morison, John H. *Life of Hon. Jeremiah Smith, LL.D.* Boston, 1845.

Namier, Louis B. "Anthony Bacon, M.P.: An Eighteenth Century Merchant," *Journal of Economic and Business History*, 2(1929), 20–70.

—— *England in the Age of the American Revolution*. London: Macmillan & Co., 1930.

Nevins, Allan. *The American States during and after the Revolution, 1775–1789.* New York: Macmillan, 1924.

New Hampshire Genealogical Record. 7 vols. Dover, 1903–1910.

Oedel, Howard T. "Portsmouth, New Hampshire: The Role of the Provincial Capital in the Development of the Colony (1700–1775)," unpub. diss. Boston University, 1960.

Page, Elwin L. "The King's Powder, 1774," *New England Quarterly*, 18(1945), 83–92.

—— "Rider for Freedom: Josiah Bartlett, 1729–1795," MS. NHHS.

Parker, Edward L. *History of Londonderry.* Boston, 1851.

Parsons, Theophilus. *Memoir of Theophilus Parsons.* Boston, 1859.

Parsons, Usher. *Life of Sir William Pepperrell, Bart., The Only Native of New England Who Was Created a Baronet during Our Connection with the Mother Country.* Boston, 1855.

Plumer, William. "The Constitution of New Hampshire," *Historical Magazine*, 14(1868), 172–185.

—— "The Constitution of New Hampshire," *Proceedings of the Bar Association of the State of New Hampshire*, n. s., 2(1904–1908), 207–244.

—— "Plumer's Biographical Sketches." 5 vols. NHHS. (Some of these are published in NHSP, XXI and XXII.)

Ratchford, B. U. *American State Debts.* Durham: Duke University Press, 1941.

Reed, William B., ed., *Life and Correspondence of Joseph Reed.* 2 vols. Philadelphia, 1847.

Rice, John L. "Dartmouth College and the State of New Connecticut," *Papers and Proceedings of the Connecticut Valley Historical Society*, 1(1876–1881), 152–206.

Ritcheson, Charles R. *British Politics and the American Revolution.* Norman, Okla.: University of Oklahoma Press, 1954.

Robinson, Maurice H. *A History of Taxation in New Hampshire.* Publications of the American Economic Association, 3d ser., vol. III. New York: Macmillan, 1903.

Rogers, Mary C. *Glimpses of an Old Social Capital.* Boston, 1923.

Sachse, William L. "John Huske's Proposals for Improving American Trade," *Publications of the Colonial Society of Massachusetts*, XLII: *Transactions* (1952–1956), 474–487.

Saltonstall, William G. *Ports of Piscataqua.* Cambridge, Mass.: Harvard University Press, 1941.

Sanborn, Edwin D. *History of New Hampshire.* Manchester, 1875.

Bibliography

Saunderson, Henry H. *History of Charlestown, New Hampshire.* Claremont, 1876.

Schutz, John A. "Succession Politics in Massachusetts, 1730–1741, *William and Mary Quarterly,* 3d ser., 15(1958), 508–520.

————— *William Shirley: King's Governor of Massachusetts.* Chapel Hill: University of North Carolina Press, 1961.

Scott, Kenneth. "Counterfeiting in Colonial New Hampshire," *Historical New Hampshire,* 13(1957), 3–38.

————— "New Hampshire Counterfeiters Operating from New York City," *New York Historical Society Quarterly,* 34(1950), 31–57.

————— "Tory Associators of Portsmouth," *William and Mary Quarterly,* 3d ser., 17(1960), 507–515.

Shipton, Clifford K. *Biographical Sketches of Those Who Attended Harvard College (Sibley's Harvard Graduates, IV–XIV).* 11 vols., in progress. Boston: Massachusetts Historical Society, 1933–

Smith, Jonathan. *Peterborough, New Hampshire, in the American Revolution.* Peterborough: Peterborough Historical Society, 1913.

Smith, Joseph H. *Appeals to the Privy Council from the American Plantations.* New York: Columbia University Press, 1950.

Spofford, Charles B. "Samuel Ashley," *Granite Monthly,* 14(1892), 141–147.

Stackpole, Everett S. *History of New Hampshire.* 5 vols. New York: The American Historical Society, 1917.

Tullock, Timothy L. "Tobias Lear," *Granite Monthly,* 6(1883), 4–14, 60–62.

Turner, Lynn W. *William Plumer of New Hampshire, 1759–1850.* Chapel Hill: University of North Carolina Press, 1962.

Ubbelohde, Carl. *Vice Admiralty Courts and the American Revolution.* Chapel Hill: University of North Carolina Press, 1960.

Upton, Richard F. *Revolutionary New Hampshire: An Account of the Social and Political Forces Underlying the Transition from Royal Province to American Commonwealth.* Hanover: Dartmouth College Publications, 1936.

Wadleigh, George. *Notable Events in the History of Dover.* Dover, 1913.

Waite, Otis F. R. *History of the Town of Claremont.* Manchester, 1895.

Walker, Joseph B. "The Controversy between the Proprietors of Bow and those of Penny Cook, 1729–1789," *Proceedings of the New Hampshire Historical Society,* 3(1895–1899), 261–292.

————— *A History of the New Hampshire Convention for the Investigations, Discussion, and Decision of the Federal Constitution.* Boston, 1888.

————— "Life of Honorable Timothy Walker," typescript, 1903. NHHS.

————— "Life of Reverend Timothy Walker." 2 vols. NHHS.

————— "The New Hampshire Covenant of 1774," *Granite Monthly,* 35(1903), 188–197.

————— *New Hampshire's Five Provincial Congresses, July 21, 1774–January 5, 1776.* Concord: Rumford Printing Co., 1905.

Watson, D. H. "Barlow Trecothick," *Bulletin of the British Association for*

American Studies, n. s., 1, September 1960, 36–49, and March 1961, 29–39.

——— "Barlow Trecothick and Other Associates of Lord Rockingham during the Stamp Act Crisis, 1765–1766," unpub. thesis Sheffield University, 1958.

Watson, J. Steven. *The Reign of George III, 1760–1815*. Oxford: Clarendon Press, 1960.

Weeden, William B. *Economic and Social History of New England, 1620–1789*. 2 vols. Boston, 1890.

Wentworth, John. *The Wentworth Genealogy* . . . 3 vols. Boston, 1878.

Whitcher, William F. *John Hurd*. Concord, 1888.

Whittemore, Charles P. *A General of the Revolution, John Sullivan of New Hampshire*. New York: Columbia University Press, 1961.

Wickwire, Franklin B. "John Pownall and British Colonial Policy," *William and Mary Quarterly*, 3d ser., 20(1963), 543–554.

Williamson, Chilton. *American Suffrage from Property to Democracy, 1760–1860*. Princeton: Princeton University Press, 1960.

——— *Vermont in Quandary, 1737–1825*. Montpelier: Vermont Historical Society, 1949.

Wingate, Charles E. L. *Life and Letters of Paine Wingate*. 2 vols. Medford, Mass.: Mercury Printing Co., 1930.

Wolff, Mabel P. *The Colonial Agency of Pennsylvania, 1712–1757*. Philadelphia, 1933.

Wood, George A. *The Public Life of William Shirley*. Columbia University Studies in History, Economics, and Public Law, vol. XVII. New York: Columbia University, 1920.

Wood, Gordon S. "The Creation of an American Polity in the Revolutionary Era," unpub. diss. Harvard University, 1964.

Woodbury, Gordon. "The Scotch-Irish and Irish Presbyterian Settlers of New Hampshire," *Proceedings of the New Hampshire Historical Society*, 4(1899–1905), 143–162.

Worcester, Samuel T. *History of the Town of Hollis*. Boston, 1879.

——— "Hollis, New Hampshire, in the War of the Revolution," NEHGR, 30(1876), 288–298.

Worthington, Harriet. "New Hampshire Churches and the American Revolution," unpub. thesis, University of Chicago, 1924. Typescript, BLDC.

Wroth, Lawrence C. *An American Bookshelf, 1755*. Philadelphia: University of Pennsylvania Press, 1934.

Wright, Benjamin F. *Consensus and Continuity, 1776–1787*. Boston: Boston University Press, 1958.

Zeichner, Oscar. *Connecticut's Years of Controversy, 1750–1776*. Chapel Hill: University of North Carolina Press, 1949.

Index

255

Index

Durand, John, 41
Durham, 80

Economic conditions, 14, 24, 47, 100, 128–135, 184–188, 219
Elections: laws and procedures, 23, 108, 122, 192–193, 233–236; to colonial house, 27, 32, 70, 77–79, 86–87; to General Court, 150, 199, 211; to presidency and governorship, 192–196, 221–222, 227
Enfield, 145
Epping, 167
Epsom, 122
Essex Result, the, 170, 172, 175
Exeter, 17, 20, 28, 67, 122, 132, 213, 235; opposition to royal government, 54, 71, 99; seat of provincial congress and state government, 102–104, 126, 150, 198; riot in, 198, 201, 202, 203, 228

Falmouth, 47, 108
Federal constitution, 206, 224; support for, 208–210, 212–213, 215; opposition to, 210–212, 213–214; ratification conventions, 213–215, 216; impact of ratification on state politics, 217–221, 235
Fenton, John, 88–89
Fisher, John, 38, 56
Folsom, Nathaniel: opposition to royal government, 79, 83, 117; in Continental Congress, 80, 102, 144; militia general, 104; state politician, 119, 136, 165, 168
Fort Dummer, 26, 27
Francestown, 98
French Revolution, 220

Gage, Thomas, 82, 84, 87, 88, 90
Gains, George, 144
General Court: organization of, 126–128, 142–144, 168, 222–225; economic policies, 128–135, 141, 186–189, 194, 198; treatment of loyalists, 131–132; and western rebellion, 150–162; instructions to constitutional conventions, 168, 170, 226; criticism of, 190–199. *See also* Council; House of Representatives; Senate
George III (king of England), 37, 45
Gerry, Elbridge, 165
Giles, Benjamin, 119, 152
Gilman, John Taylor, 212, 214, 217n, 226n, 234

Gilman, Nicholas (delegate to federal convention), 207
Gilman, Nicholas (state treasurer), 131, 133
Gilman, Peter, 17, 66, 71–72
Gilmanton, 189, 190
Goffe, John, 17
Grafton County, 88, 110, 115, 172, 218n; in western rebellion, 124, 125, 133, 146–152, 155, 162, 168
Grafton, Duke of, 10
Greenland, 74
Grenville, George, 37, 40, 41
Gulston, Joseph, 11n

Hamilton, Alexander, 220–221, 222
Hampton, 28–29, 75, 119
Hampton Falls, 17, 20, 217
Hanbury, John, 6
Hancock, John, 191n
Hanover, 50, 145, 146, 150, 158, 162, 235
Hartford, Connecticut, 50
Hartford, Vermont, 145
Harvard College, 20
Haven, Rev. Samuel, 19
Haverhill, 50, 150, 162
Hawke, Adm. Edward, 29
Hawke (town), 210
Hedges, Silas, 191n
Henniker, John, 11
Hill, Wills. *See* Hillsborough, Earl of
Hillsborough County, 115, 172, 185; civil disorder, 83, 88, 97; congresses, 100–101
Hillsborough, Earl of, 41, 46, 54
Hilton, Martha (later Martha Hilton Wentworth), 68, 69
Hinsdale, 77
Holderness, 158
Holland, John, 83n
House of Representatives
   colonial, 7, 15, 22–23, 36, 70–73, 106, 114, 116, 120; elections to, 27, 32, 70, 77–79, 86–87; criticism of, 64–65, 70–71; opposition to royal government, 71–73, 77, 79–80, 86–89, 101, 104
   under temporary constitution, 95, 112, 114–115; internal organization, 125–128; boycotted, 150
   under permanent constitution, 199, 201, 209, 224, 230
Howard, Henry, IV (Earl of Suffolk), 42, 43
Hubbard, Leverett, 189

257

Index

Hurd, John, 68, 88
Huske, Ellis, 19, 28–29
Huske, John, 37–39
Hutchinson, Thomas, 9

Jaffrey, George, 119n; commercial activities, 7, 21; colonial offices, 66, 104; during revolution, 74, 76n, 108, 137
Johnson, Sir William, 156
Johnston, Charles, 162
Jones, John Paul, 140
Judicial system: under Benning Wentworth, 16–17, 19–22; and division into counties, 20, 67, 71; criticism of, 62, 79, 196, 199; courts closed, 95, 105; efforts to reform, 230–232

Keene, 98, 99, 210, 235
King, George (later George Atkinson), 76n; member of council, 141, 142; seeks constitutional reform, 168, 170. *See also* Atkinson, George
Kingston, 119
Kittery, 83, 139

Landaff, 160
Land grants, 10, 14–16, 23–24, 37, 71
Lane, Samuel, 133, 134, 138
Langdon, John: commercial activity, 56, 117, 119, 138–139, 192; and Livius, 67; attack on Castle William, 83, 141; house representative, 87, 125–126, 128, 141–144, 165, 196; in Continental Congress, 102, 106, 109, 117; criticism of revolutionary government, 117, 124, 125, 136, 137, 142–144; seeks fiscal reform, 130, 132, 141; supports constitutional reform, 165, 167–171, 178, 200, 201, 208; presidential candidate, 192, 194, 196, 199, 221, 222; state president, 187, 194, 208, 221, 228; portrait of, 195; and federal constitution, 207, 208, 213, 214, 216; national senator, 219, 221
Langdon, Rev. Samuel, 19; describes response to imperial reform, 52, 53, 54, 62; constitutional arguments, 61; fear of Anglicanism, 63; supports federal constitution, 209, 214
Langdon, Woodbury, 56, 74, 119n, 191n; merchant activity, 43, 47, 48, 84; opposition to royal government, 53, 54, 79, 87; friendship with Livius, 67; response to revolution, 76n, 84, 116–117; in general court, 87, 141–144; delegate to Continental Congress,

143, 158; presidential candidate, 192, 193; superior court judge, 225–226
Lear, Tobias, 211, 216
Lebanon, 145
Lee, John, 43
Legge, William. *See* Dartmouth, Earl of
Libbey, Jeremiah, 204
Litchfield, 136
Livermore, Samuel: Continental Congress delegate, 158, 159; chief justice, 162, 212; supports federal constitution, 212, 214, 216, 218; national senator, 221
Livius, Peter: and mast trade, 11, 12, 48; tries to oust Gov. John Wentworth, 42–43, 56, 73, 125; appointed chief justice, 43, 74, 81; criticizes Stamp Act, 60–61; council member, 66–70, 120
Local government: in colonial period, 22, 70, 96; in revolutionary crisis, 97–100, 114–115, 120–122; relationship to revolutionary government, 133–134, 146–148, 150, 199–200
Londonderry, 3, 36, 57, 119, 197
Long, Peirce, 138
Lords of Trade. *See* Board of Trade
Louisbourg expedition, 9, 27, 29, 31
Loyalists: treatment of, 82, 88, 101, 104, 115, 137, 150; proscription and confiscation of estates, 131–132, 140, 142, 145, 174, 176, 196; and counterfeiting, 136; influence feared, 143, 173. *See also* Oaths of allegiance
Lutwyche, Edward, 57, 83n, 215
Lyme, 87, 145

McDonough, Thomas, 43
Mansfield, Earl of, 37, 39, 43
Martin, Thomas, 36
Mason, John Tufton, 11, 14, 67n
Mason (town), 105
Masonian proprietorship, 154; origins of, 14; participants, 14, 17, 27, 29, 191n; proceedings against, 39–40; challenged by "Allenites," 191, 192, 194, 195n, 197, 225
Massachusetts, 6, 56, 82, 98, 109, 116, 117, 159, 198, 211; boundary dispute with New Hampshire, 8, 9, 15–16, 21; influence on New Hampshire politics, 64, 65, 71, 72, 81, 83n, 104, 106, 212–214; Government Act, 81, 121; constitution, 170, 171
Mast trade, 5, 10–13, 41, 45, 47, 119, 129

258